Becoming a Successful Teacher of Mathematics

Becoming a Successful Teacher of Mathematics is a practical guide based on research conducted with teachers. It develops the essential knowledge, skills and understanding demanded by the DfEE requirements for courses of initial teacher training. It also offers critical insights for more experienced teachers reflecting on their practice. The book develops:

- advice on using the National Numeracy Framework;
- insights into successful strategies for teaching numeracy in primary and secondary schools;
- an understanding of effective approaches to the teaching of mathematical thinking;
- strategies for dealing with children's misconceptions in mathematics;
- an understanding of how to use ICT to enhance the teaching of mathematics;
- knowledge of effective techniques for managing and controlling classes.

By relating current initiatives to research findings and showing how these impact on classroom practice *Becoming a Successful Teacher of Mathematics* will be an essential read for students on ITT courses and their mentors, teachers with responsibility for mathematics, and providers of preservice and inservice training.

Both authors gained substantial teaching experience in secondary schools before joining the University of Wales, Swansea. They teach on the PGCE mathematics course, which has consistently received top gradings on OHMCI inspections and quality audits. **Howard Tanner's** research interests include the development of mathematical thinking skills and the place of ICT in teaching and learning. **Sonia Jones'** research interests include numeracy and interactive and conversational teaching styles. Their research with teacher inquiry groups enables them to link theories of teaching and learning with the realities of classroom life.

Becoming a Successful Teacher of Mathematics

Howard Tanner and Sonia Jones

London and New York

First published 2000
by RoutledgeFalmer
11 New Fetter Lane, London EC4P 4EE

Simultaneously published in the USA and Canada
by RoutledgeFalmer
29 West 35th Street, New York, NY 10001

RoutledgeFalmer is an imprint of the Taylor & Francis Group

© 2000 Howard Tanner and Sonia Jones

Typeset in Monotype Baskerville by Steven Gardiner Ltd
Printed and bound in Great Britain by St Edmundsbury Press, Bury St Edmunds, Suffolk

British Library Cataloguing in Publication Data
A catalogue record for this book is available
from the British Library

Library of Congress Cataloging in Publication Data
Tanner, Howard, 1951–
    Becoming a successful teacher of mathematics/Howard Tanner and Sonia Jones.
        p. cm.
    Includes bibliographical references and index.
    1. Mathematics–Study and teaching (Secondary)–Great Britain.   2. Mathematics
    teachers–Training of–Great Britain.   I. Jones, Sonia, 1953–   II. Title.

QA14.G7 T36 2000
510′.71′041–dc21   00-044650

ISBN 0 415 23068 3 (hbk)
ISBN 0 415 23069 1 (pbk)

To all the teachers who have worked in Teacher Inquiry Groups with us striving to improve the teaching and learning of mathematics.

... A wonderful thing is a Tigger ...
A. A. Milne

Contents

Figures

Tables

Abbreviations

ACCAC	*Awdurdod Cymwysterau Cwricwlwm ac Asesu Cymru* – Qualifications, Curriculum and Assessment Authority for Wales
APU	Assessment of Performance Unit
ATs	Attainment Targets
CAN	The Calculator-Aware Number project
CSE	Certificate of Secondary Education
CSMS	Concepts in Secondary Mathematics and Science
DfEE	Department for Education and Employment
Estyn	Her Majesty's Inspectorate for Education and Training in Wales
GCE	General Certificate of Education Ordinary level
GCSE	General Certificate of Secondary Education
GNVQ	General National Vocational Qualifications
ICT	Information and Communication Technology
KS	Key Stage
LEA	Local Education Authority
Ma1	Mathematics Attainment Target 1
MEP	Mathematics Enhancement Project
NNS	National Numeracy Strategy
NNP	National Numeracy Project
PoS	Programmes of Study
OFSTED	Office for Standards in Education
OHMCI	Office of Her Majesty's Chief Inspector of Schools in Wales
PAMP	Practical Applications of Mathematics Project
QCA	Qualifications and Assessment Authority
RSN	Raising Standards in Numeracy project
SEN	Special Educational Needs
STs	Standard Tasks (previously SATs)
TIGs	Teacher Inquiry Groups
TIMSS	Third International Mathematics and Science Study
ZPD	Zone of Proximal Development

Preface

These are interesting times for teachers of mathematics. A new National Curriculum has just come into force which sets challenging targets for pupils' learning. The National Numeracy Strategy (NNS) has just begun to make an impact in primary schools, demanding changes in teaching style and the introduction of new and exciting forms of classroom interaction. The extension of the NNS will move the debate forward into secondary schools, forcing a re-evaluation of traditional approaches towards teaching and learning. A new ICT curriculum is demanding that all teachers use and teach the ICT key skill in their lessons. For both newcomers to the profession and for more experienced teachers there are new issues to consider and new skills to learn.

This book is intended to be of interest to you if you are:

- a student on a course of initial teacher training such as PGCE or BEd;
- a trainee teacher on a graduate training programme;
- a novice teacher developing your practice in your first few crucial years in the profession.

It will help you to develop the essential knowledge, skills and understanding demanded by the new DfEE requirements for courses of initial teacher training.

The book addresses issues of current interest and brings you up to date on the latest research and initiatives. You will also find the book valuable if you are a more experienced teacher who is:

- responsible for mentoring students and less experienced colleagues;
- reflecting on your professional knowledge;
- following a professional training course to develop your skills;
- studying for a higher degree such as MA(Ed) or MEd;
- a head of department concerned about advancing professional practice in mathematics;
- a trainer of teachers or a provider of courses in staff development.

Our comments and advice are based on key research findings. Much of it derives from our own research conducted collaboratively with teachers in real classrooms in real schools. We are both experienced teachers (with 28 years of classroom experience between us) in addition to being established teacher trainers and researchers with international reputations in the area of mathematics education.

The book is strongly influenced by our highly successful PGCE mathematics course which we have taught at the University of Wales Swansea for the last 10 years. The course was declared a 'centre of excellence' by HEFCW in the quality assessment of ITT and was given the highest grading by OHMCI in the 1997–8 inspection.

You can use this book as a practical 'how to do it' guide to help you to learn the art of successful mathematics teaching, but we hope it will also provide critical insights for more experienced teachers reflecting on their practice.

1   The National Curriculum

A framework for teaching

INTRODUCTION

To teach mathematics in schools is a highly creative and complex endeavour. Mathematics is a body of knowledge which, although created by human beings, often seems to have a necessity of its own and to offer access to a truth which many claim to be real and fundamental. Its beauty, elegance, and precision may sometimes appear to be cold or inhuman and yet even very young children can gain great pleasure from working and solving problems within its domain.

Learning is a highly complex process and has characteristics which are both social and individual in nature. Most of us can think back to occasions when we struggled with a piece of mathematics on our own before experiencing a sudden flash of insight and the warm glow of understanding. Mathematical knowledge may often seem to have a highly personal nature as if we had created it for ourselves. However, mathematics is usually taught to large groups of pupils who are asked to arrive at a common understanding of an accepted body of knowledge.

The teacher's creative and demanding role is to mediate between the contrasting demands of mathematical knowledge, the individual pupil, and the social situation to provide a mathematical education which will meet the needs of the individual child today and the adult in a future which we may not know. The complex nature of this task requires the exercise of professional judgement and continuous, on the spot, decision making from a creative teacher in a manner which cannot be prescribed from outside the classroom.

Although teachers rightly exercise a great deal of professional freedom within their classrooms about what and how they teach, they operate within a framework of attainment targets, programmes of study, commercially produced courses and statutory examinations which constrain their choices and focus their attention. In this chapter we will analyse that framework and begin to consider some of the opportunities for effective teaching which are presented. This chapter is introductory in character and many of the issues raised here will be treated in greater depth in following chapters.

Objectives

By the end of this chapter you will:

- understand the structure of the National Curriculum for mathematics, its programmes of study (PoS), attainment targets (ATs) and key stages (KS);
- know the different forms of examination which are commonly in use at ages 16 and 18;
- be developing an awareness of the knowledge and understanding which can reasonably be expected of the average pupil at specific ages;
- be aware of the extent to which the National Curriculum and its associated systems of assessment can form a framework within which professional judgement may be exercised in the development of creative approaches to meet the educational needs of pupils.

AN OVERVIEW OF THE NATIONAL CURRICULUM

The degree of central control over the curriculum and the conduct of teaching has varied considerably, but until the last quarter of the twentieth century the trend was towards local autonomy. For example, following the 1944 Education Act there was only one compulsory subject – religious education. George Tomlinson, Labour Minister of Education from 1947 to 1951 is alleged to have claimed 'The Minister knows nowt about curriculum' (Geen 1998: 1) – a sentiment which many teachers but few Ministers have shared in the years since! Until the 1980s, Ministers concerned themselves with structural issues such as whether or not schools should be comprehensive and left decisions on the curriculum largely to the professionals.

Until quite recently, although the school curriculum was technically in the control of local authorities, in practice it was determined by head teachers in consultation with their governing bodies who could add or remove subjects or topics as they thought appropriate (Geen 1998). During the 1970s, however, a period of growing public disquiet over standards led to the famous 1976 Ruskin College speech by the then Prime Minister James Callaghan. 'The great debate' on education has continued to this day. A major committee of enquiry was set up in 1978 'to consider the teaching of mathematics in primary and secondary schools' which reported 4 years later with recommendations which were reflected in the reforms which followed and may still be seen in the structure of the mathematics curriculum today (Cockcroft 1982).

Governments first began to take central control of teaching and learning in schools during the introduction of the new GCSE examinations. These were first awarded in 1988 and replaced the old O levels and CSEs. This required no legislation because, although the certificates were awarded by independent examination boards, they were countersigned by an Under Secretary in the Department of Education and Science. This previously unrecognized power enabled the then Secretary of State Keith Joseph to influence greatly the nature of the new GCSE. He was thus able to begin to control the curriculum and to some extent the style of teaching in secondary schools through the format of the new examination (Daugherty 1994).

The 1988 Education Reform Act which followed was one of the biggest single pieces of legislation of the twentieth century and provided the legal framework for the National Curriculum. Although the teaching unions were involved in an acrimonious dispute about pay and conditions at the time, both GCSE and the National Curriculum were generally welcomed by the profession in principle, although some were concerned that it was too prescriptive. There were also concerns about practicality because, although the curriculum was intended originally to require only 60 per cent of available time, it demanded that all pupils study ten subjects (eleven in Wales as a consequence of the inclusion of Welsh). As it was phased in during the late 1980s and early 1990s it became increasingly clear that it was overloaded and that some of the suggested plans for its assessment were impractical (Tanner 1992b).

Many amendments were made to the curriculum and its associated assessment during the first few years and, following a union boycott of the assessment arrangements, the Government ordered a full-scale review (Dearing 1993). This resulted in a new, simplified curriculum which was introduced in September 1995 with a promise that in the interests of stability there would be no further change before the year 2000.

The new curriculum for the year 2000 and beyond aims, first, to provide opportunities for all pupils to learn and to achieve and, second, to promote pupils' spiritual, moral, social, and cultural development preparing them for the opportunities, responsibilities, and experiences of life (DfEE/QCA 1999b: Foreword). These two aims are interdependent because, as we will discuss in later chapters, the social and moral development of pupils influences their learning potential significantly. Clearly a centrally imposed curriculum is unable to achieve these aims by itself – motivated, professional teachers with effective practical skills are required to interact with children and mediate between curriculum aims and pupils' individual human needs and ambitions. The curriculum does, however, fulfil four significant purposes:

> to establish an entitlement for all pupils;
> to establish standards and expectations;
> to promote continuity and coherence; and
> to promote public understanding.
> (DfEE/QCA 1999b)

Task 1.1 The scope of the curriculum

The National Curriculum is expressed in terms of subjects. Imagine a typical school week of 25 hours spread over 5 days (i.e. 5 hours per day).

a   Try to decide which subjects you would teach to a middle-ability year-9 class in an inner-city school.

b   Should it make a difference if the class is of very high or very low ability?

c   Should it make a difference if the school is in an affluent suburb?

d   What proportion of the time have you granted to mathematics? How do you justify this?

Advice which had been offered to schools at the start of the decade had empha-sized the rights of all children to access a curriculum which was broad and balanced no matter what their race, class, or sex. Without this entitlement enshrined in law, there was a concern that the curriculum for some pupils might be based on stereotypical and sometimes impoverished expectations. For example, girls might not be encouraged to study physics, boys might not learn foreign languages, inner-city pupils might not be expected to appreciate litera-ture, high-ability pupils might not experience design technology, low-ability pupils might be discouraged from learning about science. Thus the demands of high culture, expressed through a traditional subject structure, are imposed nationally regardless of local conditions.

The National Curriculum does not dictate the hours to be granted to each subject, or even whether the subjects are taught separately from each other, but it does specify an entitlement which should be provided for the vast majority of pupils. In certain circumstances it is possible to 'disapply' up to two specified National Curriculum subjects for any one pupil but in such circumstances the Qualifications and Curriculum Authority (QCA) must be informed.

The curriculum is divided into four key stages associated with various ages and school years. At each key stage certain 'core' and 'foundation' subjects must be studied as shown in Table 1.1.

In addition to the subjects above, all pupils must study religious education. English, mathematics and science are described as 'core' subjects and occupy a privileged place in the curriculum. Pupils are expected to study core courses to GCSE level. In Scotland, Wales, and Northern Ireland different National Curricula apply, reflecting the different cultural aims, ambitions, and contexts of those nations. For example, in Wales, Welsh is a 'core' subject in Welsh medium schools and a foundation subject in all other schools. As control of education has been devolved to the constituent national assemblies of the United Kingdom, further divergence is to be expected in the years to come.

The National Curriculum for mathematics has been the subject of significant disputation and political argument during its short history and consequently has been through several transformations. The disputes still continue and are gener-ally focused on the nature of the subject itself and our aims in teaching it. As men-tioned above, mathematics has a privileged position in the curriculum and it is appropriate for you to pause and consider why that might be.

Task 1.2 Aims of mathematics teaching

This task asks you to consider three issues:

a   Why should mathematics be a core subject?
b   What is mathematics essentially about?
c   What should mathematics teaching emphasize?

The privileged position occupied by mathematics in the national curricula of most

Table 1.1 The core and foundation subjects for each key stage.

Key stage		KS1	KS2	KS3	KS4
Ages		5–7	7–11	11–14	14–16
School years		1–2	3–6	7–9	9–11
English	(Core)	✓	✓	✓	✓
Mathematics	(Core)	✓	✓	✓	✓
Science	(Core)	✓	✓	✓	✓
Design and technology		✓	✓	✓	✓
ICT		✓	✓	✓	✓
History		✓	✓	✓	
Geography		✓	✓	✓	
Modern foreign languages				✓	✓
Art and design		✓	✓	✓	
Music		✓	✓	✓	
Physical education		✓	✓	✓	✓
Citizenship				✓	✓

DfEE/QCA (1999a).

countries is due largely to its perceived usefulness. Unfortunately, since the 1970s, it has become increasingly clear that employers, school inspectors, and others are dissatisfied with the inability of school leavers to transfer the knowledge and skills taught in mathematics lessons to other contexts in the workplace and in everyday life (e.g. DES 1979). Research has shown (Lave 1988; Nunes *et al.* 1993) that in 'real life' situations school-learned procedures are unlikely to be used. Furthermore, much of the mathematics which is taught to all children in secondary schools has no obvious justification in everyday life although it is used as a tool by a minority of students at higher levels. For example: when did you last factorize a quadratic equation in the supermarket?

Mathematics is an essential part of our culture and deserves a place in the curriculum for its own sake. We can enjoy its elegance and beauty in the same way as we might enjoy fine art. Mathematics teaching will have failed if pupils never experience the joy of mathematics. People enjoy solving problems. However, it should not justify its core position on those grounds alone. Mathematics provides a window for looking at the world and a framework for solving problems. In a democratic society all citizens require insight into such processes.

The debate continues to this day between those who see mathematics as a form of high culture, emphasizing abstract algebra and formal proof, focused inwards on itself (e.g. Gardiner in Neumark 1995) and those who see it as a practical and useful human construction gaining its status from its power to explain, organize, and change our world (e.g. Burton 1994). We would not wish to underemphasize either aspect, but we recognize that it is not yet fulfilling its potential as a powerful problem-solving tool for many of our pupils.

The following 'indispensable' aims for teaching mathematics to all pupils (DES 1985) influenced greatly the development of the new GCSE examination and the National Curriculum orders for mathematics. It was suggested that teaching at all levels should offer opportunities for pupils to experience:

mathematics as an essential element of communication;
mathematics as a powerful tool;
an appreciation of relationships within mathematics;
an awareness of the fascination of mathematics;
imagination, initiative, and flexibility of mind in mathematics;
working in a systematic way;
working independently;
working cooperatively;
in-depth study; and
confidence in their own mathematical abilities.

(DES 1985)

The aims were generally well received, although it was clear to many that turning such aims into a practical curriculum was going to require considerable development in school practices.

Like the other academic subjects, mathematics in the National Curriculum is described in terms of PoS and ATs. The PoS set out what should be taught to pupils and the ATs set out expected standards of attainment. The orders are not intended to dictate to schools how to teach the subject or how to arrange their teaching – it is for schools to determine how to plan to include the PoS within their curriculum (DfEE/QCA 1999b). However, although QCA claims that overall the latest programmes of study are less prescriptive, the new mathematics orders are far more detailed than previous orders. Detailed advice about the organization of teaching and learning in primary schools is also provided by the National Numeracy and Literacy Strategies.

Task 1.3 defining the PoS and ATs

For much of its existence mathematics has been expressed through five PoS and four or five ATs.

a   If you were to divide the mathematics curriculum into four or five elements for teaching and assessment, how would you do it? Make a list of your own four or five titles for PoS and ATs.

The earliest version of the orders for mathematics had fourteen PoS and ATs (DES/WO 1989). This unmanageable excess was reduced to five PoS and ATs in the 1991 proposals (DES/WO 1991) and although the format and number of components has changed over the intervening years, the underlying pattern remains. The essential elements of the taught curriculum are: using and applying mathematics, number, algebra, shape and space, and handling data. However, as there is very little algebra towards the lower levels of the NC and there is little number work at the higher levels, practical difficulties soon arose about achieving balance between the elements of the subject in assessment and examination. A single, double-weighted AT for number and algebra was introduced in the 1995

(DFE/WO 1995) orders to account for this. In the latest version of the curriculum in England (but not Wales) the PoS have also been merged. The new mathematics orders in England define the subject as shown in Table 1.2.

Table 1.2 The programmes of study and attainment targets in England.

PoS	Topic	AT
	Using and applying mathematics	Ma1
Ma2	Number and algebra	Ma2
Ma3	Shape, space and measures	Ma3
Ma4	Handling data	Ma4

DfEE/QCA (1999b).

'Using and Applying Mathematics' (known as Ma1 – mathematics attainment target 1) deals with a number of interrelated processes associated with mathematical thinking. These processes underpin both the learning of new mathematics and the application of existing mathematical knowledge to real-life situations (SCAA 1994: 14). At its heart these processes are about problem solving and investigation both in the application of mathematics and within mathematics itself. The aim of this AT was to focus attention on such problem-solving processes as well as on the content of mathematics. The non-statutory guidance for the National Curriculum (CCW 1989) emphasized this dual nature:

> Mathematics is both a body of knowledge and a process of enquiry, a 'product' and a 'process'.
>
> (CCW 1989: A1)

The position and nature of 'Using and Applying Mathematics' was fiercely contested from the outset and remains an area of hot dispute today. The dispute highlights two positions on the nature of mathematics. On the one hand are those who see mathematics as a body of knowledge consisting of facts and rules to learn off by heart and reproduce in examinations. On the other hand are those who see it as a human construction for making sense of the world, emphasizing creativity, investigation, and problem solving. We make no apologies for taking the latter position. Clearly mathematical investigation and problem solving cannot exist in isolation from the body of mathematical knowledge. Unfortunately, however, it is all too possible to teach mathematical content (badly) in such a way that challenging problems, mathematical investigations, and real problems are not experienced. The PoS for Ma1 demanded that pupils be given opportunities to:

a use and apply mathematics in practical tasks, in real-life situations, and in mathematics itself;
b work on problems that pose a challenge;
c encounter and consider different lines of mathematical argument.

(DFE/WO 1995: 11)

Supporters of the existence of a distinct programme of study for Ma1 wished to emphasize the importance of this aspect of mathematics to avoid it being overwhelmed by an emphasis on content alone. The latest version of the National

Curriculum in England (but not Wales) has dropped Ma1 as a PoS, but has retained it as an AT. The new orders include the statements from the old PoS for Ma1 in the context of each of the other PoS. The demands of the AT remain largely unchanged and it begins by emphasizing that attainment should 'be demonstrated through activities in which the mathematics from the other ATs is at, or very close to, the same level' (DfEE/QCA 1999b). Each PoS demands that pupils should be taught to solve problems, communicate mathematically, and develop skills of mathematical reasoning in that area.

Assessment of the National Curriculum in KS1, KS2, and KS3 (key stages) is judged against ATs which describe the knowledge, skills and understanding which pupils of differing ages and abilities might exhibit on a hierarchy of eight levels plus a further level for exceptional performance. The original 1988 design was based on ten levels, but national qualifications such as GCSE and GNVQ are now the main means of assessing attainment in KS4 so the higher levels have been dropped.

Assessment is based on *criterion referencing*. This means that it is based on the fulfilment of specific criteria rather than competition with other pupils. Each level of an AT consists of a series of statements of things pupils can do. Records and evidence of each separate statement of attainment for each pupil are neither desirable nor practical. Teachers should develop familiarity with the statements of attainment at each level so that they can then use their professional judgement to

Task 1.4 Judging an appropriate level for teaching

You require a copy of the National Curriculum for mathematics to complete this task. You may find it at:

>   http://www.accac.org.uk/publications/ncorders.html
>   (Welsh orders)

or   http://www.nc.uk.net (English orders)

In order to begin planning lessons, you must first begin to appreciate the level of prior knowledge which you might be able to expect from your class. Think of a middle-ability class of 11-year-old pupils at the start of year 7. (In most parts of the UK, this will be when they start secondary school.)

a   Write down what you hope that most pupils in the class would be able to do without the help of a teacher in the area of number, fractions, and decimals.

b   Now write down what you think they would be able to do with the help of a teacher during a lesson.

c   Level 4 is the target for the majority of 11-year-old pupils at the end of KS2. Compare your list for (a) with level 4 and your list for (b) with level 5 in the AT for number and algebra.

Table 1.3 Expected range and targets for each key stage.

	KS1	KS2	KS3
Age at end of key stage	7	11	14
Range of levels within which the majority of pupils are expected to work	1–3	2–5	3–7
Expected attainment for the majority of pupils at the end of the key stage	2	4	5/6

DfEE/QCA (1999b).

choose the level description which seems most appropriate at the end of each key stage. This teacher assessment stands as the official record of pupils' attainments in the foundation subjects. In the core subjects, however, the teacher assessment is complemented by externally set and marked tests (Standard Tests or STs). (Teachers still call these tests SATs although the term has been dropped officially following threatened litigation from the USA where the name SAT is copyright.)

The levels cover a wide range of ages and abilities so each level is quite broad. As a rough rule of thumb, each level represents approximately 2 years of development for the average pupil as may be seen in Table 1.3. The level of attainment now expected for the majority of pupils was previously expected of the average pupil and represents a challenging, though realistic target for the profession to achieve.

Level 5/6 is the target for the majority of pupils at the end of KS3. In KS4, although the curriculum is defined by the PoS, assessment is through national examinations: GCSEs, GNVQs, and NVQs.

ASSESSMENT AT 16

In 1986 the GCSE (General Certificate of Secondary Education) was introduced to replace the dual system of the GCE O level (General Certificate of Education Ordinary level) and CSE (Certificate of Secondary Education) examinations. O levels were designed to be taken by approximately the top 25 per cent of pupils in the ability range, and CSE examinations by the next 40 per cent (Cockcroft 1982). O levels were regarded as the high-status examinations as they were required in order to continue to A-level studies and hence to university. CSE was often seen as a second best, and pupils allocated to such groups suffered from a lack of status and motivation. The two examinations had different syllabuses and assessment arrangements and teachers had to decide, often when pupils were just 13 years of age, for which course they should be entered.

A CSE Grade 4, the performance to be expected from a pupil of average ability, could be achieved with only 30 per cent of the marks (Cockcroft 1982). Thus, in order to gain an external qualification in mathematics, many pupils were obliged to study a range of topics which were conceptually too difficult and perhaps inappropriate for them. Cockcroft suggested that lower attaining pupils for whom CSE was not intended should follow a restricted syllabus so that they could develop understanding of their mathematics and confidence in their ability to use it appropriately. It was hoped that pupils who studied a course better matched to their attainment and rate of learning would achieve not only greater self-confidence in their mathematical abilities but also greater mastery of the mathematics (Cockroft 1982: para. 473). Whilst the topics proposed in Cockcroft's Foundation list had a strong emphasis on relevance to everyday life, topics were drawn from many areas of mathematics including geometry and probability.

Some schools adopted the Mode 3 CSE in an attempt to provide their lower attaining pupils with a relevant and worthwhile course. In this version of the examination, schools were able to write their own syllabuses and examination papers to meet the needs and interests of their pupils. Thus teachers at this time could have significant control over the content and assessment procedures of a nationally recognized qualification. Others entered pupils for CSE arithmetic rather than mathematics.

The introduction of the GCSE, however, brought for the first time *national* criteria for the aims, content, assessment objectives, and techniques of an examination at this level. Whilst it was claimed that this had the advantage of standardizing the experiences of pupils (SEC/OU 1986), it reduced teacher influence on the teaching and examination process, and control moved from the teachers and the examination boards to centralized, government-appointed committees.

The original purpose of GCE was to select the brightest pupils in a cohort to proceed to further studies. The examination therefore was designed to discriminate between the candidates and to compare their performance with the mean score or that at any given percentile. In such a norm-referenced system, the grade awarded to a candidate depended to some extent on the performance of the other candidates. In contrast, GCSE aimed to identify what a candidate could do and was intended to be criterion referenced. Detailed statements of attainment were not produced, however, instead a series of grade-related criteria described what was required of candidates achieving certain grades. The grade awarded to a candidate therefore was to be measured against a prespecified standard and would be unaffected by the performance of others.

GCSE introduced a number of innovative assessment practices. It required a widening of assessment techniques to include assessments of a pupil's practical and investigative skills, mental mathematics, and their ability to respond orally to questions and tasks.

> Examinations in mathematics which consist only of timed written papers cannot, by their nature, assess ability to undertake practical and investigational work or ability to carry out work of an extended nature. They cannot assess skills of mental computation or ability to discuss mathematics nor, other than in very limited ways, qualities of perseverance and inventiveness. Work and qualities of this type can only be assessed in the classroom and such assessment needs to be made over an extended period.
>
> (Cockcroft 1982: para. 532)

Mental tests, aural tests, practical and investigational coursework tasks were introduced to complement the written examinations. Coursework tasks could be 'pure investigations' (e.g. what is the connection between the numbers of lines and the number of points of intersection?), or more practical problems such as cal-

O level	CSE	GCSE
A	:	A
B	1	B
C	:	C
D	2	D
E	3	E
:	4	F
:	5	G
:	:	:
U	U	U

Figure 1.1 O levels, CSEs, and GCSEs.

culating the costs and associated profit for an ice-cream stall at a school fete. These tasks were intended to become an integral part of mathematics teaching throughout secondary school. Suitable tasks for GCSE could be set and assessed by the class teacher. Initially, it was possible for coursework to contribute up to 50 per cent of the total mark. More recent changes limit the permitted contribution of coursework to the present 20 per cent, paralleling the 20 per cent of the curriculum assessed by Ma1.

The style of questions in the written examinations also changed from those which were based on the reproduction of memorized algorithms to those which placed a greater emphasis on application of mathematics to contextualized, non-standard problems.

Such requirements reflect a much wider view of mathematics. Mathematics is seen not as a fixed body of knowledge to be transmitted to pupils but as a more creative process in which mathematical thinking is emphasized and an ability to apply mathematics to problems and to real-life situations is required. This view is paralleled in the inclusion of Ma1 in the National Curriculum. However, for some teachers this represented a significant and contentious change in their thinking about the nature of mathematics as a subject. Changes of this nature had been argued for previously with varying degrees of success by, for example, the Cockcroft Report (1982) and DES (1985), but whilst changes in curriculum could be safely ignored by teachers, changes in the ways their pupils were assessed could not (Tanner 1989). Because of the need for development of new teaching and assessment practices to meet these innovations the compulsory use of coursework was delayed until 1991, 3 years after the first written examinations at GCSE. However, although coursework is now a compulsory part of all GCSE schemes, since 1992 an exception has been allowed in mathematics and teachers must choose between coursework and an additional timed written paper.

Mathematics is often thought to be the easiest of all subjects to assess as the answer is either right or wrong, that it cannot depend upon subjective judgement (SED 1979). Questions such as '$7 \times 8 = ?$', or 'solve $x^2 + 5x + 6 = 0$', which require only short, factual answers or the application of an algorithm, can be marked consistently (and quickly). The mark awarded is unlikely to vary irrespective of who actually marked the work. Whilst such questions can be assessed reliably, their validity is limited as they only test lower order skills. The introduction of more open-ended problems where pupils were able to apply a range of approaches increased the validity of the assessment of pupils' mathematics but risked decreasing its reliability. Systems of moderation had to be set up to develop consistency of judgement by teachers who were required to assess their pupils' coursework and to address questions about the appropriateness of a substantial element of the assessment in public examinations being made by teachers (Daugherty *et al.* 1991).

Meetings were held within the school to ensure agreement across the department. External monitoring by the examination boards aimed to ensure consistency of judgements across schools. The introduction of coursework increased the 'backwash validity' of GCSE as such practices were introduced into classroom teaching in preparation for the examination (Wiliam 1992). Thus, as had been intended, the nature of the GCSE examination changed teaching styles in schools (Tanner 1989).

There was no clear policy statement on the range of ability for whom the GCSE was intended (Daugherty *et al.* 1991). If GCSE had been intended merely to replace GCE and CSE with a common examination then it would have applied to pupils in the top 60 per cent of the ability range. As many as 90 per cent of pupils, however, were achieving at least one CSE and so a similar percentage of pupils might have been expected to study for GCSE. In 1999, 88 per cent of 15-year-old pupils in England achieved at least one GCSE, with 48 per cent gaining five or more GCSEs, at grades A*–G (DfEE 1999b).

The GCSE examinations are intended to reward positive achievement: to enable pupils to demonstrate what they do know rather than what they do not. In order for pupils from a wide range of ability to demonstrate achievement

GCSE	NC
A*	10
A	9
B	8
C	7
D	6
E	5
F	4
G	3
U	2
	1

Figure 1.2 GCSE and the National Curriculum. (Source: NCC 1989.)

there has to be some form of differentiation within the syllabus and its assessment. In mathematics, the syllabus and examination papers are 'tiered' to allow pupils to follow a course at an appropriate level. An example of a current tiering system is given in Table 1.4. Only a limited range of grades are available in a tier, and each tier is focused on a target grade which is awarded to candidates who achieve about two-thirds of the marks available. Most pupils therefore may study a course in which they can attain success in the majority of topics.

Table 1.4 Tiering at GCSE.

Tier	Grades
Foundation	D–G
Intermediate	B–E
Higher	A*–C

Adapted from ACAC/SCAA (1995).

The 2000 version of the National Curriculum for England (DfEE/QCA 1999b) reintroduces Cockcroft's suggestion of a restricted syllabus for lower attaining pupils through the division of the mathematics content into higher and foundation sections. Although all pupils are still required to study mathematics until the end of KS4, concerns remain about the suitability of GCSE for lower attaining and less academic pupils. Graduated assessment schemes such as the SMP Green Scheme (SMP 1985) are designed specifically for such pupils. The curriculum is divided into short modules so that short-term targets can be set for pupils. Each module is assessed and the tests can be retaken several times if necessary. The pupils know what is expected of them and can build credit towards their final grade. In some respects this is similar to the recent modularization of A-level courses.

More recent developments in external courses pre-16 include the introduction of General National Vocational Qualifications (GNVQ) into schools. These courses, as their title implies, have a practical application and include such courses as engineering, business, and leisure and tourism. The courses are school based and provide an alternative to purely academic study. They allow certification of knowledge and skills developed in a vocational area. Key skills such as application of number are an integral part of all GNVQs and so provide opportunities for the development and assessment of pupils' mathematical abilities.

For pupils who are working below foundation level, entry-level awards such as the Certificate of Educational Achievement (CoEA) are a meaningful option. These allow accreditation of work at NC levels 1–3 and provide access to the higher level courses.

All courses are now to be subsumed into a National Framework of Qualifications as shown in Table 1.5.

Qualifications post-16

A variety of options now exist for those students who wish to continue their studies post-16. In addition to A levels, from September 2000 students may also study for Advanced Subsidiary (AS) qualifications. An alternative to the academic

Table 1.5 Relationships between families of qualifications.

Levels and qualifications	Entry	Foundation	Intermediate	Advanced	4	5
Vocational	Common	Level-1 NVQ	Level-2 NVQ	Level-3 NVQ	Level-4 NVQ	Level-5 NVQ
General vocational	To all	GNVQ foundation	GNVQ intermediate	GNVQ advanced		
General	Families	GCSE (grades D–G)	GCSE (grades A*–C)	GCE A/AS level		
		←	Key skills		→	

QCA (1999).

pathway offered by AS/A levels is provided by the vocationally orientated GNVQ. The aim of the reforms is to lead to broader A-level programmes and improved vocational qualifications which are underpinned by key skills and rigorous standards (QCA 1999).

The original GNVQ level-3 awards were based on twelve units and were ranked as equivalent to two A levels. Under the new arrangements this linkage is made clearer and in addition to the older twelve-unit awards, GNVQs will also be available as six-unit awards from September 2000. A six-unit award is equivalent to an A level. This is intended to encourage students to mix and match GNVQs with other qualifications, including A levels.

For foundation and intermediate GNVQs, the grades remain as pass, merit, and distinction. At advanced level, an A–E scale is used, comparable with A level. Grade E is broadly equivalent to pass, C to merit, and A to distinction.

Assessment is through a combination of internal and external requirements. Generally, one-third of the overall assessment will be externally set and marked. At advanced level, GNVQs will also be available as three-unit awards, equivalent to an AS level, to encourage students to mix and match GNVQs with other qualifications, or pursue GNVQ study part time, possibly mixed with employment.

From September 2000, each A-level course will contain six units. The first three units, to be taken in the first year of study, will make up an AS course. Unlike the old 'Advanced Supplementary' which was set at A-level standard but on a restricted syllabus, the new AS will be set at a standard to be expected of students at the end of their first year of advanced-level study. Students will be able to study a range of subjects to AS or to A level to broaden and enhance their post-16 studies. The units may be assessed in stages or at the end of the course. All A-level courses must include a final synoptic examination which would normally contribute 20 per cent of the marks. Students will be permitted to resit assessments once only, unlike some current schemes which allow a number of attempts.

Key skills

Key skills are claimed to be the skills needed to succeed in work, education, and everyday life. There are six key skills:

communication;
application of number;
information technology;
working with others;
improving own learning and performance;
problem solving.

Currently, key skills in application of number, communication, and IT are compulsory for all GNVQ students. However, in future all post-16 qualifications must include opportunities to develop the students' key skills of communication, application of number, and IT.

A new qualification in key skills is to be awarded for the first time from September 2000 and is open to all post-16 students, trainees, and employees in schools, colleges, training organizations, and at work. It will be awarded to candidates who achieve a pass in the three key skills of communication, application of number and information technology at any level from 1 to 4. The award will be profiled to show what each candidate knows, understands, and can do in each skill.

AS/A-level mathematics

The last awards of the old style A and AS syllabuses will be made in August 2001. The new mathematics courses are based on a modular structure set within the three broad areas of pure mathematics, mechanics and statistics. A wide range of combinations of units is allowed within these areas. The pattern offered by WJEC (Welsh Joint Education Committee) is typical; 6 units are offered in pure mathematics, 3 units in mechanics, 3 in statistics and 1 in mechanics and statistics. Allowable combinations of 3 units lead to AS level and 6 units to A level. A range of subject titles is available according to the units selected. The study of additional units can lead to further AS level and further A level awards.

Task 1.6 Understanding the new courses in mathematical subjects at A and AS levels

Examine the details of the units available and the allowable combinations in the WJEC system. You will find specifications and specimen materials at:

http://www.wjec.co.uk/gmaths.html

Study the precise syllabus requirements and in particular consider the position of proof and the attitude to calculators.

The syllabuses are very similar in content to current courses. There is an emphasis on being able to apply pure mathematics to problems and to model situations. However, there is a much greater emphasis on the capacity to develop increasingly rigorous arguments and proofs. The use of calculators is restricted to simple scientific devices in some papers (pure 1 and 2) with graphical calculators allowed elsewhere (see appendix three of the document for details). The appropriate use of technology is encouraged during teaching but restricted in examinations.

Modular courses are available in which students are able to gain credit during the course, but at least 20 per cent of each scheme is allocated to a synoptic assessment which addresses the candidates' understanding of the connections between the different aspects of the course. The motivational impact and the improvement in attainment for modular courses is now well documented (WJEC 1999).

CONCLUSION

The mathematics education community has experienced a period of considerable change over the last two decades. Those of us who lived through the period probably remember it as a period of almost continuous change, confusion, and political interference. However, the end result is not as bad as many of us had feared, and in very many ways represents a significant improvement over the old system of GCEs and CSEs which rejected or ignored roughly 25 per cent of the population producing large numbers of unmotivated and eventually unqualified young people.

Many of us regret the passing of teachers' professional power and regard the development of strong central control of the curriculum and its assessment as dangerously totalitarian. However, in the end, teaching is an essentially human pursuit which remains out of the direct control of the bureaucrats and pen-pushers. Teaching remains a highly creative and complex endeavour and we march to higher orders than those found in National Curriculum documents. In the end we are driven by the needs of the children in our care and we teach only that which we feel will benefit them.

Many of the structural changes which have been made to courses and examinations over the last two decades have helped to improve the quality of the mathematical learning experience for large numbers of pupils. We summarize a few below.

Summary

- Far more children now have the opportunity to access a broad and balanced curriculum;
- there has been an increase in the opportunities for pupils to acquire formal certification of their achievements;
- an increased emphasis on positive achievement rather than failure;
- more appropriate courses have been developed for the less able;
- far more young people are being motivated and challenged by examinations;
- far more young people are now able to leave school with a sense of achievement having gained appropriate qualifications;
- within mathematics, a focus on mathematical processes and not just the memorization of knowledge has made courses more relevant and interesting;
- in particular, far more young people are developing a confidence in their ability to use the mathematics which they know to solve problems in real-life situations, and also in order to learn further mathematics.

2 What makes a good mathematics lesson?

INTRODUCTION

Debates over the nature of good mathematics teaching are as old as teaching itself and, in spite of government pronouncements to have found the philosopher's stone of perfect school organization and classroom pedagogy, are likely to continue for as long as schools exist. This is partly because there is no consensus about what it means to be a mathematically educated adult and partly because of the very nature of teaching and learning. Teachers and learners are individuals with their own backgrounds, personalities, and ambitions. Methods which work well for one teacher sometimes fail for another. The preferred style of learning for one pupil may be different from that of another. An approach which works well with most of a class may fail totally for a significant minority. Good teachers cater for the needs of individuals as well as groups by continuously modifying their approaches in response to the feedback they are receiving from learners.

However, although we must be cautious about describing the nature of good mathematics teaching because of the limitations expressed above, educational research has provided clear evidence from a variety of different sources about a number of features and approaches which are common to most successful lessons. For the last 15 years our own research has been focused on teaching and learning in mathematics classrooms (e.g. Tanner and Jones 1994a, b, 1995a, 1997, 1999a, b). We have analysed and recorded interactions between teachers and pupils in hundreds of classrooms and in this chapter we will try to lead you to understand why some particular teaching activities should be described as good practice.

Objectives

By the end of this chapter you should:

- be aware of two different types of mathematical understanding – relational and instrumental – and their characteristic features;
- know how different forms of learning lead to different forms of understanding;
- be aware of the different characteristic elements which constitute mathematical knowledge and how different teaching and learning approaches are appropriate for their development;

- understand why certain key elements should be present in effective mathematics teaching at all levels.

UNDERSTANDING AND MATHEMATICS

Mathematics is a difficult subject to learn, and an even more difficult subject to teach well. This is partly because it has many hierarchical characteristics, which often demand a familiarity with lower level concepts and skills before more advanced ones may be grasped (Cockcroft 1982: para 228). In fact, learning a new piece of mathematics often seems to demand that a previous skill has been learned to the point of *automaticity*. By automaticity we mean that the answer to a question leaps into the learner's mind without conscious effort or strategy on their part.

Task 2.1 Simplifying fractions

Imagine that you are being taught to simplify fractions.
  Simplify the fraction 49/63.
  How did you do it?
  If you said divide numerator and denominator by 7, ask yourself how you worked out that 7 was the common factor.

The last question may well be difficult to answer as many readers will have experienced the number 7 coming to mind involuntarily. However, pupils or readers who have not yet developed their multiplication number bonds to the point of automaticity will not have experienced this. For these learners, an explanation from a teacher that both the numerator and denominator will divide by 7 may well only lead to the response 'Where did the 7 come from?'.

Mathematics is also difficult because it is about solving problems (Cockcroft 1982). We define a problem as being a situation which one cannot solve immediately by a routine process. A problem is thus solver and situation specific. For those pupils who do not know multiplication number bonds automatically, simplifying 49/63 may be a problem, although for you it was probably routine. In problem situations, knowing how to get started is often one of the most difficult parts of the problem. Fortunately if pupils understand the concept of dividing numerator and denominator by the same number to simplify a fraction, there is a general strategy which they may have met in other contexts which will eventually lead to solution. They may recognize that they can work systematically and exhaustively beginning with simple cases first; that is, try division by 2 then 3, (4), 5, (6), 7... This will eventually lead to a solution although it is not the most efficient approach. They may even bring their knowledge of factors into play and realize that if dividing by 2 failed then there is no need to try 4 or 6 thus improving their efficiency.

Clearly, there is a real advantage in skills being automatic when they are being used in work at a higher level, but even in the case of the very simple illustration used above it is clear that there are other aspects to the learning of mathematics than the application of automatic skill.

Task 2.2 Simplifying bigger fractions

Simplify the fraction 6890/7420.
Make a note of the strategies you tried – even if you abandoned them.

We imagine that this example began to take on some of the characteristics of a problem for many readers. Some may have used systematic working. Others may have chosen to decompose into prime factors first. Many will have resorted to using a calculator. Some readers will have known a routine process to follow at once but many others will have used a mixture of formal and informal approaches. Others will have considered the problem boring and, having failed to engage with it at an emotional level, just read straight on. Clearly doing mathematics is a much more complicated process for most people than just following the routines they learned in school. There are conceptual, strategic, and emotional considerations involved in bringing knowledge and skills into use in problem situations. Teaching must take these considerations seriously if mathematics is to justify its claims as a useful subject.

Several of the respondents to the Cockcroft Committee of Enquiry into Mathematics Teaching suggested a return to techniques of rote learning. This was defined as being 'in a mechanical manner, by routine ... without proper understanding' and was soundly rejected by the Committee who believed that it should never be necessary 'to commit things to memory without at the same time seeking to develop a proper understanding' (Cockcroft 1982: para 238). Given our earlier emphasis on the importance of developing automaticity in the use of some mathematical skills we need to consider the nature and significance of mathematical understanding.

Mathematical understanding is difficult to define precisely in any given context. It is an internal state of mind, usually held to a degree rather than absolutely and cannot be viewed directly. We infer that pupils understand concepts when they answer particular questions correctly, but we are never absolutely certain that misconceptions do not remain untouched beneath the surface. The depth of understanding which is challenged by a question depends on the extent to which the question parallels examples used during instruction. Although it is generally accepted that understanding a concept implies an ability to make use of it in a variety of settings, including unfamiliar or problem situations (Cockcroft 1982: para 231), practices in many classrooms and the construction of exercises in some textbooks suggests either that understanding is not sought or that alternative interpretation is being placed on the word (Cornelius 1985; Tanner 1989).

Two distinct interpretations of mathematical understanding are suggested by Skemp (1976) in his seminal article: 'Relational understanding and instrumental understanding'. The difference between the two forms is illustrated through analogy with different forms of knowledge of the geography of a locality. Instrumental understanding is equivalent to knowing large numbers of fixed local plans, whereas relational understanding is equivalent to having a mental map of the town. In instrumental mathematics:

> what has to be done next is determined purely by the local situation. (When you see the post office turn left) ... In contrast, learning relational mathematics consists of building up a conceptual structure (or schema) from which its possessor can (in principle) produce an unlimited number of plans for getting from any starting point within his schema to any finishing point.
>
> (Skemp 1976: 25)

Classrooms in which teachers aim for instrumental understanding have very different characteristics from those aiming at relational understanding. Some of the features are listed in Table 2.1 based on Skemp's (1976) comments and our observations of lessons.

The value of relational understanding in problem solving is self-evident. However, quick results, in terms of recall, are certainly obtained by teachers who aim for instrumental understanding using drill-and-practice methods, divorced from application. However, this is almost certainly at the expense of adaptability to new tasks, and it is adaptability which is at a premium in real-life problem solving.

Both forms of understanding are still to be found in mathematics classrooms today, in spite of years of advice from inspectors, advisors, and teacher trainers that instrumental understanding is far too limited an objective for education (e.g. Cockcroft 1982; DES 1985; NCC 1989; DFE/WO 1995; Straker 1997).

There are several reasons for the persistence of instrumental mathematics in schools. Three are listed by Skemp (1976):

1   Within its own context, instrumental mathematics is usually easier to understand ...
2   So the rewards are more immediate and more apparent ...
3   Because less mathematics is involved one can often get the right answer more quickly.

> (Skemp 1976: 23)

However, instrumental mathematics succeeds *only* in its own context. When a new problem is met, pupils are lost. It is difficult to apply outside school because real-life problems are messy and not formulated like school questions. It doesn't even work very well in examinations. Certainly since the introduction of GCSE and National Curriculum testing, examiners have become quite skilled at asking questions which probe for a deeper understanding, leaving children who have only an instrumental understanding totally lost. Consider, for example, this assessment of basic numeracy which is typical of KS2 formal examinations:

$$
\begin{array}{r}
23 * 5 \\
-1 * 87 \\
\hline
738
\end{array}
$$

Table 2.1 Distinctive features of instrumental and relational classrooms.

Instrumental	*Relational*
Maths is a series of rules, laws or algorithms to remember by heart	Maths is about relationships and asking "Why?" or "What if . . .?"
This is the rule . . . Now do twenty of the same sort to make it stick	Examples are not all the same – there is a slightly new trick each time
Good teachers tell you how to do each step of the procedure	Good teachers ask you what you think the next step ought to be
There isn't any time for practical work: just learn the rule	Practical tasks are used to develop understanding
Pupils ask "Show me one like it" at the start of every new exercise	Pupils ask "Does that work for negative numbers too?"
When pupils meet a new sort of problem they don't know what to do	New sorts of problem are met every day and pupils have a range of strategies to help them cope

Pupils who have learned a standard algorithm for subtraction without considering *why* it worked or developing any sense of place value would be unable to cope no matter how efficient they were at repeating the standard procedure in class.

We have recently studied classroom practices in twenty schools in South Wales which were identified as performing much better than would be expected using value-added measures of performance. In essence, we selected the schools to study by looking at the standard of pupils on entry and predicting what their performance should be on exit based on national norms. We found that, amongst other factors, particularly successful schools emphasized relational rather than instrumental understanding (Tanner *et al.*, 1999).

One possible explanation for the continuation of instrumental approaches in spite of the evidence and advice is that some teachers experienced nothing better when they were pupils and have only a limited understanding of mathematics themselves. Under pressure of examinations and a desire to demonstrate that they have completed the syllabus, some teachers and textbooks occasionally resort to instrumental approaches, particularly when a mathematically valid justification appears to be too complex for the pupils in question. For example, consider this division of fractions example taken from a popular series of books.

Task 2.3 Dividing fractions

To divide one fraction by another, turn the second fraction upside down and multiply:

$$\frac{5}{8} \div \frac{3}{4} = \frac{5}{8} \times \frac{4}{3} = \frac{5}{2} \times \frac{1}{3} = \frac{5}{6}$$

Consider how you would respond if a pupil asked 'Why do we turn the second one upside down?'

Do you know a sensible answer or a better way to do it?

Now try and think of an example of division of fractions being used in a real-life context.

Many readers of this book will have been happily turning upside down and multiplying for years without considering why. However, if the teaching of fractions is approached in an instrumental manner it generates a large number of rules which have to be accepted without understanding, almost as if they had appeared by magic. Unfortunately, when the basis for rules is magic rather than understanding, the danger is that pupils forget them, confuse them with each other and apply them in inappropriate contexts. Detailed large-scale studies of children's errors and misconceptions which were conducted in the 1970s and 1980s, when the instrumental teaching of the four rules of fractions was common, revealed this to be the case (Hart 1981; Foxman 1985). These studies revealed also that only 30 per cent of 15-year-old pupils were able to calculate:

$$3/4 \div 1/8$$

even though this example may be solved by informal methods.

From the beginning of the National Curriculum the real difficulty of the topic was recognized and multiplication and division of fraction by fraction was removed from the curriculum of most pupils in KS3 by setting 'calculating with fractions' at level 8. However, recently reactionary political forces have insisted on its return to the KS3 programme of study for teaching although it does not appear directly within the attainment targets for assessment.

We doubt, incidentally, if any readers managed to think of an example of division of fractions in a real-life context. When we ask this question of non-mathematicians we usually receive an answer of the form 'What is 1/3 of 21?' which is of course, a multiplication, demonstrating a misconception.

There seems little point in teaching such a topic without aiming for understanding. The instrumental approach we offered above is based on the properties of the multiplicative inverse and teachers have often considered this to be too hard to explain to Y7. However, it is not necessary to abandon our aim to teach for relational understanding. In most topics it is usually possible to find an approach which is intellectually honest and understandable. As you may not have seen an approach based on a relational approach, we offer one here which we have found to be successful.

Example

$\dfrac{5/8}{3/4}$ Multiply numerator and denominator by 4 to simplify the denominator

$\dfrac{5/2}{3}$ Multiply top and bottom by 2 to simplify the numerator

$5/6$ is the answer

This approach has the advantage of using and reinforcing one of the key concepts in fractions, namely leaving a fraction unchanged if the numerator and denominator are multiplied by the same number. It resonates with techniques used in other areas of mathematics such as multiplying both sides of the equation by a common factor leaving the equality unchanged. Because of its association with preexisting knowledge and strategies, it is likely to contribute towards the development of interconnected and organized information which is less likely to be forgotten or wrongly remembered. It is the interconnectedness of information that builds secure knowledge. Relational approaches are based on the development of interconnected knowledge structures based on big ideas rather than large quantities of trivial content (Glaser 1995; Prawat 1991).

Developing interconnected knowledge structures

Unfortunately, the development of such interconnected structures is more easily said than done and we have a great deal of evidence that teaching often fails to make contact with the learner's preexisting knowledge. In such cases, knowledge is sometimes built upon weak foundations and not really believed or used outside of school. Research shows that children have conceptual frameworks or models which are often independent of the teaching to which they have been exposed and that these intuitive or naive structures can be both very different from 'official' models and very resistant to change (Berry and Graham 1991; Pozo and Carretero 1992). For example, when Berry and Graham (1991) presented sixth-form students with 'concept questions' which challenged them because of their slightly unusual format, many of them resorted to 'common sense' or naive approaches which bore no relation to the mathematics they were able to use successfully when answering standard problems. It is worth briefly considering at this point what might be happening as children meet new information and construct new knowledge.

The psychology of Piaget uses the term 'assimilation' to describe the process by which individuals perceive new information. During assimilation a learner perceives information using a preexisting conceptual structure. Assimilation, thus, always reduces new experiences to already-existing conceptual structures (Piaget 1972, 1980a, b). Learners try to resolve differences between their old ideas and new ones without conceptual change if possible. They would like to maintain their old ideas as well as taking on the new ones. An individual might choose to ignore or distort the properties of the new ideas to avoid change, leading to the continuation of naive concepts after teaching. However, the need for ideas to make sense is a strong motivator. If the discrepancy or 'perturbation' between the old structure and the new is too great, learners may modify their mental structures to take account of the new – this is known as 'accommodation' and is the mechanism by which significant new knowledge is constructed.

As such new constructions are created, the learner needs to test them for viability in the real world or the classroom. This might be done in several ways; for example, by comparing ideas about the knowledge with the teacher's ongoing explanation, by putting the knowledge forward as a question for the teacher to rule on, by using the new knowledge to answer a teacher's question or by successfully using it to solve the questions in an exercise. Such restructuring and viability testing is hard work and learners sometimes avoid possible problems by choosing to keep school work and real life as separate systems. Inconsistencies will only be perceived through a process of reflection. Reflection is thus at the heart of the thinking process.

Some learners are naturally 'mindful' and choose to reflect as a matter of personal style (Salomon and Globerson 1987); others only reflect when teachers create occasions for collective reflection (Cobb *et al.*, 1997; Tanner and Jones 2000). That such reflection often does not occur is well documented (e.g. Lave 1988; Berry and Graham 1991). The physical world, the social world outside school, and school-taught mathematics often remain discrete and sometimes incompatible subsystems.

TEACHING AND LEARNING THE ELEMENTS OF MATHEMATICS

It is worth noting that whilst some aspects of mathematics require deep reflection and mental restructuring other aspects of mathematics require different approaches. Mathematical knowledge includes a number of distinct aspects or elements which require different teaching approaches to develop to best effect. Cockcroft (1982) divided the subject up into facts, skills, conceptual structures, and general strategies. This was taken further by DES (1985) who added personal qualities and attitudes. We continue by considering mathematics teaching and learning under five headings: facts and conventions, skills and routines, conceptual structures, techniques and results, mathematical processes and thinking.

Facts and conventions

The essential feature of this form of mathematical knowledge is its essentially arbitrary nature. We include here conventions such as pound being written as lb or facts such as $2.2\,\text{lb} = 1\,\text{kg}$ which describe the relationship between essentially arbitrary conventional systems. Some definitions fall into this category, such as the ratio definitions of sine, cosine, and tangent in a right-angled triangle, and although there is a conceptual structure associated with the use of the knowledge, the definition is essentially arbitrary or, as in this case, historical. Such facts and conventions must be learned in such a way that their retrieval is automatic in appropriate circumstances. Mnemonic devices for learning such facts include rhymes and doggerel such as:

2.2 pounds of strawberry jam weighs about a kilogram

which has the advantage of linking the numbers to an imagined real-world situation where the information might be required. Other devices include nonsense words such as:

SOHCAHTOA

to remind pupils of the definitions:

$$\sin \alpha = \frac{\text{opposite}}{\text{hypotenuse}}, \quad \text{etc.}$$

It is important to help the learner to associate the chosen mnemonic with the situation in which it might be used. SOHCAHTOA is no use without knowledge of the association between sides and letters. Thus it should be learned in tandem with the lettering convention for right-angled triangles.

Even though learning such facts requires no conceptual development, effort is still required on the part of the learner. Pupils will not make the effort unless they are motivated to do so. Most teachers use short tests or quizzes in combination with rewards and punishments to ensure that the effort is made. One strategy which we have often found to be effective is to invite pupils to invent their own mnemonics along the lines of 'Some old horses can always hear their owners' approach', 'Silly old Harry climbed a high tree of apples', etc., and offer a prize to the pupil producing the best mnemonic and poster diagram.

The facts and conventions considered so far have been arbitrary. There are other conventions which are either not arbitrary or which have a conceptual aspect to them. For example, a negative number multiplied by a negative number is positive. When asked by a group of teachers to provide a metaphor to justify $-1 \times -3 = +3$ Lerman (1999) replied 'What else could it be?'. Our number system is defined in this way in order to preserve pattern and to extend the laws that hold for the natural numbers to the integers. If presented with the question in the right way, even quite young children are able to arrive at the same conclusion. It is an important lesson to learn that definitions are made with a sense of pattern in mind.

Example

$$3 \times -3 = -9$$
$$2 \times -3 = -6$$
$$1 \times -3 = -3$$
$$0 \times -3 = 0$$
$$-1 \times -3 = ?$$

What would you like the next answer to say?
   Well, let's define it that way.

Similarly, although the order of operations when calculating is a matter of convention rather than mathematical necessity, there is a logic to the order, with the more powerful operations taking priority. This is the point at which we think the use of mnemonics becomes dubious. BODMAS (Brackets, Of, Division, Multiplication, Addition, Subtraction) strikes us as a mnemonic which reduces a principled operation to mindless rule following.

Skills and routines

Skills and routines are the well-established procedures or algorithms which we use again and again. Examples include operations with basic number facts and the standard algorithms for basic arithmetic. They are so familiar to us that we use them automatically and with little or no conscious effort, but they are not arbitrary. They include the basic skills beloved of politicians, but may include a lot more besides. For example, there are many routine procedures which occur in algebra. The solution of linear simultaneous equations or differentiation of polynomials is probably routine for many readers of this book.

Information-processing models of cognition compare the human mind with a computer and talk of our long-term memory consisting of unlimited amounts of organized knowledge which we pull into short-term memory for processing. Research has demonstrated that the capacity of our short-term memory is quite limited – perhaps between four and seven items (Simon 1978, 1980, 1989). As we suggested earlier in the chapter, we often work very efficiently when we are able to conduct some of our operations automatically, leaving our limited cognitive processing capability free to focus on other aspects of a task. As we develop as mathematicians, procedures and techniques which used to demand our full conscious control are reduced to automatic routines. It must be an aim of mathematics teaching to ensure that such automatization occurs.

However, as we also indicated above, mere routine following is not sufficient for problem solving, the real-life application of knowledge, or the development of new knowledge. The pupil must also be able to deconstruct routines back to their fundamental principles, returning the process to conscious control to modify and adapt it when necessary.

Thus teaching approaches must include two elements: relational understanding and practice. In order to be of use, skills and routines must be practised in a range of situations, where they might commonly be applied. Therefore we would suggest that pupils should not be asked to practise the same sort of example twenty times, but rather to practise the skill or routine in as many different contexts as possible, requiring the use of conscious control rather than rote learning. Furthermore, as far as possible, the focus of the teaching should be on the principle which is being applied, not the routine which is being followed. As well as routine procedures, we must help children to develop conceptual structures.

All too often, teachers who wish to offer pupils immediate success take the approaches such as mnemonics and rote-learning techniques which are appropriate for teaching arbitrary knowledge and apply them in situations where the development of deep conceptual structures should be our aim.

For example, we have met many teachers using the mnemonic FOIL to teach multiplication of brackets in algebra such as: $(a + b)(c + d) = ac + ad + bc + bd$. FOIL stands for First, Outer, Inner, Last and allows the pupil to decide which terms to multiply without thinking mathematically or developing any principled knowledge. Like most instrumental approaches it succeeds in its own context for as long as the question is formulated exactly as expected. Unfortunately when the same children are asked to expand $(a + b)(c + d + e)$ they often get the wrong answer $ac + ae + bc + be$. The principle involved is that each term in the first bracket must be multiplied by each term in the second – and that works in all cases. Good teaching of skills and routines focuses on the teaching of principles and conceptual structures not just skills and routines.

Conceptual structures

Conceptual structure has two different meanings in this context (cf. Backhouse *et al.* 1992). First, there are the key ideas of mathematics such as: factor, multiple, tangent, derivative, etc. along with the processes associated with them such as divide, multiply, differentiate, etc. These are usually defined in mathematics according to a convention. However, it should be noted that the tidy and rigorous definitions are very much the finished product of mathematical activity and have often been arrived at only after much modification (Lakatos 1976).

Second, to a psychologist, conceptual structures must be constructed by the learner and interconnect elements of knowledge. The term used by Piaget, Skemp and others is 'schema' (plural schemata). A schema is a more or less coherent collection of mental objects and the processes for manipulating them (Dubinsky 1991) along with some sense of the range of contexts in which they might be applied.

Teachers come to the classroom armed with the official language, definitions, and structure of mathematics. They know the words, their meanings, and how to use them in speech and action. Pupils, on the other hand, come with a variety of naive common-sense structures, individual misconceptions, and their own language which is sometimes very limited. How do they communicate?

Slightly different positions on how this interaction occurs are taken by the schools of psychology based on Piaget and Vygotsky. Piaget's approach is summed up as:

The mind organises the world by organising itself.

(Piaget 1937: 311)

As we discussed earlier in this chapter, Piaget's emphasis is on individual learners organizing their own thought structures. They will not learn just because they have copied down a mathematical definition. Learners have to consider how the new information fits into what they already know and, if necessary, amend their existing knowledge to make sense of it. This requires effort from the learner. Although teachers can signal which aspects of the information to consider, only the learner can *decide to make the effort* to do the necessary reflection and restructuring. It is an illusion that ideas, concepts, and even whole chunks of knowledge can be transported from a speaker to a listener.

Even if a teacher has provided a clear and accurate exposition of a concept, we can never be sure that the learner has read the intended meanings into the words which were used. We impose our own meanings on whatever others say or write (von Glasersfeld 1991: xiv).

Vygotsky (1962) emphasizes the role of language in the learning process. He suggests that although teachers cannot transmit their concepts directly to the learners, children form their own meanings around the words teachers use. These meanings are then compared with the teacher's official interpretations during discussion and questioning.

This process often *appears* to be one of negotiation whilst the learners construct and reconstruct their own meanings as they test their ideas, intuitions, and half-formed concepts against the teacher's official version.

Even when an official definition is presented to pupils, perhaps in the form of a note, the meaning or sense which pupils make of it will depend on what they already know. From a pupil's perspective, a definition will be 'meaningful, connected, and easy to learn' only if the pupil 'already knows enough about its contents to provide connections', and is able to use familiar facts and images to make the meaning apparent (Howe 1999: 70). This usually means that examples of the use of the concept have to be experienced in a familiar context before the definition begins to make sense.

Concept development usually moves through three stages: the enactive, the iconic, and the symbolic (Bruner 1968). In the first stage, pupils build on knowledge which is concrete in that it is secure or well known or perhaps founded in the physical world through the use of materials which can be manipulated. The iconic stage involves diagrams or internal pictures, or a sense of pattern by means of which we can see relationships. Finally, the symbolic stage is reached in which generalizations are achieved through the use of symbols.

You can help pupils by showing them how to connect the knowledge to be acquired to what they already know. What is needed are activities which connect readily to a pupil's assumed secure knowledge but are also conceptually linked to the new material. The key idea is to build up from the child's preexisting knowledge. The following example illustrates a logical progression for pupil tasks within a lesson aiming to develop understanding about volume of a prism (see also Chapter 3).

Example

A sequence of pupil tasks to develop understanding about volume of a prism:

1   Use multilink cubes in small groups to produce prisms of specific dimensions and count cubes to find volume (Enactive).

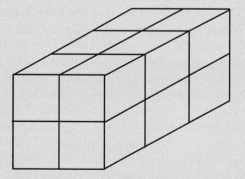

Figure 2.1 Making cuboids.

2　From diagrams of prisms which have dimensions too big to make sensibly in class, calculate volumes from the patterns identified in 1 (Iconic).

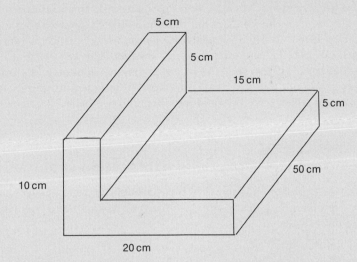

Figure 2.2 Calculating volumes.

3　Justify in words why the calculation used should give the correct answer. Generalize to any prism and write in words and symbols (Symbolic).

Write a definition of a prism and modify in discussion to improve rigour.

Clearly, some children would begin with a higher level of preexisting knowledge than others and be able to miss out steps. It is worth noting, however, that we think that the formal-concept definition should be the last element in the chain and not the first.

Good teachers do not tell pupils too much directly. Exposition by the teacher in the literal sense of exposing the subject has its place in the teacher's repertoire; for example, when summarizing, providing an overview for the lesson, or offering a mathematical argument which pupils are not yet able to make for themselves. Exposition provides pupils with an opportunity to hear mathematical language used precisely in context. However, it should be used sparingly as a means of telling because too much exposition can leave you talking to yourself rather than your class.

We distinguish here between telling by *exposition* and telling by *explanation* (see Love and Mason 1992, 1995). During exposition, pupils listen to the words of the teacher. During explanation, teachers listen to the words of pupils and build on them. Teachers ask questions during explanations in order to find out what their pupils are currently thinking so that they can base their next utterance on the pupils' responses. This is what makes explanation hard for novice teachers. In explanation you have to listen to pupils and respond, not just plough on through a prepared lecture. We will discuss how teachers can manage this while leading a whole class in Chapter 5.

Good teachers prepare themselves by setting up linking tasks to prompt perturbations and then give pupils a chance to try out their half-formed ideas without fear of humiliation. They listen to what pupils say, focus on key aspects, rephrase comments which are unclear, and adapt pupils' answers. The key element of an explanation is that it works from the bottom up, beginning from a child's current level of understanding and leading them forwards. Consequently, pupils build conceptual structures which have personal meaning and are believed rather than just known.

Task 2.4 Observing explanation

Ask your mentor to identify a teacher who is particularly good at explanation. Arrange to observe a lesson with the intention of analysing how new concepts are developed.

Make a note of the following:

- questions which aim to identify prior knowledge;
- questions or tasks which aim to link prior knowledge to the new material;
- any physical equipment, visual aid, or practical activity used to link the new material to real-world knowledge;
- occasions when pupils are given an opportunity to explain or justify an idea to others, either in a group or to the whole class.

Ask the teacher to explain why that approach was taken.

Techniques and results

Techniques are standard procedures for solving classes of mathematical problem which still demand a significant amount of conscious control in operation. Examples include the solution of simultaneous linear equations, using trigonometry to find missing sides in right-angled triangles, or integration by parts. As mentioned earlier, whether a particular procedure is a technique requiring significant conscious control or a standard routine requiring little conscious effort will depend on the individual, but in all cases our intention is to reduce techniques to routines in the longer term.

Results are statements connecting concepts which are so significant that we require pupils to memorize them. Some results are so significant as to have the title 'theorem' (e.g. Pythagoras' theorem). Others are not so grand, but are no less necessary, such as $\frac{1}{2} = 0.5$. The National Curriculum for England (DfEE/QCA 1999b) and the National Numeracy Strategy (DfEE 1999a) include detailed lists of results like this which are non-arbitrary but should be learned by heart so that they can be treated as facts. Caution is needed here. If too much priority is placed on the learning of such non-arbitrary results as if they were arbitrary conventions, there is a danger of a return to a level of meaningless rote learning not seen since the nineteenth century.

It is important to remember that whilst the knowledge that $\frac{3}{8} = 0.375$ might confer a marginal advantage in mathematical efficiency in very specific circumstances, it will confer no such advantage without a corresponding relational understanding of the nature of fractions and decimals. Although it is often useful to reduce many of the results we have derived to the level of facts and to reduce the techniques we are developing to the level of routines, this is not the real business of mathematics teaching. We automatize in order to free our minds to use mathematics in the solution of problems and for that we often need a sufficiently deep conceptual understanding of the results and processes to be able to deconstruct them for use in changed circumstances. Mathematics is rarely only about getting an answer to a problem – mathematics is about getting answers and being able to justify why the answer is correct.

When teaching techniques we need to consider three aspects of understanding: first, when to use it; second, how to use it; and third, why it works. Similarly when teaching results we need to consider three aspects of understanding: first, it must connect with pupils' schemata; second, we must consider the context in which it might be used; and third, we must convey why the result is correct.

Mathematical processes and thinking

In recent years, mathematical reasoning and proof has received less emphasis in the secondary-school curriculum than it deserves. However, it is a key aspect of mathematical thinking and forms a significant part of Attainment Target 1 (AT1) which represents one of the three process strands in each programme of study (PoS).

The three strands are: problem solving, communicating, and reasoning. In addition to its focus on the strategies and processes of problem solving and the development of mathematical language and communication, AT1 describes targets for the development of formal ideas of reasoning and proof. Even at level 2, the average 7-year-old is expected to be able to 'explain why an answer is correct'. By level 7, 16-year-old pupils are expected to:

> justify their generalisations, arguments or solutions, showing some insight into the mathematical structure of the problem. They appreciate the difference between mathematical explanation and experimental evidence.
>
> (DfEE/QCA 1999b: 87)

Formal mathematical proof is a difficult concept to grasp, and we progress towards it in stages which are illustrated within AT1. At the lowest level we should be ensuring that pupils at least verify that a result is correct by testing it on a particular case. They should then be encouraged to extend testing to a range of cases, choosing values with some sense of intuition, such as: does it work for zero, negative numbers, rational numbers, non-right-angled triangles, etc.?

Some results may be approached through the process of inductive generalization. For example, pupils drawing triangular numbers (1, 3, 6, 10, 15,

21 ...) may often be led to recognize that the formula $n(n + 1)/2$ seems to work for all the cases they have drawn so far. They may then hypothesize that it will fit with larger numbers and test their hypothesis on a few further cases. However, it is important for pupils to realize that satisfying a large number of cases does not constitute proof for all cases. However, it is possible to prove this contention through the use of a diagram:

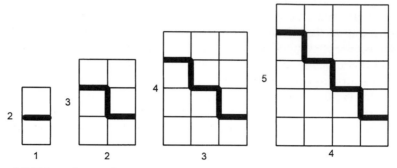

Figure 2.3 Triangular numbers.

Teachers can justify rules to pupils at a range of levels. At the lowest level a result may be demonstrated. Inductive generalization may be very convincing and provide useful insights and number sense, but it does not constitute a proof. Although pupils might not be able to produce a formal proof of a result for themselves, a teacher might often be able to lead pupils to understand a proof and the nature of proof itself.

For example, consider the result that the angle sum of a triangle is 180°. This is often introduced to pupils in years 6 or 7 by tearing the corners off randomly drawn triangles and demonstrating that the angles fit together on a straight line. This is demonstration and not proof, although few pupils realize this. An alternative approach which leads towards an understanding of proof is to ask pupils to use paper clips to hold three differently coloured pieces of paper together and cut out three congruent copies of a random triangle. The three triangles may then be tessellated as shown:

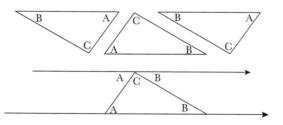

Figure 2.4 Angle sum of a triangle.

Again we are only demonstrating rather than proving, but the class may then discuss the question 'Why should the three angles always fit like that?'. The resulting mathematical discussion depends only on alternate angles and leads to the traditional Euclidean proof in a way that year 6 or 7 pupils are likely to be able to understand. Notice that although we end up with a symbolic proof, we began with physical materials and concrete concepts to provide the child with a firm foundation on which to build their own understanding and an opportunity in discussion to hear mathematical arguments and to test their ideas under the guidance of the teacher.

The names of the strands within AT1 which describe the processes of mathematics have changed their names over the years and, as discussed in Chapter 1, there has been amalgamation of the PoS for number and algebra, but the diagram given in the non-statutory guidance for the National Curriculum, originally published by the Association of Teachers of Mathematics (1989) is still useful in indicating the range and complexity of the domain.

AT1 links the contexts, processes, and content of mathematics. Some of the mathematical activities which might be involved are listed in the various versions of the non-statutory guidance which have been produced over the years and include:

Problem-solving strategies explore connections in mathematics; select appropriate strategies; develop flexible approaches; planning and organizing; designing; reviewing progress; checking the sense of results; and presenting alternative solutions; and evaluate the effectiveness of strategies.

Communication describing; discussing; explaining; interpreting; talking; questioning; recording and presenting; examine critically, improve, then justify their choice of mathematical presentation; present a concise, reasoned argument using precise language.

Reasoning and proof predicting; testing; hypothesizing; generalizing; justifying; arguing; reasoning; conjecturing; defining; proving and disproving; explore, identify, and use pattern and symmetry; distinguish between practical demonstration, proof, conventions, facts, definitions, and derived properties; recognize the importance and limitations of assumptions.
(Summarized from: NCC (1989: D2); CCW (1989: B18); CCW (1992: A12); DfEE/QCA (1999b); and ACCAC (2000).

These activities are supposed to be based in practical tasks and real-life problems as well as in mathematics itself. The intention is that pupils will be taught the skills of problem solving and explaining or justifying the results to others in a variety of mathematical contexts.

Clearly we would not expect to see all of these aspects of mathematics in one lesson! However, good mathematics lessons will always contain some of the mathematical process skills and knowledge shown in Figure 2.5.

A careful examination of the strands reveals that the problem-solving processes which are being discussed here are ill defined out of context. It is not possible to demonstrate a skill in mathematical problem solving without a mathematical problem to solve – and that problem may well demand the use of mathematical facts and conventions, skills and routines, conceptual structures, techniques and results. The National Curriculum expects these processes to 'be demonstrated through activities in which the mathematics from the other ATs is at, or very

CONTEXT

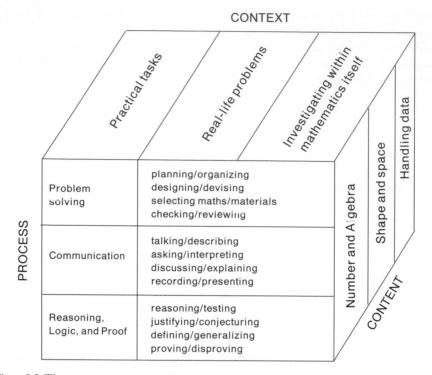

Figure 2.5 The process, content, and context dimensions of using and applying mathematics. Adapted from ATM (1989).

close to, the same level' (DfEE/QCA 1999b). In problem solving there is always a 'gap' which must be closed between the learner's current knowledge, conceptual structures, techniques and processes, and the path to a viable solution (Ausubel 1969; Tanner 1987). The gap may be in content or processes, but there is always something new learned when a problem is solved. If the 'gap' is in both aspects, then overall it may be too wide for pupils to cross without significant help.

It is characteristic of the processes listed above that they demand significant pupil autonomy in their operation. This does not preclude support from teachers and others – far from it – the National Curriculum demands that these processes be *taught* not just stumbled across during problem solving. The processes of mathematical thinking described in AT1 *can* be taught (Tanner and Jones 1995c, 2000) and we will discuss how such teaching might be organized in Chapters 5 and 7. However, it is clear that if teachers overdirect activity or restrict tasks to close repetition of recently taught algorithms the opportunity to meet and solve genuine problems will be missed.

If pupils are to learn to use such processes then lessons must include opportunities for them to take responsibility for planning and executing their work. They should be given opportunities to create short chains of deductive reasoning and explain their reasoning to others and develop their own proofs (DfEE/QCA 1999b). In order to do this they should meet an appropriate range of unfamiliar problems with teacher support. These should include practical tasks, investiga-

Table 2.2 Open and closed tasks.

Closed task	More open task
Find the area of a triangle with base 10 cm and vertical height 8 cm	How many different triangles can you make with an area of 40 cm^2 and whole number sides?
Use Pythagoras' theorem to calculate x	Investigate right-angled triangles with whole-number sides
Draw the graphs of: $y = x + 2$ $y = x + 3$ $y = x + 4$	Investigate the effect of choosing different values for m and c in $y = mx + c$ on your graphic calculator
Find the mean and standard deviation of these ten examination marks: 2, 16, 3, 4, 9, 11, 4, 7, 11, 12	Write two different sets of ten examination marks which have a mean of 5 and a standard deviation of 2

tions in real life and within mathematics itself. These problems must be sufficiently open to allow for the selection of one strategy from many, flexibility in the use of different approaches, discussion, mathematical argument, and comparison of solutions (NCC 1989). The non-statutory guidance for the National Curriculum (NCC 1989) offers a number of closed tasks and suggests more open versions which allow opportunities for process skills to be developed. We list a few similar examples in Table 2.2.

Task 2.5 Creating open tasks

Choose a 'standard' topic in the mathematics curriculum such as averages, fractions, decimals, etc. and try to make up an open task which would do the same job but allow the use of mathematical process skills.

For more ideas, we suggest that you examine some of the resources produced by the Association of Teachers of Mathematics in the *Points of Departure* series (Hardy *et al.* 1986).

CONCLUSION

Our objectives for this chapter included the identification of a number of aspects of mathematics teaching which should be present in good mathematics teaching. We hope that you now realize the wide range of activities which should appear in good mathematics teaching. Obviously these need not all be present in any one lesson, but we believe that to be effective, mathematics teaching should include an appropriate balance between these features. Although it was written in 1982, the guidance offered below remains a clear checklist for teachers trying to provide their classes with an appropriate range of learning opportunities. Mathematics teaching at all levels should include opportunities for:

- exposition by the teacher;
- discussion between teacher and pupils and between pupils themselves;
- appropriate practical work;
- consolidation and practice of fundamental skills and routines;
- problem solving, including the application of mathematics to everyday situations;
- investigational work.

(Cockcroft 1982: para 243)

We will focus on how lessons might be planned to include such features in Chapter 4. However, before you can hope to develop the learning opportunities suggested above, you must learn how to manage your classroom to ensure that the environment in your classroom is conducive to effective learning and it is to this which we now turn.

Summary

- Mathematical understanding may be categorized as relational or instrumental;
- although instrumental understanding often appears to provide quick and easy success, it is fool's gold and relational understanding is the only worthwhile goal;
- five elements of mathematics have been identified:

    - facts or conventions: are arbitrary and require automaticity so mnemonics are useful;
    - skills and routines: require automaticity but good teachers focus also on principles and conceptual structures;
    - conceptual structures: demand personal meaning, so must be built on concrete foundations and explained or negotiated rather than exposed;
    - techniques and results: must connect with schemata, be associated with context, and justified or proved;
    - processes and thinking: include problem solving, communication and proof, and demand significant pupil autonomy and the challenge of open tasks in a wide range of contexts.

3 Managing the mathematics classroom

Recent reports in the media have portrayed schools as ill-disciplined places where pupils are out of control. Whilst such attention-grabbing headlines may make for good sales figures, just pause for a moment and reflect on how accurately such images match with your own school experiences. In contrast to the headlines, more objective evidence from research studies and school inspections describe standards of pupil behaviour as good or very good in the vast majority of schools (see e.g. OHMCI 1996). The ability to manage pupils effectively is, however, a major concern for new teachers and rightly so, as effective teaching and learning is dependent on a disciplined classroom. In this chapter we shall discuss how teacher behaviour influences pupils, and identify strategies for the development of effective class management and control techniques.

We hope that reading this chapter will prove useful to you either if you are a novice teacher still learning how to establish your own style of classroom management, or if you are an established teacher or mentor concerned about how to support other members of staff in your own department.

Objectives

By the end of this chapter you will:

- be aware of teacher behaviours which lead to the establishment of authority;
- be aware of teacher behaviours associated with good classroom management;
- be able to identify critical points in lessons for behaviour management;
- understand why pupils misbehave and how teachers should respond to misbehaviour.

School and classroom culture

Each school has its own distinctive culture or ethos and a teacher's discipline strategy is constructed within the wider school context. Most schools have effective policies on behaviour and discipline (OHMCI 1996) and part of your induction as a new teacher will be to familiarize yourself with the policies of your school. In a study of schools in which pupils were outperforming in mathematics, the following common characteristics were observed:

- a clear focus on academic achievement;
- an emphasis on pupils' self-esteem;
- an expectation of high achievement by all pupils;
- all pupils were valued and respected;
- discipline policies had been developed collaboratively by staff, often in consultation with pupils;
- staff agreed with the school discipline policy and operated it consistently;
- a clear structure of rewards and punishments that was known to both staff and pupils;
- an expectation of sociable behaviour.

(Tanner *et al.* 1999)

It should be noted that not all the schools in the study were in leafy suburbs, and some were working in areas of high social deprivation. If you are long established in your school you may wish to perform the next task as if through the eyes of a newcomer and reflect on your practices.

Task 3.1 Policies and practices

Obtain a copy of the discipline policies for your school and department.

Which of the above characteristics can be discerned in your school's policies?

What features would you look for in the classroom as evidence of the extent to which policies are transformed into practice?

In many classrooms, the school or departmental rules are clearly displayed and referred to by teachers. Pupils' work is often displayed on the walls. Merits or commendations are given to pupils for good effort or achievement, and such information is frequently conveyed to the parents. The atmosphere within the classroom is one of mutual respect, with a sense of shared purpose, led by the teacher.

Most novice teachers will work closely with a 'mentor' during their training. As a novice, your mentor will provide you with a role model, initially to copy, and hopefully to adapt, as you develop your own teaching style. Similarly, your early attempts at developing effective management strategies will be supported by working within those already negotiated between the mentor and the class.

During the first few weeks of school experience many student teachers share a class with their mentor. This provides an excellent opportunity for the student to observe how to respond to pupils and for mentors to coach students who are making inappropriate responses. During lesson observations, students should analyse carefully how experienced teachers use rules and routines to handle their classes. It is extremely helpful to students if experienced teachers spend a few minutes reflecting back on a lesson to help the student identify critical interventions. Talking through the results of a structured observation by a student often provides a useful focus. Some observation tasks are provided later to help you to identify key aspects of classroom management.

Students teaching in collaboration with their mentors also raises questions about how the responsibility for classroom management is to be shared. If the mentor always responds to events this will diminish the status of the student; however, the mentor is likely to spot misbehaviour before an inexperienced student. You should discuss in advance how the responsibility for responding to incidents will be shared. It is often helpful for mentors to delay their interventions in order to allow a student to practise exerting authority.

FIRST MEETINGS WITH YOUR CLASSES

First impressions matter! Teaching is often compared with acting, and behaving like a teacher from the start will help to persuade pupils that you deserve the respect accorded to established teachers. This is the advantage which experienced teachers have when beginning in a new school. Just like students they need to establish their authority, but everything about their behaviour says that they expect respect.

Body language, or non-verbal communication, sends very powerful signals. It can convey status and authority and influence pupils' attention and interest. If your body language is in conflict with your verbal instructions it is often the non-verbal message which dominates (Robertson 1981). Non-verbal messages may be transmitted in a number of ways. Experienced teachers assume a relaxed, confident posture. They position themselves where they have a clear view of all pupils, especially when addressing the whole class, and they move freely around the classroom. They vary the tone and volume of their voice to emphasize points and to prevent a monotonous delivery. Similarly, their facial expressions and gestures help to clarify and to reinforce their speech. A raised eyebrow may be used to signal disapproval, or a smile to convey praise. Most importantly, frequent use is made of eye contact for a wide variety of purposes – to monitor the class for attention, for sign of a failure to understand, to reprimand silently a pupil who is off task.

Pupils and teachers have to develop a shared understanding of the expected standards of work and behaviour. This negotiation begins at the first meeting and continues until agreement is obtained. This usually takes several weeks and, with more challenging classes, may continue through the first term or even longer! The pupils will define the situation if the teacher does not (Hargreaves 1972). Discussion with your mentor and observation of a range of classes will help you to establish realistic expectations and standards for particular classes. Remember that memories of your own school days are likely to be based on the experiences of an able and well-motivated pupil, and are possibly also rose tinted.

Expectations and behaviours established during these first few weeks are often very difficult to modify later. Because pupils are uncertain about you at the start of school experience they will be watching your reactions and evaluating your attitudes. They will be predicting what the relationship between you and the class will be. Expect the pupils to test your standards; for example, by asking you seemingly innocuous questions such as 'Did you see the match last night?'. How would your response differ if you were asked this at break time compared with during a lesson?

During break time, the question is likely to be a genuine query. By continuing the conversation you discover more about the pupil's interests and begin to develop a rapport. To be asked during the lesson, however, is an attempt to discover how much off-task behaviour you are prepared to tolerate. An appropriate response would be to raise an eyebrow and look pointedly at the work the pupil is meant to be undertaking, accompanied, if necessary, by a verbal reminder of the task – 'Work!'. Novice teachers have to learn to recognize probing challenges for what they are and gently but firmly resist them.

Experienced teachers take advantage of this initial uncertainty to establish on-task and cooperative behaviour patterns. Begin firmly – relax later.

Establishing rules and routines

By taking immediate charge of the classroom, teachers ensure that they have the right to make the rules. Students need to know what their mentor normally requires and to base their rules and expectations on those already established. Rules must be clear and consistent. Make sure that your class knows what you require. The class will scrutinize your behaviour to judge how you enforce the rules you have set, so make sure that your rules are reasonable. Decide in advance how you will deal with transgressions, and behave consistently and fairly.

After some time a basic consensus may develop between pupil and teacher as to the roles they expect one another to play. The teacher's personal authority then begins to take the place of formal authority. If you are observing a teacher who has developed a good relationship with a class over a period of time they are likely to be relying on their personal authority. A teacher in this position can do things which would be disastrous for a student. While it is part of good rapport between teacher and pupils for some social interchange to take place, the need for you to establish authority must take precedence. Friendly relationships between teachers and pupils should be treated with caution.

Establishing your authority

Teachers are assumed to have authority initially because of their status as teachers. If you act as if you have such status then pupils will tend to behave accordingly. Act as though you are comfortable and relaxed in the classroom, look happy and at ease, not nervous and anxious. Move around the room and exercise your right as a teacher to look at pupils' work, or even to take a pupil's pen and replace it on the desk. Use strategies such as 'hands up' to control who speaks and when. Arrange the class as you see fit, and move pupils if you are unhappy with the way they are working (Robertson 1981).

Teachers have many common expectations of appropriate behaviours and use similar routines to reinforce their classroom rules. If you employ the same routines this will convey to the pupils that you know what is expected and so help to reinforce your 'teacher status'. Student teachers often underestimate the effort that experienced teachers put into establishing themselves with a new class. Remember when you are observing lessons, that you are watching classes which have already been socialized into an agreed way of working with the teacher. You will probably have to be more formal than their usual teacher.

Task 3.2 Focused Observation 1 – Learning the rules and routines

Arrange to observe a number of different teachers with different classes. Observe just one aspect (e.g. entry, exposition, questioning, distribution of equipment, dismissal) in any one lesson. Use the prompts below to help you to focus on the significant events. Discuss the aspect to be observed with the teacher in advance of the lesson and offer to discuss your observations afterwards. For each aspect of the lesson, what features were common to many teachers?

Entry:
When and how are the class allowed into the room?

☐   before the teacher?   ☐   lined up outside?   ☐   as pupils arrive?

Where is the teacher during the entry?
What exactly does the teacher do or say during the entry?
When are pupils allowed to sit?

Exposition:
Where is the teacher positioned during the exposition?
How does the teacher gain the pupils' attention?
Are the pupils allowed to talk/question?
For how long does the teacher talk before asking questions?

Dismissal:
What (exactly) happens when the bell rings?

Are there set routines?

☐   pack up and sit quietly   ☐   wait for silence

☐   stand behind chairs?

Do the pupils leave as a class?

Creating a classroom atmosphere which encourages learning

The way in which a teacher behaves in the classroom can pre-empt misbehaviour and encourage learning. Kounin (1970) compared the classroom management techniques of teachers whose pupils spent high and low proportions of class time on academic work. The techniques used by the more effective teachers are discussed below.

Kounin analysed teachers' use of 'desists' – their interventions to modify inappropriate behaviour. His first, and somewhat surprising, finding was that when pupils misbehaved the quality of the desist – the wording of the reprimand – was not important. What was far more influential in altering pupils' behaviour was the correct timing and targeting of the response.

Imagine a classroom incident which starts with Alison whispering to Sue, who then starts to doodle on Alison's book, whereupon Jane leans over to see what is happening. At this point the teacher rebukes Jane for talking. By not responding at the start the teacher has allowed a chain of events to develop which involved more pupils and increased in severity of disruption. The original instigator of the sequence is also, somewhat unfairly, not targeted with the rebuke. A teacher who responded in such a fashion would not be described as 'with it'. We are sure that you can remember being in awe of teachers who seemed to have 'eyes in the back of their heads'; such teachers communicate to their classes by their actual behaviour that they know what is going on. Kounin found that teachers who were 'with it' were able to pre-empt misbehaviour.

Effective teachers were also able to 'overlap' their activities; that is, to deal with two different events at the same time. For example, whilst the teacher is marking the work of one pupil another pupil asks for help. The teacher raises his hand to signal 'Wait' whilst continuing the marking. As soon as this is completed the teacher turns to the other pupil and asks 'Now, what's the problem?' Effective teachers do not become so immersed in dealing with misbehaviour or teaching a group that they are unable to monitor the rest of the class. Maintaining 'withitness' helps to develop the skills of overlapping. Pupils interpret the display of such skills as signals that the teacher is in control of the classroom (Kounin, 1970).

Maintaining the pace and flow of a lesson

Misbehaviour is less likely when pupils are occupied with their work. Opportunities for misbehaviour occur most frequently at the transition points when the lesson changes from one phase to another; for example, after pupils have copied an example from the board and have then to start an exercise. The way in which the teacher manages such transitions is significant. The following were identified by Kounin (1970) as common managerial faults which impeded the flow of the lesson.

Thrusts

The teacher issues instructions before scanning the class and gaining the pupils' attention. Imagine a scenario where pupils are working quietly on an exercise. The teacher suddenly announces: 'OK, let's mark the exercise now' (and immediately continues with) 'The answer to number 1 is $x = 6$; number 2, $x = 4$; number . . .' Many pupils missed the start of the announcement and were, therefore, unprepared to start marking. As a result there was a flurry of 'Miss, what was number 1?', accompanied by pupils talking to each other to ascertain the answers.

Flip-flops

Where a transition is made to a new phase or topic but then the teacher reverts back to the topic just left. For example, having started the class on an exercise the teacher remembers that question 3 requires further explanation and has to regain the pupils' attention.

It is when transitions are poorly signalled that many novice teachers create situations in which their lack of withitness is demonstrated and in which pupils begin to misbehave because of the teacher's actions. For example, most teachers demand that pupils are completely silent during expositions and explanations except when contributing an answer to a question. During the exercise phase of the lesson, however, most teachers allow pupils to talk quietly as long as the conversation is on task. If pupils believe themselves to be in 'exercise phase' when the teacher thinks it is 'exposition phase' they will misbehave without intention, and attract undeserved punishments. Similarly, if some pupils falsely believe the phase to be 'exposition' and yet observe the teacher condoning 'quiet talking' they will consider the teacher to lack withitness.

How could such a situation arise? We have observed 'thrusts' and 'flip-flops' creating exactly these circumstances. We have observed novices explaining a point to a small group of pupils during an 'exercise phase' but doing so from a dominant position near the blackboard in a loud voice, confusing some other pupils into thinking an exposition was occurring. We have observed novices attempting to deal with a common misconception which had arisen during an exercise session by talking to a class without first calling them to order. Several pupils were talking during what had become an 'exposition phase' without their noticing it.

The use of effective strategies to manage transitions contributes to a smooth, well-paced lesson and hence limits the opportunities for misbehaviour.

Task 3.3 Focused Observation 2 – Observing transitions

Arrange to observe a lesson and focus only on the transitions.

Make a note of the exact phrases used by the teacher immediately before moving a class from exposition phase to exercise phase.

Make a note of the exact phrases used by teachers on moving a class from exercise phase to exposition phase. Where does the teacher stand?

Are different words for demanding quiet used in the different phases? What are they?

Different teachers use their own phrases and mannerisms, but we have found these phrases to be particularly common immediately prior to a transition to exercise:

Has everyone got all the equipment they need?
Does everyone know what they are supposed to do?
OK . . . ? Everyone start the worksheet now. Work quietly.

At this point there should be no questions or hands up. All the heads should go down and work should begin. Experienced teachers stand at the front scanning for a few moments, looking for problems before beginning to circulate.

At the transition to exposition we have often heard:

> Pens down, stop talking and look to the front.
> Everybody pay attention to me. Silence please.

This is best done from a dominant position in the classroom. One of our colleagues even trained his classes that when he stood silently by the left-hand side of the board with his chalk held up that they had to fall silent, put their pens down and pay attention. This usually took less than 20 seconds and was very impressive to observe – very 'with it'. Experienced teachers wait for absolute pin-drop silence. Novices usually begin talking too soon.

CLASS MANAGEMENT IN A TYPICAL MATHEMATICS LESSON

The following lesson was taught by a mentor and observed by the student. Descriptions of key parts of the lesson are taken from the student's notes. Extracts from the debriefing discussion after the lesson between student and mentor are inserted into the description to indicate critical points within a lesson for effective class management and control. The discussion suggests some strategies which you could plan as part of your lesson preparation.

Topic: volume of prisms (year-7 top set)

Context

In the last lesson, the class revised areas of plane shapes and are now to proceed to find the volumes of prisms.

Entry

Some questions are written up on the board in advance (e.g. *Find 3^2*, *What is the area of a rectangle of length 9.2 cm and width 4 cm?* As the pupils arrive Ms T stands at the front of the class watching them enter the room. Eye contact is made with several pupils, sometimes accompanied by a smile, occasionally by the use of a name (e.g. if the pupil is talking). As the pupils settle, Ms T announces 'OK then, you know what to do – back of your books, questions are on the board.' She continues to scan the class.

Student: I could see the effectiveness of the 'authority position' at the front during their entry. You were able to settle the noisy ones as soon they came in.

Mentor: Yes, just a look is often all they need. The questions on the board help too. All of my classes know my routine. They come in, there's some work on the board, they get on with it. It allows me chance to deal with any latecomers before I have to start teaching. It also starts the pupils thinking about maths, and sets the scene for the lesson.

Register

As the pupils work on the questions, the teacher scans the class and marks off the pupils who are present. A head count provides a double check. Absentees are checked on by asking questions such as 'Where is Alison today?' of her friends.

Mentor:　How do you normally take the class register? I find that taking the register by scanning and counting heads does not interrupt pupils' work. Also, by appearing to spot the absentees, I give the impression of being 'with it'. You do, however, need to know the pupils' names – you could check on these by referring to the class seating plan.

Student:　The only way I'd seen before was to call the register aloud for pupils to answer to their names.

Mentor:　That is traditionally done at the start of the lesson with the class silent and otherwise unoccupied. That situation is much harder for a student to achieve and to control, and any misbehaviour by individual pupils is very obvious. Develop your managerial skills before you place yourself in such an exposed position.

Transition to exposition

Ms T scans the class noting a couple of pupils starting to lift their heads and look around. She then announces, 'One more minute' and, after a brief pause, she moves to the board, picks up the chalk as if about to write, then announces in a loud clear voice,

OK, pens down, sit up straight and pay attention.

She pauses and scans. Within a few seconds nearly all the class are looking at her ready to continue.

Put your pen down James, look this way Sarah.

After this command, targeted at individuals, all the class fall silent and pay attention, including two other miscreants who were not named!

Hands up, who thinks they know the answer to question 1?

Pupils are called on by name to supply answers. At the end Ms T asks the pupils who had every question right to put their hands up and she says 'Well done' to them.

Mentor:　The warm-up questions are revision so the pupils should be able to do them fairly easily. I monitored the progress of the class and when some of the pupils were finishing I gave a one-minute warning. This helped pace the lesson by holding the pupils accountable for working to time. It also alerted them to the imminent change of activity. The pauses between the instructions allowed the pupils time to comply with the requests and prevented thrusts and flip-flops.

Student: Why didn't you just call out the answers?

Mentor: Firstly, calling on them for the answers holds pupils accountable for their learning; and secondly, it gives me an overview of the degree of success of the class.

Main teaching activity

There follows another brief pause during which Ms T scans the class making eye contact whilst moving across to her desk where she picks up a large cuboid made from multilink cubes.

Now, the first problem we're going to look at today is how can we find the volume of this?

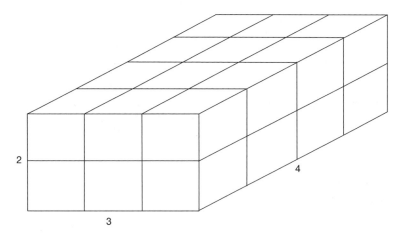

Figure 3.1 Volume of a cuboid.

The meaning of 'volume' is developed mainly through question and answer. Ms T is positioned at the front of the class but moves around holding up the shape so that all pupils have a clear view. She uses gestures to clarify properties of the shape in response to the pupils' answers. Initially, most pupils count the cubes but Ms T sets a challenge:

Can anyone find a quicker way than counting every cube?

Three different ways of finding the volume are suggested by pupils depending on which face is taken to be the base. Ms T then holds up an L-shaped prism and asks the pupils to think silently as to how they would work out its volume. Pupils are asked to explain their methods. A number of different prisms are drawn on the board and pupils are to explain how they would find their volumes.

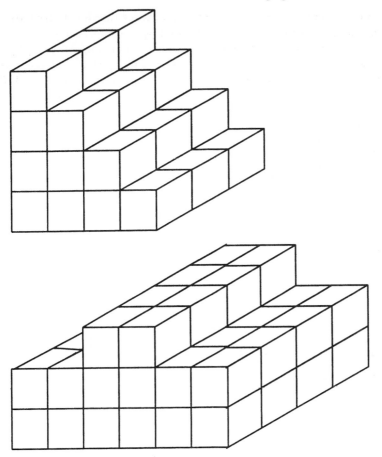

Figure 3.2 Volume of prisms.

Finally Ms T asks pupils to describe how they could explain the method for finding the volume of a prism to an absent pupil. The formula is negotiated through discussion and Ms T then starts writes the final version on the board. Someone starts whispering. Immediately Ms T turns and stares in the direction of the sound, then resumes writing.

Student: I enjoyed that, but when I was in school I think I was just given the formula and told to do the exercise.

Mentor: Showing them the model and posing a challenge stimulated interest in the new task. I was trying to build up their concept of volume through the use of concrete materials and also to link it to the work we've done on area. I always aim to develop relational understanding because then maths makes sense. Just being given a formula doesn't help them to apply their maths to other situations and it reduces maths to an impossible list of things to learn. Did you notice how involved they were? If you can make them think and participate in the lesson rather than just passively listening and copying down notes they learn more, and there are fewer discipline problems. I know that Kirsty tried to talk when I was writing the formula, but a look is usually enough to bring them back on task. It takes time to build up that rapport, though, and at the start you have to be very firm with them. They have to know that they are safe when they are trying to explain their methods to you and I am very hard with anyone who dares to comment if someone makes an error. I'm trying to convince them that you don't learn if you are afraid of making errors.

Transition to exercise

Again, Ms T scans the class and announces:

> In the front of your books, copy down the heading, the date, and the examples. Then start the worksheet. You should be able to finish the first five questions by 10 past.

After checking that they are all writing we both give out the worksheets.

Mentor: Plan when and how to distribute the worksheets or equipment just before they will need them. Make sure it's clear what they have to do. Setting a target time for doing a number of questions is a good way of pushing the pace along. Notice also how few questions they can get through when they are working alone compared to the number we went through on the board as a class.

Exercise

The pupils start to work. Initially there is silence but after a few minutes there is quiet discussion related to the worksheet. After scanning to make sure everyone has settled, Ms T circulates monitoring pupils' work. One girl has a hairbrush on her desk, Ms T points to it with her finger and raises an eyebrow quizzically at the pupil. The girl mutters an apology and replaces it in her bag. Quiet comments are made to individuals, a word of praise, some additional help, a remark on the layout of their work. After two pupils have asked for help with question 4, Ms T returns to the front and stops the class. 'Listen everyone (pauses and waits for silence) ... a couple of you are having trouble with question 4. Everybody read question 4 please ...'

Student: Are they meant to work in silence on the exercise? Some of them started talking after the first few questions.

Mentor: The first few questions in an exercise should be similar enough to the examples for everyone in the class to attempt on their own. This facilitates a smooth transition. The questions then progress in difficulty to maintain a level of challenge for all pupils and hence pre-empt misbehaviour due to boredom. At this stage the pupils often help each other by discussing their work. I did my own worksheet for this topic because the exercises in the textbook were not suitable – they were essentially all the same question with different numbers!

Student: What happened with number 4?

Mentor: The twist in that question was that the sides were given in different units. I thought it might wake them up, however, once I'd been asked about it by two pupils I decided to discuss it with the class. That avoided 'fragmentation' – having to explain it several times over to individuals. Of course, if I hadn't been circulating I'd not have noticed the difficulty soon enough to alert all the class to it. Circulating also gives you the chance to monitor progress, neatness, and to have a quiet word with anyone who is not up to standard.

Marking the exercise

After most pupils have reached question 5, Ms T returns to the front. 'Stop working please and get ready to mark your answers' (pauses, waiting for silence, and scans) ... 'Jo, pen down ... thank you. Now, question 1 (pause) ... Anna?' After all the questions have been marked Ms T asks for a show of hands to indicate who has them all correct. Lots of praise is given followed by 'Anyone who isn't sure ask me in a moment. Now, we should be able to finish the exercise by the end of the lesson, but be careful on number 9 – there's a catch!' Pupils start reading number 9. One calls out asking 'Is the catch ...' but Ms T raises a finger to stop him and says 'That's for you to work out *when* you get to it.'

Plenary

About 10 minutes before the end of the lesson, Ms T stops the class and marks the remainder of the exercise. Then she asks the pupils:

> Think back, what have you been working on this lesson? How would you explain what a prism is to someone who was absent from today's lesson? And how would you explain to them how to find its volume?'

Several accounts are offered. Ms T repeats them, emphasizing key aspects and inserting correct terminology (e.g. 'uniform' cross-section). Then she asks, 'What warnings would you give other pupils before they tried these questions? Which bits did you find difficult?' Again, several hands go up and pupils' comments include checking that the units are the same, and being careful with decimal points. Ms T comments approvingly.

Ending the lesson

> OK, everyone, get out your homework diaries and copy this down from the board.

Ms T writes the homework on the board and then scans the class. Then she says in a loud, firm voice:

OK, pens down when you've finished and sit up straight. (Pause) Any questions about the homework? Right, some questions now to make sure that you know what you've learned ... This side (indicating one-half of the class) – what's 3^3?

The questions continue until the bell rings. Ms T scans the class:

Well done, everyone, some good work this lesson. OK, this row looks ready, off you go ...

Mentor: Allow time for the homework to be set, written down and any queries dealt with a few minutes before the bell is due. Question and answer can then be used to review the main points of the lesson, perhaps in a quiz situation – these two rows versus those two rows. Pupils always respond well to a competition! The quiz could be extended by using mental mathematics questions, etc., and the activity can be easily curtailed at the bell. The winning rows may of course then be dismissed first, alternatively, the groups who worked the hardest, sat most quietly, etc. Don't miss the opportunity to praise the class for their efforts, high standard of work, etc. There's usually something positive you can say and they remember that ready for coming in to the next lesson.

Effective class management creates a smooth, well-paced lesson in which opportunities for misbehaviour are avoided. However, whilst good discipline skills are essential they are not sufficient for effective teaching. As a new teacher you will also be trying to develop a classroom culture in which pupils expect to behave well and are motivated to learn.

PROMOTING POSITIVE BEHAVIOUR

There are fewer discipline problems in lessons where the pupils are involved with their work (Kounin 1970; OHMCI 1996). How can you encourage pupils to become interested in and enthusiastic about your lessons? Think back to the distinctions drawn in the last chapter between instrumental and relational views of mathematics. An instrumental approach allows pupils swift success with a task but risks disillusionment later as the number of formulae and algorithms to be memorized increases. To achieve relational understanding takes more effort from both the teacher and the learner, but results in connected knowledge that 'makes sense'. What are the likely effects of both types of approaches on pupils' motivation?

Task 3.4

Think of a class that you have observed. Make a list of the strategies which were used to motivate and interest the pupils. What other strategies could you add?

Pupils may be motivated to undertake a task because of the rewards they will accrue from its successful completion. These rewards may be external – such as a page of 'ticks', the award of a 'merit', or a good grade in a forthcoming examination. The rewards do not relate directly to the task itself, the motivation is extrinsic. Such motivation might also have a negative character – pupils do the work because they wish to avoid the consequences – a reprimand, a detention – which would result from its non-completion. Alternatively, pupils may be motivated to undertake a task because they are interested in the task itself – they *want* to find out the answer. Such intrinsic motivation is stimulated by tasks which relate to pupils' interests or where the teacher has provoked their curiosity. Which types of motivational strategies did you include in your list?

Strategies for generating motivation in your lessons

Intrinsic motivation

Mathematics is intrinsically interesting. It is full of seemingly strange connections and results; for example, why does the Fibonacci series appear in the patterns in a sunflower head? Starting a lesson by drawing attention to such connections can intrigue pupils. People enjoy solving problems and puzzles often engage interest. Look at the number of books of puzzles at railway stations and the enduring popularity of crosswords, etc.

Consider whether you can frame the task as a puzzle or a challenge to be investigated. For example, *A rectangle measuring 4 cm by 4 cm has its area numerically equal to its perimeter. Are there any other rectangles like this?* Another technique is to ask pupils to (dis)prove a 'mathematical rumour' which you have heard. For example, *I've been told that a quadratic equation can have three different types of roots. Is this true? Why?*

Challenging pupils' misconceptions can also stimulate a keen interest in the lesson. For example, before teaching the multiplication of fractions or decimals ask, possibly with reference to some examples on the board, what happens to numbers when you multiply/divide them?

A variation on intrinsic motivation is to challenge the pupils' capabilities. For example, 'The topic today is quite a difficult one but you've done so well this term I think you'll be able to cope with it.' Notice the implied confidence in the pupils' abilities and the use of praise. Variation in the type of question set within an exercise, with an appropriate level of difficulty, can maintain the pupils' interest in the task.

Extrinsic motivation

Not all tasks have strong intrinsic appeal for every pupil. A set of questions reinforcing the equivalence of fractions and percentages might supply essential practice but is hardly exciting. In such cases consider whether the task can be re-packaged as a game (e.g. percentages-and-fractions dominoes), or as a class competition. The 'Mastermind' format works well – divide the class into four groups and have four sets of questions on cards. Every pupil from each group in turn is questioned. If they respond correctly their group gains two points. If they 'pass' or are incorrect then the question is offered to the rest of the class for a bonus. The promise of a game or contest later in the lesson provided that the class has worked hard is an effective incentive.

Pupils respond well to credible praise, both oral and written (Watkins 1997). A smile or word of approval encourages pupils and indicates that you are aware of their progress. A complimentary comment on a pupil's book is an easy and effective way to convey your praise to the pupil and also, if you request that it is shown to the parent for signature, to the parents as well. Such communications are appreciated by older as well as the younger pupils. Many schools now have formal merit systems to encourage and reward pupils although they tend to be used less frequently and less consistently than sanctions for misbehaviour (OHMCI 1996). As a novice teacher you will be alert to early signs of misbehaviour by your pupils but do not overlook opportunities to *catch them being good* as the old adage says.

Your attitude to the pupils

Every aspect of your teaching behaviour: the quality of preparation of your lessons, the neatness and legibility of handouts, the attractiveness of wall displays, the way in which you address the class; all of these transmit messages to pupils about the esteem in which they are held and the value which you place upon teaching them. If your work is untidy and inaccurate then you have provided neither a model nor an incentive for pupils to do better. Poorly prepared lessons and inappropriate tasks will result in poorly motivated pupils and disruptive behaviour. The prompt marking and return of pupils' work indicates that you consider their work to be important and worthy of your time. Pupils respond positively, in terms of work and behaviour, to teachers who demonstrate a genuine interest in them as individuals (OHMCI 1996).

Pupils who enjoy their work have little incentive to misbehave. Enjoyment is generated by tasks that are of interest to the pupils and provide a level of attainable challenge. Motivation to undertake the task can be enhanced by communicating your enthusiasm for mathematics and an appropriate use of rewards and incentives. Showing a genuine interest in the pupils as individuals, their progress, and a desire for them to succeed builds rapport and leads to the development of an effective learning environment. However, some misbehaviour has to be expected and effective teachers are skilled at dealing with it appropriately.

Dealing with misbehaviour

The bulk of misbehaviour is minor in character; for example, pupils talking, being out of their seats, or not getting on with the work set (Kyriacou 1986). Effective teachers are judged not by an absence of such problems but by the ways in which they deal with them (Elton 1989). To an unskilled observer it might look as if these lessons are incident free because the teacher preempts incipient disruption with a look or gesture, which is often unnoticed by anyone other than its recipient.

Misbehaviour is not easy to define. It is dependent on context and, within limits, what is considered to be misbehaviour varies from teacher to teacher. What is a problem to one teacher may be seen as a minor irritant or just high spirits by others (see Kyriacou 1986; Fontana 1994; McManus 1989). Observation of lessons and discussions with your mentor will help you to establish what can be tolerated and at what point misbehaviour requires action. Your mentor will have established classroom norms, the class will be probing to ascertain the extent to which you are able to maintain these standards. Before you start teaching significant parts of lessons know what the school rules and procedures are and discuss with your mentor some strategies that you could use to deal with transgressions.

Three main causes for misbehaviour have been identified: inappropriate teaching, low attainment, and threats to pupils' self-esteem (see e.g. Kyriacou 1986; Fontana 1994; McManus 1989). These causes are often interrelated.

Lessons which pupils perceive as irrelevant, uninteresting, or at an inappropriate level of difficulty (either too hard or too easy), are not going to engage pupils' interest or effort. Work that is continually too difficult results in pupils experiencing repeated failure. Such a lack of success may be accounted for by the pupil in two ways, either the pupil becomes demoralized 'I can't do maths' and stops trying, or the blame is placed on your poor teaching, which leads to hostility towards you and the subject (Fontana, 1994). The position of mathematics as a core subject in the curriculum lends status to you as its teacher and motivates pupils to achieve success. Unfortunately, for those pupils who experience repeated failure in mathematics, not only are they learning that they 'cannot do' a subject but that they are failing in a subject of major importance. Inappropriate work, therefore, places low attainers in a 'catch-22' situation – if they attempt the work then they risk further failure with a consequent blow to their self-esteem, if they don't attempt the work then they risk boredom and retribution from the teacher (Kyriacou 1986). To avoid being placed in such situations the pupils misbehave. Pupils may also misbehave to gain increased attention, increased excitement, or for the pleasure of maliciously teasing the teacher (Robertson 1981). Good teachers try to identify why pupils are misbehaving and address the causes where possible.

Effective teaching and good planning are the best strategies for the avoidance of problems. When misbehaviour does occur then you have to respond decisively and appropriately.

Task 3.5 Dealing with misbehaviour

What sorts of misbehaviour have you seen (or do you remember from your school days)? How did teachers deal with the misbehaviour? Which were the most subtle strategies used? What sort of hierarchy was there to the teacher's responses?

Teachers' initial responses to misbehaviour are often non-verbal, or are quietly spoken, low key, and avoid drawing class attention to the incident (McManus 1989). Pupils who are talking may be silenced merely by the teacher staring at them. Carefully used, a humorous comment is often an effective means of refocusing attention on tasks. More severe responses such as verbal reprimands, and occasionally punishments, are used when the initial desists have been ineffective, or in response to more serious misbehaviour such as rudeness, dumb insolence, or defiance (Fontana 1994).

The characteristics of effective verbal reprimands have been described by several studies (see e.g. McManus 1989; Kyriacou 1986). Effective reprimands are correctly targeted at the main culprit, tend to be short, are delivered in a firm tone of voice, refer to established rules and procedures, and do not invite a response from the pupil: 'John, sit down and get on with your work.' As with desists, the verbal instruction should be reinforced by the teacher's body language; for example, by making eye contact with the culprit accompanied by a momentary pause before continuing with the task in hand.

Effective reprimands avoid attacking the pupil's self-esteem – it should be the behaviour you object to not the pupil: 'This work is not up to standard – you normally do much better than this' expresses your concern but also indicates that it is within the pupil's capability to achieve the level you are demanding.

The third level of response to misbehaviour is formal punishment. A wise teacher will have thought through a carefully graded series of desists which fall short of formal punishment. These should represent a consistent and predictable scale of escalation to ensure that you do not fall into the trap of using formal punishments too quickly when dealing with minor infringements and having nothing left to use on more serious challenges to authority. Punishments should be used sparingly to maintain their effect, but as with all control interventions, timing is everything. A small action taken early is always better then a larger intervention made later after a problem has grown greater.

Task 3.6 Planning effective desists

Write a carefully graded list of ten or more desists which you have seen used in the classroom. Your list should begin with the lowest possible intervention you can imagine and build gently to the point where a punishment might be necessary. Our suggested list appears at the end of the chapter.

If a punishment should become necessary, it should:

- be directed at one or two individuals – never at whole classes;
- take place as soon after the event as possible;
- be reasonable (1,000 lines is not reasonable even if he did forget his pencil twice!);
- be in line with school policy (e.g. after-school detentions require 24 hours notice);
- be unpleasant for the pupil – sitting in a warm classroom at break on a cold, damp morning might not be seen as too much hardship!

You will probably be able to remember a few punishments from personal experience; however, suitable examples include:

- demerits (if the school has such a system);
- additional work to be done at home;
- 'mindless activity' such as writing out multiplication tables;
- detention at lunchtime or after school;
- exclusion from class – having to work in the mentor's group;
- reporting the misconduct to 'significant others' (e.g. the tutor or head of year).

At this last stage of punishment, we may enter the school's official system of consequences which usually moves through a number of progressively more significant stages on route to eventual exclusion from school. Senior members of staff will determine procedures at this stage and you should not threaten consequences which you cannot deliver. If misbehaviour is extreme you should act only on the advice of your mentor or an appropriate senior member of staff.

Note that any form of physical punishment is illegal.

During a punishment or a reprimand, sarcastic comments should be avoided as they obstruct the eventual development of an effective working relationship between you and the pupil. They provoke an unwillingness to work, hostility, and may lead to a confrontation.

Experienced teachers avoid confrontations where their authority is directly and publicly challenged. Confrontations may be triggered by: intimidation of the pupil physically or verbally, public embarrassment (e.g. sarcastic remarks), or, occasionally, the pupil might just be having a bad day and is inadvertently provoked (Kyriacou 1986).

In such situations try to stay, or at least to appear, calm, by switching to a low tone and avoiding pointing or threatening gestures. Offer the pupil an escape route; for example, by stating that you will discuss it at the end of the lesson and then moving swiftly on with the planned work as if to signal that you are unperturbed but have decided not to waste any more time on the incident. Avoid dealing with the problem in front of the class audience if possible. If the pupil is unwilling to settle and trouble continues then ask the pupil to go and work with the mentor or, *in extremis*, send another pupil to fetch help.

After the lesson discuss the incident with the pupil in a low-key manner. Try to ascertain why the pupil reacted so adversely. If you were in part to blame then apologize – even teachers can have bad days! The outcome must allow both of you to continue working together. If, in the unlikely event that you are unable to reach agreement as to what constitutes reasonable behaviour and expectations, then seek further help.

CONCLUSION

Class management is a skilled and complex process which is fundamental to, and is reinforced by, effective teaching. Its complexity is exacerbated by the speed at which incidents and responses occur in the classroom situation. There is little time to 'think on your feet'. An essential part of the learning process for you as a novice teacher is, therefore, to reflect back on your management of the lesson. It is then that you can identify any errors and make a mental note of more appropriate strategies. Discussion with your mentor can help you to analyse how an incident arose and thereby to preempt similar episodes in future. To any incident there is always a variety of possible responses: students can usually only think of one or two, your mentor will be able to suggest others. Consideration of the effectiveness of your response will help you to use more suitable alternatives in future.

In the early stages of teaching your classes, your focus must be on establishing your authority and developing expert use of the strategies outlined here. Whilst you do this you are likely to rely heavily on very controlled teaching situations (e.g. the exposition/exercise format of lessons with straightforward 'closed' tasks which are more easily managed). However, when you reach the stage of being in control you should pause to reflect: Are you yet able to make apposite use of all six of Cockcroft's teaching and learning strategies which were discussed in the last chapter? Good discipline is essential but will be of little value if your teaching is ineffective.

Summary

- The majority of children are well behaved and the majority of misbehaviour is trivial in nature;
- misbehaviour can be prevented or minimized by good planning and effective classroom management;
- effective teachers are 'with it' and anticipate where problems might occur;
- transition points in lessons should be carefully planned to minimize opportunities for disruption;
- good control strategies support rather than replace effective, inspiring teaching.

Our graded list of desists to use during exposition

- A sour look;
- pausing in exposition;
- moving towards the pupils who are off task whilst continuing with the explanation;
- directing a question towards a pair of off-task pupils during an explanation;
- naming a pupil (i.e. saying 'John!' and then continuing the exposition);
- naming a pupil and stating the rule which has been broken (e.g. 'John, you know that you are not allowed to talk while I am speaking to the whole class.');
- writing a pupil's name on the corner of the board (for later action);
- telling a pupil to see you at the end of the lesson for further unspecified action;
- threatening an unpleasant consequence (e.g. 'John, I'm letting you sit next to Brian at the moment, but if you don't behave I'll have to think again.');
- threatening to move a pupil if a behaviour is repeated;
- moving a pupil to sit at the teacher's desk or an empty desk if one is available;
- threatening to use a small punishment if a behaviour is repeated.

Please note: any threat must be followed through if made.

4 Planning and evaluating a mathematics lesson

In this chapter we shall discuss the factors which have to be considered before you start to plan a lesson and analyse some different approaches to planning. The planning process will be illustrated by extracts taken from a lesson planned and taught by a mentor and observed by the student. Issues to do with longer term planning will then be considered.

Objectives

By the end of this chapter you should:

- be aware of the key issues to be considered when planning a lesson;
- be able to set appropriate aims and objectives;
- begin to develop the skills necessary for effective planning;
- begin to appreciate the relationship between lesson planning and broader curriculum planning documents (e.g. schemes of work, National Curriculum, National Numeracy Framework).

Why is planning necessary?

Experienced teachers rarely need to plan their lessons in the kind of detail which is demanded of students. In the last chapter, when discussing how to develop your authority as a teacher, teaching was compared with acting. The analogy is useful again here. Experienced teachers have 'acted' the lesson many times before. They know their role, their speeches, and their actions. They can predict, from bexperience, how the pupil audience will react: which parts pupils will find difficult, and which props would be helpful to explain the plot. Novices do not have such a stock of prior experience on which to draw. For novices, detailed lesson planning is part of the process of creating professional expertise.

Preparing a plan in advance of the lesson has two main advantages for a novice teacher. First, it helps to clarify and to structure your thoughts about what it is you are trying to teach and how you intend to achieve it. Second, showing your plan to a mentor or colleague gives them an opportunity to suggest how the lesson could be improved.

Unlike watching a play, learning is not a spectator sport. Pupils are expected to take an active part and, whilst so doing, may exhibit unanticipated difficulties with the topic. In such situations, teachers are able to respond appropriately and to improvise successfully by drawing on their previous experience and professional expertise. It is far more difficult for students to 'think on their feet'. Discussing your plan with a mentor will help you to prepare for such eventualities and to avoid difficulties.

What does planning a lesson require?

In preparing to teach any part of a lesson you have to combine three areas of knowledge and expertise: your knowledge of mathematics as a subject, your pedagogical knowledge (what you know about effective teaching and learning), and your knowledge relating to the effective management and control of pupils. Whilst a novice teacher might be relatively confident in subject knowledge, the other two areas of expertise will be developed mainly during their training and as they start teaching.

To teach even a small part of a lesson effectively, however, you need to be competent in all three areas. Knowing how to do the mathematics yourself is not sufficient, you also have to be able to attract and sustain the pupils' attention, to motivate them to undertake the tasks, and simultaneously to implement an appropriate sequence of activities which will result in effective learning by the pupils of the specified objectives for the lesson. Both planning a lesson and teaching it are extremely complex tasks requiring the integration of a wide range of skills.

This is where planning and teaching with a mentor is an invaluable part of a novice teacher's professional development. Part of the mentor's role is to support students or newly qualified teachers as they develop and extend their pedagogical skills. Although mentors cannot be expected to plan every lesson collaboratively with novice teachers, the occasions when they find the time and opportunity to engage in joint planning are greatly valued by novices.

There are a range of strategies through which mentors can enable novices to focus closely on particular parts of the planning/teaching process. For instance, the novice might attempt to plan one aspect of the lesson (e.g. the exposition on a new topic). The novice would then discuss the plan with their mentor and amend it as necessary before teaching that aspect as part of a collaborative lesson. Alternatively, a novice might plan an entire lesson jointly with the mentor and then assume responsibility for teaching it using the mentor as in-class support. In both scenarios, the presence of the mentor is likely to inhibit any discipline problems and hence allow the novice to focus on their presentation and interactive teaching skills. As expertise develops in all three areas novices can progressively assume a greater degree of responsibility for planning the lesson and teaching each of its component parts. We shall next examine some possible starting points for planning a lesson.

Approaches to lesson planning

There is a debate as to whether lesson planning should start with the identification of clear aims and objectives for the lesson or with the selection of appropriate tasks and activities.

Specifying precise objectives at the outset of planning a lesson can indeed help you to focus clearly on what exactly it is that you wish to teach, and hence to select appropriate activities and tasks. However, by so doing, you risk emphasizing easily observed outcomes at the expense of more important goals, and this approach may inhibit your creativity in response to unplanned but valuable learning opportunities which arise in the course of the lesson (Stenhouse 1975).

We would not wish you to restrict yourself through the misuse of narrow behavioural objectives; however, when you teach a lesson you take the class on a journey. Unless you know where you intend to go from the start you are unlikely to arrive there at the end. One question which you ought to ask yourself both in your planning and in evaluating your teaching is:

> What will they know at the end of the lesson which they did not know at the start?

We do not mean to imply by this question that your objectives should be limited to easily observable facts, skills, and techniques – far from it. We believe that even when lessons are focused on the processes of mathematics and the development of mathematical thinking skills, you should be clear as to which of these will be developed by the selected tasks.

Jones (1999) claims that experienced teachers often start to plan their lessons by selecting tasks and activities – their choice of tasks, etc. being guided by their implicit objectives for the lesson. However, it is our experience that lessons which lack clear objectives are often unsuccessful. After all, if you do not know what it is you are trying to achieve, what path will you take to get there? Whilst experienced teachers are often able to rely on implicit objectives with which they select their tasks and activities, novice teachers are less able to do this. The danger is that in the absence of explicit objectives, the implicit objective may become 'Get through exercise 17b without any trouble.' Now whilst exercise 17b may be well matched to some educational objectives, they may not be appropriate for this class, who may find them much too easy and learn little, albeit in a quiet and orderly lesson.

We believe that the task should be selected to meet the aims and objectives for the lesson and not vice versa.

The novice teacher would be wise to regard aims and objectives as a framework around which lesson activities are planned but that these may be modified as part of the planning and teaching process (Holt 1996). The danger is that in the early stages of your development as a novice teacher, you are likely to be focusing on your performance in the classroom rather than the pupils' learning (Furlong and Maynard 1995). In such circumstances novices sometimes create activities which fill time and keep classes busy rather than ensure pace and progress in learning. Returning to aims and objectives during the planning process can often be helpful in returning your focus to the learning outcomes of your pupils.

We suggest a planning process which starts by attempting to outline lesson objectives but that these should then be used as a framework to guide your choice of teaching and learning activities. Identification of suitable activities may in turn, however, modify your original choice of objectives for the lesson as your aims and objectives are tempered by the practical issues which arise from the activities.

PREPARING TO PLAN A LESSON

Before you attempt to write a lesson plan, a range of preparatory information needs to be gathered. Each aspect of this is discussed below.

What is the topic?

The topic will usually be given to you (e.g. 'Start linear equations with 7Q'), but what exactly does this mean? Which aspects of the topic are you expected to teach? What have the pupils already covered? You may have clear memories of studying that topic whilst you were a pupil but be careful to adapt your expectations and approaches to match the age and abilities of the particular pupils you are to teach. Discussing the topic with the class teacher will help you to set realistic objectives.

You should also consult the department's scheme of work. This should indicate the work which has already been taught and may provide a rough guide to how many lessons the topic is expected to last. It should also indicate which resources are available to help you to teach the topic. Study them, as they will suggest the scope and range of the work that you should expect the pupils to cover. They may also suggest some interesting teaching approaches for you. Note any 'key points' highlighted by the text as these may indicate important mathematical issues which you might otherwise have overlooked because of their familiarity.

The resources will also be good starting points for revising your own subject knowledge. Remember, you will need to be confident in front of the pupils, not just able to do the calculations but also able to explain how and why. Try out some of the questions to refresh your memory and, whilst you are working, try to identify the main mathematical issues that you will need to explain to the pupils. Try to anticipate which aspects are likely to cause difficulties. Make a note of these and discuss them with your mentor. You will need to prepare a variety of explanations for any difficult points.

It is also good practice for you to consult the National Curriculum for each new topic you teach. Where in the programme of study may the topic be found? What level is it? Which other topics in the same strand are at the same/higher/lower levels? Locating the topic within the wider curriculum will help you to identify what the pupils may be expected to know already and which aspects may be too difficult for them at present.

How does this topic link to other areas of mathematics? Which of these links would you wish to make explicit to the pupils by the end of the lesson?

After you have worked through this section of the prompt sheet your subject knowledge of the mathematics which you have to teach should be sound. Next we focus on the pupils who are to learn the mathematics.

To whom, where and when?

Usually a student will have observed and assisted the teacher with the class before planning a lesson for them. This gives you a chance to get to know the pupils, to learn their names and to gain an impression of the level and pace of their usual work. Find out how able the pupils are. At what National Curriculum levels are they working? Are there any particularly slow or fast workers, or pupils with special needs? Are there any particular class management and control issues associated with the class? Your observations should be used as a basis for discussion with the teacher about how much work should be covered in a lesson, and at what pace. This will help you to plan appropriate targets.

Establish how long the topic is expected to take – is it just one lesson, part of the lesson, or perhaps the work for the week? When are you to teach it and how much time will you have to prepare any additional resources which you may wish to use?

Check on the room in which you will be teaching and on any resources which will be available – will there be a whiteboard, an overhead projector (OHP), does the layout of the room enable you to circulate freely, to call pupils out to the board, etc.

Why should this piece of mathematics be taught?

Teaching is much easier if the pupils want to learn what you are trying to teach them. What justification can you provide to the pupils for expecting them to learn this mathematical topic? Is it relevant to their everyday lives or does it link to other school subjects? As well as such external motivations, can you justify the mathematics intrinsically – can it perhaps be presented as a puzzle, or as a statement which intrigues the pupils because it conflicts with their previous conceptions?

How will you teach the topic?

By now you should be starting to develop some ideas about the content you wish to cover and the capabilities of the pupils. Your lesson observations, examination of the resources, and discussions with your mentor should have suggested some teaching approaches and activities which could be used. Now reflect back on the discussions in Chapter 2 about what constitutes a good mathematics lesson. Are your activities aimed at developing instrumental or relational understanding? Will you start with practical examples and then develop the abstract symbolism?

Over the course of a term you must try to ensure that your lessons achieve a balance between a number of contrasting factors. You should ensure that your lessons cover all the aspects of mathematical thinking discussed in Chapter 2 from facts and skills through to processes and the development of mathematical thinking. You should pay particular regard to the range of learning opportunities listed in Cockcroft's paragraph 243 (Cockcroft 1982). In particular we think you should consider the balance between tasks which are:

open versus closed;
short versus extended;
applied versus pure;
individual versus collaborative.

Detailed advice on the selection of activities may be found in the non-statutory guidance for the National Curriculum (NCC 1989; CCW 1989).

On pp. 62–9 all of these issues are summarized as a series of prompts to help you to plan a lesson. You don't have to write answers to every prompt under the Mathematical content section. The prompts are there to help you think around the topic before forming your aims and objectives for the lesson. The prompt sheet is suitable for use whether you are planning all or just part of a lesson.

As a result of working through the prompt sheets you will have two forms of written output. One will be an outline plan of the lesson. The normal length of this will be about one side of A4. It will include the main features of the lesson plus approximate timings for each of the phases (see the example of a plan given on p. 66 below). This overview is what you will refer to as necessary during the lesson. In addition to this, however, you will also have copious background notes which should include all the worked examples which you intend to use during the lesson and the answers to any exercises.

Task 4.1

Work through the prompt sheets and try to answer the questions as if you were to teach area of a triangle to a Y8 (year-8) class (some sample answers are given to start you off). Then compare your draft plan with the example plan which follows afterwards which was prepared by an experienced teacher.

A LESSON PLANNING PROMPT SHEET

Basic information

What do you want them to have learned by the end of the lesson(s)?

e.g. how to work out the areas of triangles.

How long have you got to do it in? Where? When? What resources are available?

e.g. Y8, set 2, period 3, in room 17, no suitable books.

How able are the pupils? Are there any particularly slow or fast pupils?

e.g. a reasonable class, about level 5 on average, but a wide range, from levels 4 to 6.

Mathematical content

> *Think:*
> *Is there a technique or skill which they don't have now which you want them to have by the end?*
> *Is there a concept underpinning the technique or skill?*
> *What misconceptions might they have?*
> *Are there any conventions they will have to learn?*
> *Is there any special language?*
> *Are there any definitions you want them to learn?*
> *Are there any results they will have to learn? Can you justify or prove the results?*
> *Are there any other areas of maths which this links with?*
> *What is the simplest example you want the least able pupils to cope with by the end?*
> *What is the most complex example you want the fastest pupils to be able to cope with?*
> *Can you write any of the questions in problem form? And can the problems be reversed?*
> *Are there any useful investigations which would help to teach the topic or to provide 'open-ended stopper' questions during practice?*

Designing your worksheet

The design of the worksheet is a central part of the lesson planning process. Its contents will depend on the overall aims and objectives for the lesson, the time available within the lesson plan, and the range of ability of the pupils. Exercises from textbooks rarely meet all of these criteria without adaptation.

Your worksheet should address each of the following features:

- it should be attractive to look at, interesting but uncluttered;
- clipart may be used to add interest but it should relate to the mathematics;
- question 1 should be accessible to all pupils, perhaps very similar to the examples taught;
- the questions should progress in difficulty;
- the questions should be varied in character (e.g. by requiring the use of a skill in a number of different contexts);
- excessive repetition is unhelpful;
- the final question should be a stopper question (i.e. a question which is more extended than usual to challenge and extend the more able pupils).

THE LESSON PLAN PROFORMA

Aims and objectives

Now try to write down your aims/objectives for the lesson(s).

Teaching and learning activities

> *Think:*
> *Is the learning going to be active or passive?*
> *How can you involve the pupils in the learning?*
> *Are you starting with the concrete and moving to the abstract?*
> *Can you include any practical activities?*
> *Might the use of IT make the concept easier to understand?*
> *Are there any visual aids which you could make to help them understand?*
> *When are they going to talk mathematics in your lesson?*

Lesson content

Write down: factual information, worksheets and handouts, OHPs, board diagrams, the main questions you are going to ask, definitions to be given, etc. Write out your examples as they will be set out on the board. *Exercise 3b* does not provide sufficient information – indicate the type of questions, possible problems, etc.

Resources

Now make a list of all the equipment and materials which you expect to use in the lesson.

The overall plan

> *Think:*
> *In what order are things going to be done?*
> *How long will each section take?*
> *What will the introduction be like?*
> *How will you end it and pull all the ideas together?*
> *Is any homework going to be set?*

Write down your sequence of activities with approximate timings showing who is doing what, when, and for how long. Transition points should be clearly identified and strategies prepared for any anticipated class management issues. Make a note of what you will set for homework.

Fine detail

> *Think:*
> *Read through your plan and check that you know the following.*
> *What (exactly) are you going to say? What questions are you going to ask?*
> *Of whom?*
> *What (exactly) are you going to do?*
> *What are you going to write on the board or on the OHP?*
> *Have you planned how this will be set out?*
> *What are pupils going to write in their books and how will they set their work out?*
> *How will you evaluate your success in teaching this topic?*
> *What was it you were trying to teach anyway?*

The following lesson plan was written by a mentor to illustrate to the student what was expected. The lesson was then taught by the mentor with the student's assistance. The post-lesson debrief discussed the extent to which the planning had supported the teaching and also the reasons why the teacher had, on occasions, deviated from the plan.

Task 4.2

Read carefully through the plan below. How clear a picture do you have of what would happen in the lesson? What other information would you need to evaluate the effectiveness of the planning? What other details would you have to consider as part of your planning before you were to teach such a lesson?

Lesson plan – area of a triangle

Y8 set 2 (NC levels 4–6) (Monday 10.00–11.00).

Aims

By the end of topic, pupils will have developed their concepts of the area and perimeter of plane shapes and will be able to apply their knowledge confidently to the solution of problems.

Objectives

- To justify that the area of a triangle is half that of its parallelogram;
- to use the formula to calculate areas of triangle in a variety of orientations;
- to calculate the areas of composite shapes.

Assumed prior knowledge of pupils

Able to calculate area of a parallelogram (taught last lesson).

Possible misconceptions

- Perpendicular height = slant height;
- the base of a triangle has to be a horizontal line;
- area = perimeter.

Resources

Pile of books/pack of cards to demonstrate shearing of rectangle into parallelogram.

Paper triangles for templates

Worksheet on area of triangles and composite shapes.

Plan

10.00   Supervised entry, two puzzle questions on board:
        What is the biggest rectangular area I can enclose with a piece of string 18 cm long?
        What is the biggest perimeter I can get around a shape made from twenty-five squares of side 1 cm? (Each square must touch the next along at least one side, not just a corner)

10.05   Stop class – pens down, listen, etc. Call on pupils with hands up to offer answers to mark questions – emphasize difference between area and perimeter and units of length and area.

10.08   Introduction to main lesson – questions to revise prior knowledge:
        Last lesson we were working out areas of which shapes? . . . Who can come out to show us, using this pile of books, how we found the area of a parallelogram from the area of this rectangle? . . . And the formula we used then was? . . . What tricky lengths did we have to remember not to confuse? . . .
        Stick card parallelogram to board – base not horizontal. Pupil to board to explain which lengths to measure and then proceed to calculate area.

10.15   Demonstrate why the area of a triangle equals half the area of a parallelogram: unstick parallelogram, show *diagonal* drawn on reverse, *What fraction of the area of the parallelogram is the area of this triangle?* Demonstrate by cutting and overlaying. Draw around one triangle on board, then use it as template to complete the parallelogram. Pupils calculate area as before.
        Distribute card triangles to pupils. Pupils to board, draw around triangles, complete parallelograms, measure, calculate areas. (Collect in triangles)
        Question: *Is there a quicker way?* – lead to formula.
        Three examples on board, second with redundant measurements given,

third – composite shape. Question pupils to reinforce formula and method.

10.25   Worksheet – first five questions by 10.35. (Monitor progress)

10.35   Stop class, Q & A to mark answers. Problems?
        Class discussion of number 8.

10.40   Worksheet. Circulate and mark.
        (Extension questions if necessary)

10.50   Q & A to mark sheet.
        Plenary: *What have they learned this lesson?* Use pupils to summarize justification of method, formulae, and the difference between area and perimeter (using answers to number 10).

11.00   Praise for good work. Merits? Dismissal by rows.

Debriefing discussion

Student: How long should it take to plan a lesson? I tried going through that prompt sheet yesterday and it took ages. I did look at some books and found some exercises but if I'd really had to plan the whole lesson I'd have been up all night!

Mentor: At this early stage, I'd say it will take at least 3 hours to prepare a 1-hour lesson. But before you panic, it does get much quicker! This is partly why, of course, you should start by planning just parts of a lesson.

Student: How much detail should I include? Is what you did enough?

Mentor: Initially you have to prepare almost everything. My plan was more detailed than I needed but I wanted to give you an indication of what I was going to do. What I did was really just a running order – something you could glance at in the lesson. That is what you take into the lesson with you but you need to do far more preparation than that. You need to think very carefully about your explanations and your key questions. Try not to write a script, but make a list of the main points so that you can check quickly that you have covered them all before moving on. You also need to work through the exercise in advance, note any problematic questions and plan how you would explain these. You need to have the answers to the questions too.

Student: Your board work always looks neat whereas I'm always struggling for space.

Mentor: That's planning too. Do a rough sketch of the board and plan how you will set out your notes. Remember the pupils will copy it exactly as you write it.

Student: I noticed that you'd written things like 'pens down', why was that?

Mentor: Many class-management problems occur when you change from one activity to the next. As a student you should be noting each such transition point carefully in your plan. You actually need to think through how *exactly* you are, for example, going to gain the pupils' attention when they are doing an exercise and you want them to mark their work.

Student: Why did you put the timings down? You didn't always keep to them.

Mentor: Estimating how long each phase of the lesson will take helps to pace the lesson and stops you spending too long on any one activity. It helps avoid class-management problems too. The timings, just like the plan itself, are only there as a guide, however, and sometimes you will have to modify things on your feet. For example, when I noticed that a group of pupils were struggling with question 6, I went through it with the class. After that, of course, the timings and part of the plan went out of the window! The important part is to evaluate, after the lesson, why you had to change your plan and learn from this for the next time.

As we hope the above extracts make clear, planning is a complex and lengthy process. The outcome of good planning, however, is a smoothly organized, well-structured lesson which leads to effective learning.

Evaluating your lessons

There are so many different factors to be monitored whilst you are teaching a lesson that there is little opportunity for you to 'think on your feet'. (Interestingly, the only other job which requires a comparable number of interactions is that of an air-traffic controller – Watkins 1997.) During a lesson, teachers have to make instant decisions – how to respond to an incorrect answer, or to a pupil who does not understand an explanation, with little time to think through alternative approaches or the consequences of their response. Under such pressure, it is not always possible to respond most effectively.

This is why lesson evaluations are so important. Reflecting back after the lesson allows you to analyse the significant points in the lesson and to consider alternative approaches and responses. These issues can then be considered as you plan and teach future lessons. Initially, debriefs with your mentor or tutor will help you to identify the important features but acquiring the skills of effective self-evaluation is an important part of your professional development.

All lessons should be followed by a realistic, written evaluation. No lesson is ever perfect and you should try to identify your strengths and weaknesses. The four main aspects to evaluate are:

- the effectiveness of your planning – lesson structure, choice of activities;
- your teaching skills – explaining, questioning, discussing;
- the extent to which the pupils achieved the learning objectives;
- the pupils' behaviour and your class-management skills.

All self-evaluations should answer the question:

> *If I were to teach this lesson again, what would I do differently and why?*

Longer term planning

As you move on to planning whole topics rather than just individual lessons, your focus should widen. You need to take an overview of your pupils' mathematical experience. For example, to what extent does the curriculum you provide for your pupils meet the aims of mathematics teaching, the statutory requirements of the

National Curriculum, or the requirements of external examinations? Such questions should also be addressed in your department's scheme of work – the longer term planning document within which your shorter term planning is situated.

Within your planning there are three key issues to be addressed (DfEE 1999a). First, what mathematics do your pupils already know? How can your teaching link with this prior knowledge and develop it?

Second, your planning should enable pupils to experience progression in their mathematical studies. This progression is not just a vertical, hierarchical development as pupils meet harder ideas within the same topic. Mathematics can also be seen as a network of concepts connected to form a coherent structure. In this sense progression requires pupils to make mathematical connections across topics as you develop the links within mathematics (CCW 1989). What other mathematical topics should this work link with?

Third, how does this mathematical topic relate to other subjects within the curriculum or to everyday life? Is there potential to develop the literacy, numeracy, or ICT key skills in this topic?

In the early stages of your teaching it is likely that the lessons and tasks will be aimed at a limited range of abilities. Increasingly, however, you will need to take account of the wide range of abilities and aptitudes that are to be found, even within classes which are set, and to differentiate your teaching approaches and learning activities appropriately. At this stage it might be helpful to pause and to reflect on how many of Cockcroft's (1982) list of recommended teaching strategies you have been able to incorporate into your teaching so far, and to what extent you would consider that your teaching represents good practice (cf. Chapter 2).

CONCLUSION

In many ways, planning a lesson is similar to developing a piece of mathematics. Although the finished product appears concise and logical, its development is a creative interaction between objectives, tasks, and practicalities in the quest for an effective learning experience. In the next chapter we will consider how you may develop a range of effective teaching and learning approaches.

Summary

When planning a lesson you should:

- be able to state what the pupils will know by the end of the lesson that they did not know at the start;
- revise your own mathematical knowledge and identify which aspects the pupils are likely to find difficult;
- list your main teaching points and key questions;
- prepare alternative methods of explanation;
- aim for relational rather than instrumental understanding;
- ensure that you have utilized an appropriate range of teaching and learning strategies;
- evaluate each lesson critically and set yourself targets for improvement.

5 Effective teaching approaches

INTRODUCTION

So far we have discussed the nature of a good lesson in terms of its mathematical content and the nature of the understanding for which we should be striving. We have discussed the teacher behaviours associated with good classroom management and the establishment of authority. We then examined the issues which arise in lesson planning and led you through the process of planning a lesson. We now intend to look more closely at some of the common teaching strategies which are available to you and to focus on those which have been found to be most effective in particular situations. In particular we focus on teaching behaviours and intentions in three forms of classroom organization: whole class, group, and individual.

We do not intend to dictate a particular teaching approach which should be employed in all circumstances – in fact we believe that to concentrate for too long on a single approach is likely to lead to boredom and loss of motivation for both pupils and teachers! Our advice to you is that you should become a 'magpie'. You should observe, evaluate, and analyse every approach that you see used in school, whether it is used in a mathematics classroom or elsewhere, and steal the brightest and the best. Good teachers have a wide range of styles and approaches which they select according to the occasion and their objectives.

Objectives

By the end of this chapter you will:

- be more aware of the nature and pedagogical intent of some common teaching strategies;
- understand what teacher behaviours make such strategies effective and why;
- understand when it is appropriate to use particular strategies in the context of whole class, group, and individual activities.

WHY DO TEACHERS ASK QUESTIONS?

One of the most common actions which a teacher takes is to ask a question. However, questioning is also one of the most subtle skills for the novice teacher to learn. Although in everyday life people generally ask a question because they wish to know the answer to that question, this purpose of questioning is probably used least often in teaching. As you may recall, in Chapter 2 we distinguished between exposition and explanation on the basis that explanation made purposeful use of questioning; similarly, you may also recall that in Chapter 3 we included asking a question as one of our desist strategies. The subtle art of questioning is the art of teaching. In a real sense, learning to teach is learning to ask questions.

Teachers' purposes for questioning are complex and have been divided into several categories over the years; for example, stimulating pupils to think, testing knowledge, and exercising control (Backhouse *et al.* 1992) or genuine, testing and focusing (Pimm and Johnston-Wilder 1999). We will discuss questioning for *control, recall and practice, supporting learning*, and *evaluation*, but we warn you in advance that questions often fulfil multiple purposes.

Control

We begin with control as this form of questioning is probably one the most commonly used in school and will certainly be a major focus of attention for the beginning teacher. We expressed the view in Chapter 2 that exposition alone would be insufficient to hold the attention of a class for more than a few minutes. Explanation, on the other hand, can hold pupils' attention for much longer if it is clear that they are being held accountable.

Control is exerted through questioning in two ways. First, teachers often respond to the early stages of misbehaviour by directing a question, which develops their explanation, to an off-task pupil. In this way they are able to deal with misbehaviour in its early stages without disrupting the flow of their argument or risking a confrontation. Second, questioning during exposition or explanation is used for *alerting*. Kounin's (1970) research, which we discussed in Chapter 3, found that the best classroom managers arranged their questioning so that pupils were constantly in expectation that they might be asked a question about the lesson. They were thus held *accountable* for their learning during any exposition or explanation. For example, consider these two ways of asking this simple recall question during an explanation:

John – how many sides does a hexagon have?

How many sides does a hexagon have? (*Pause*) John?

Although the first version of the question will alert John, perhaps bringing him back on task after the naming, only John needs to listen carefully. Other members of the class may allow their attention to wander. In the second case, all the class have to think of an answer until a pupil is named. (We are assuming here that the teacher is controlling who is to answer and not allowing calling out.)

Recall and practice

Recall of facts and conventions and practice of fundamental skills and routines is often provided during questioning. Many teachers use quick short-response questions which practise old work as a warm-up at the start of lessons. Others deliberately plan to pack away slightly early and use competitive questioning in a game format to fill in time usefully while waiting for the bell. Regular reminders of old work through this form of quick practice aids retention and encourages the development of automaticity.

When questioning is used as a warm-up activity, it is often linked to the theme of the lesson and used to set the scene or recall previous work. This can serve to boost pupils' confidence prior to beginning new work, or the questions can act as an 'advance organiser' (Ausubel 1968) to help the class link the new ideas to their existing knowledge. So, in a lesson introducing percentages for example, questions might include reminders of useful techniques such as:

Does anyone remember how we can write $\frac{3}{5}$ as a decimal?

Such questioning often includes links to real-world knowledge such as:

Can anyone tell me where they have seen the word percentage before?

As with most questioning, each question may fulfil more than one purpose. Although the main aim of the questioning may be to set up advance organizers for new ideas, teachers also use such question-and-answer sessions to refine their judgements about pupils' prior knowledge and any possible misconceptions which exist prior to teaching. Information gained here will be used to modify their plan for the lesson. This is not to say that experienced teachers do not plan in advance. The plans of experienced teachers are often unwritten but more complex than those of novices and rely on decisions which they anticipate making in response to the feedback they receive from their classes (Tanner *et al.*, 1999). Their teaching often occurs during such interactions. Although novices need to plan in far more detail than experienced teachers, they must retain and develop sufficient flexibility to refine their teaching in the light of continuous feedback they should aim to receive from classes. To become effective teachers, novices must learn how to interact with classes and teach through their questioning.

Supporting learning

Supporting learning through questioning is not new. The resulting interaction is sometimes referred to as Socratic dialogue after the Greek philosopher Socrates (BC 469–399). More recently the term '*scaffolding*' (Bruner 1985) has been used to describe the support which a learner can draw from structured questioning by a more experienced person. Questions can be used to lead a person through a problem, argument, or proof. Such a dialogue may have the teacher acting as a 'vicarious form of consciousness' (Bruner 1985: 24–5) taking most of the strategic decisions and guiding progress in order to reduce the total cognitive load on the pupil. However, if too much of the decision making, or to put it another way – the hard work, is done by the teacher and the pupil is left with simple low level recall questions to answer then, instead of teaching through questioning, this reduces to simple *alerting* during exposition. Learning requires mental effort. If too much of the load is carried by the teacher, the potential for real learning is curtailed. The trick is to provide just enough support to allow the pupil to progress through their own efforts.

It is helpful to distinguish between two forms of support which might be provided by the teacher through questioning: *funnelling* and *focusing* (Bauersfeld 1988; Wood 1994). In *funnelling*, it is the teacher who is involved in using thinking strategies and carrying out the demanding tasks to lead the discourse to a predetermined solution. Unfortunately, the social processes of the classroom may hide the mathematical structure which is presented. The pupil may not notice or begin to build a mental picture of this structure unless he/she chooses to reflect on regularities in the actions performed. Only the most mindful pupils do this. If these are the only type of question used in your classroom then learning of deeper structure and problem-solving processes is likely to be limited (Bauersfeld 1988).

Funnelling questions often begin with 'What?' or 'How many?' and lead to short answers based on the recall of facts or conventions such as:

> How many grams are there in a kilogram?
>
> What is seven times eight?

We are not suggesting that there is anything wrong with such questions; in fact, in our research into high-value-added schools we often saw such questions used to set the scene or to alert and involve classes (Tanner *et al.* 1999). They are a necessary part of a teacher's questioning technique but they are not sufficient if used alone.

In *focusing*, the teacher's questions draw attention to critical features of the problem which might not yet be understood. The pupil is then encouraged to resolve any perturbations which have thus been created (Wood 1994: 160). The distinction is often quite subtle, and very difficult to translate to a whole-class situation, requiring skill and sensitivity on the part of the teacher. Examples include:

> Do you think that will be true for all values of x?
>
> Can you always get the lowest possible new denominator by multiplying the old ones?
>
> Can you explain why your formula works?
>
> When would you be likely to use this?

Focusing questions often ask 'When?' or 'Why?' or 'Explain' and demand a longer more reasoned response. This provides an opportunity for pupils to practise and be supported in learning the processes of mathematics as well as the content.

Questions can support learning by helping pupils to overcome a difficulty they have met without telling them how to do act. Sometimes questions with this intention direct the pupil towards an error or towards a profitable place to investigate such as:

> What is different about the units in this question?
>
> Have you thought about congruent triangles?
>
> Do you remember when we met one like this last lesson?

However, questioning need not lead quite so directly to an easy answer. Questions can be used to stimulate learners to think for themselves. The best question is one which pupils might have thought of themselves if only you had given them the opportunity. For example:

> Explain your plan to me.
>
> Talk me through what you have done so far and what you might do next.
>
> OK, pause a moment, before you go any further, and think.

Asking pupils to explain their plan focuses their attention on the need for a plan! Sometimes just 'talking things through' with a teacher or another pupil helps learners who are 'stuck' to clarify their thoughts sufficiently to proceed. It does not always work, but when it does the resulting achievement belongs to the pupil, building self-confidence and a deeper understanding (Backhouse *et al.* 1992). It is during reflection that learning often occurs, but opportunities for reflection may seem sparse during the bustle of classroom life (Wheatley 1991). Asking a question at the right moment can stimulate a pupil to pause and reflect, to monitor their progress in a problem or re-evaluate a plan.

Evaluation

Some questions are to gain feedback to evaluate teaching and learning. Effective teachers assess their pupils continuously. It was characteristic of teachers in the high-attaining schools we studied that they described the abilities and progress of individuals when they discussed their lessons. They were able to give quite precise information about individuals. This continuous-assessment information was used formatively to plan future teaching.

Continuous assessment gained a bad name amongst teachers during the early days of the National Curriculum when it was suggested that such assessments should be formally recorded. We are not suggesting that teachers attempt to formally record such data. The value of such data lies in its immediacy, its continuously changing character and its use. The best teachers question continuously to evaluate the impact of their own teaching and use that information to act on the spot. They modify and adapt their teaching in action as appropriate, and plan tomorrow's lesson to build on today's. Most importantly, however, the best teachers continually reflect on the evaluations they make of their pupils' learning with a view to improving their teaching.

If questioning is to be used to support teaching and learning, it must be managed effectively. We have already suggested above that we think teachers should be able to manage questioning so that they are able to decide who is to answer. We think that this is necessary for several reasons:

- so that less able/more able pupils can be challenged appropriately;
- so that the quieter pupils have a chance to join in;
- so that the teacher can deliberately select wrong answers when it seems helpful to challenge a misconception;

Task 5.1 Focused observation of the purposes of questioning

Watch question-and-answer sessions led by a variety of teachers and try to assess and record the main purpose of each question against this list:

Control/alerting;

Recall/practice;

Supporting learning through funnelling;

Supporting learning through focusing;

Evaluation;

Other.

In particular notice how often the teachers ask questions during an exposition or explanation.

Of course, most questions will be multipurpose and you should make a judgement as to their main purpose.

Discuss your results with the teacher concerned and ask if they usually use as many questions as you have recorded.

- so that a range of possible solutions to a problem can be selected in an order of increasing complexity, allowing as many contributions as possible;
- so that the questioning session remains quiet and controlled while you establish your authority.

The traditional means of controlling question-and-answer sessions is ask for 'hands up'. We believe that beginning teachers would be wise to aim to use this technique in a fairly formal manner while authority is developed. It is easy to develop a more informal style later if you wish, but you should still be able to achieve sufficient control to achieve the objectives above when appropriate. You should decide which classes to try to use 'hands up' with after consultation with your mentor.

In our research into high-attaining schools we saw a range of successful questioning styles. Some teachers used a mixture of formal and informal approaches, sometimes allowing pupils to call out answers to encourage participation but on other occasions saying 'Now, hands up, who can explain ...' when they wanted to control response. Answers from pupils who answered out of turn in such situations were ignored. Persistent offenders were reminded of the rules and when necessary threatened with punishment. Correct answers were not always judged as such at once, but were often offered to another pupil saying 'Is she right?' or to a third pupil saying 'How did he get that answer?'.

Incorrect answers were treated in an identical manner to correct answers in the first instance, but often led to a class discussion, managed by the teacher, in which a range of alternatives were compared. These discussions often proved to be valuable learning opportunities, as misconceptions were addressed directly

Task 5.2 Focused observation on managing questioning

Arrange to observe several lessons with a range of teachers, years, and abilities, and focus solely on the management of the questioning. Try to find out:

How the teacher controls who is going to answer a question?
Is there a ritual established (e.g. 'hands up')? If so is it always used or do teachers sometimes break their own rules?
How does the teacher indicate if 'hands up' is required?
Are pupils called to answer by name, pointing, or other means?
How does the teacher deal with pupils who call out answers 'out of turn'?
What does the teacher do when a pupil gives a correct answer?
What does the teacher do when a pupil gives an incorrect answer?
What does the teacher do when a pupil does not know the answer or refuses to answer?

and perturbations established in the minds of some pupils. Whilst such situations were not entirely predictable, we found that experienced teachers were able to use their knowledge of common misunderstandings to construct questions which were likely to root out misconceptions.

In choosing whom to ask for a response, teachers explained that they used a variety of considerations, but that they did not restrict themselves to those pupils who had their hands up. To do so would allow children to withdraw from the lesson if they wished. All teachers claimed to be keeping a rough mental check that all were being asked to join in, and our observations confirmed that this was the case.

All the teachers we observed had developed differentiation strategies to cope with the range of ability which is present even in set classes. They were able to match questions of appropriate difficulty to different pupils when necessary to ensure that all pupils could participate effectively.

In the majority of schools we observed, teachers had developed a culture in which conjecturing was encouraged. There was no shame in an incorrect response – rather mistakes were expected as a part of learning. Children seemed keen to participate in interactive teaching and learning.

INTERACTIVE WHOLE-CLASS TEACHING

In the high-attaining primary and secondary schools which we researched (Tanner *et al.* 1999), the dominant teaching approach included many features which could be described as interactive whole-class teaching. Teaching approaches varied according to the age and ability of pupils, the topic being taught, the constraints of the physical environment and the pedagogical preferences of the teacher. However, many characteristic strategies and themes applied across the majority of the lessons observed.

One feature which was common to many of the lessons in the high-performing schools which we researched (Tanner *et al.* 1999) was children coming to the board. One positive aspect of this was that pupils were actively involved and motivated to participate. In the lessons we observed, all pupils were expected to take a turn at the board on a regular basis, maintaining alertness. When pupils were at the board, exchanges were managed by teachers to ensure that presenters were offered polite attention and respect. However, it was obvious in the lessons, which we observed, that pupils were interested in what their peers had to say and paid close attention to the proceedings. A culture of mutual respect had been established in these classrooms making it safe for pupils to present in front of their peers. Although this strategy clearly had advantages in terms of motivation and active involvement of pupils, it is not likely to be the act of writing on a board itself which facilitates learning – it is far more likely to be the demands made of the pupils while they are at the front and the contributions made by teachers and other pupils to assist the development of mathematics.

Typically, in both primary and secondary schools pupils were required to explain and justify their work to other pupils – often while working at the board. One secondary teacher gave out 'the pen of doom' several times in one lesson and demanded that its recipient talk and explain while writing on the board. He claimed to his class 'If you can explain it then you know you understand it.' Several of the teachers expressed their aim in such situations as 'Getting the point over without telling – leaving them the joy of working it out for themselves – but giving the support they need to make sure they get there'.

In one lesson we observed, three Y10 pupils were selected to solve a trigonometry problem on the board as they entered the room and their classmates were taking their seats and getting their bags out. By the time the class had settled down, three different solutions were on the board. The authors were then challenged to justify their solutions. The solutions were then thrown open for discussion by the class. During discussion, it became clear to the class which solution was correct. The teacher then told the class how many marks would be allocated for this question in GCSE and invited them to allocate marks. The resulting discussion allowed the teacher to make important points about showing clear working and precision in mathematical language. Clearly this was a teacher-led activity, and although the mathematical contributions all came from members of the class, it could not have occurred without teacher intervention, leadership, and control.

In this example, as with so many others that we observed in the successful schools, the teacher's role was the most significant in the discourse. The teacher was in control at all times, leading and driving the lesson forwards, challenging the pupils, supporting, probing, and encouraging and, perhaps most important of all, focusing the attention of the class on what was significant in the activity and what they were learning through their participation in the lesson. Often this was achieved through rebroadcasting what a pupil had said, sometimes with minor amendments to clarify or change the emphasis. This needs care and sensitivity to ensure that teachers do not 'steal the pupil's voice' and make them say something they did not intend.

The lessons in the most successful schools had effective endings or plenary sessions during which the main points were summarized. Plenaries were planned in advance in most cases and offered opportunities for pupils to report back on progress and to reflect on their learning. This was usually driven by focusing questions from the teacher, but in many lessons the class had obviously come to expect such a session. For example, one Y6 class were not surprised when their teacher asked towards the end 'Well, how was it for you?'. She accepted comments relating to the difficulty of the work, personal concerns about success and failure, patterns which had emerged, and the design of the worksheet. However, she used supplementary focusing questions such as 'Which bits were hardest? Why?', 'What mistakes did you make that you won't do again?', 'What have you learned?' Other teachers asked questions like 'What was important about today's lesson that you are going to remember?'. Others made links to ongoing developments and made announcements like 'Tomorrow we will . . . so tonight I'd like you to think about . . .'

Although plenaries were generated from ideas and issues raised by pupils, they were far from random. Good lessons have clear objectives, and teachers knew in advance what they wanted plenary sessions to include, often to the extent of sometimes having a formal definition which was to come out at the end.

The main feature of effective interactive whole-class teaching is that teachers are listening to pupils' developing ideas and helping them to build their own schemata. The learning process includes the discussion, negotiation, and justification of important ideas as opposed to the simple presentation of a finished product and saying take it or leave it. Whether pupils are at the board or speaking from their desks, they are expected, not only to do mathematics, but also to talk about their mathematics, justifying why any claims they make might be true and putting forward their own ideas. Whole-class discussion and mathematical argumentation has a long tradition in some of our best schools, but it is sometimes difficult to manage in a class of thirty. To be successful, the approach requires pupils to articulate their mathematical ideas and unfortunately the culture in some schools does not support this at present.

SMALL-GROUP WORK

If the school culture encourages pupils to be passive, rather than active learners, it is sometimes difficult at first to get pupils to volunteer extended mathematical speech. This is sometimes compounded by poor discipline or an ethos in which a wrong answer might result in public humiliation. Even when discipline is not an issue, adolescent pupils are sometimes embarrassed about speaking in public at first, and even A-level mathematics students may sometimes be shy about contributing. In such circumstances, small-group work can be used to encourage children to talk about their mathematical ideas in a safer restricted environment, building their self-confidence, before contributing to the whole class.

For example, we observed a teacher end a lesson by setting a challenging question to a Y9 class, who had been working on mode, median, and mean.

Write a set of ten percentage examination marks such that they have a mean of 50%, a median of 40%, and a mode of 60%.

He then divided the class into five teams of six and challenged them to get as many solutions as possible within the next 10 minutes without the use of calculators. The class set to the task with great enthusiasm. While they worked, the teacher circulated, listening to discussions, correcting any conceptual errors, but not arithmetical ones. Each group had a group leader and a secretary/checker.

A spokesperson for each team was then invited out to the board to list their solutions. A point was then awarded for each solution. Teams could challenge any solutions they thought were incorrect. A correct challenge gained one point from the challenged team. An incorrect challenge lost a point to the challenged team. While solutions were being written up rapid mental calculations took place in each team. Challenging teams had to justify their claim and team members had to defend their solution.

Finally, the teacher offered two bonus points for any teams which could explain a strategy which would help a team to win a game like this. Several were offered and discussed. The whole game lasted 25 minutes, and during that time every pupil had calculated literally dozens of examples of mode, median, and mean. However, the teacher had also succeeded in creating a situation where the pupils were willing to challenge and defend a mathematical point of view in public. The work rate was considerably higher than when they had been doing standard exercises in the first half of the lesson.

Although the game aspect of this situation undoubtedly helped to raise enthusiasm, research suggests that even without this aspect, pupils who are presented with challenging questions to discuss in small groups respond positively. For example, Berry and Graham (1991) have demonstrated that the use of 'concept questions' and small-group work in the teaching of A-level mathematics can generate effective discussion in otherwise quiet classes (see Chapter 6).

A combination of small-group work, challenging questions, and interactive whole-class teaching can help to generate a high work rate and enthusiasm for the task in hand. However, mathematics should not always be a group activity. There comes a time when mathematics must be done alone. Whilst some such practice may be achieved through homework, the conditions for this are unequal and uncontrolled, so some individual work must be conducted in school.

INDIVIDUALIZED LEARNING

In the 1970s and 1980s much effort was put into generating resources for mathematics lessons which could be used on an individualized basis. School Mathematics Inner London Education Authority (SMILE), Kent Mathematics Project (KMP), the Schools Mathematics Project SMP (11–16), and Dyfed Mathematics are some of the best known schemes. Many teachers believed that such schemes provided a ready-made solution to the difficulties involved in providing differentiated resources for classes which contained a wide range of ability (whether designated mixed ability, band, or set). The assumption was often made that because pupils had a wide range of background knowledge from which to begin building new knowledge, the ideal solution would be an individualized one, with each child following a personal programme of work and proceeding at their own rate. This assumption is often built into computer-based-teaching software also.

However, it is a false premise that pupils can only learn when the task they are offered is at *exactly* the right level for their personal background knowledge and experience. Children are actually able to learn when a task comes within *range* of their ability. Theories of whole-class teaching are often founded on this 'learning zone' (Newman *et al.* 1989) which is based on what Vygotsky calls the 'Zone of Proximal Development' (Vygotsky 1978: 86) and is commonly referred to as the ZPD.

> The zone of proximal development . . . is the distance between the actual developmental level as determined by independent problem solving and the level of potential development as determined through problem solving under adult guidance or in collaboration with more capable peers.
>
> (Vygotsky 1978: 86)

Vygotsky is describing three possible levels of difficulty for pupil tasks. First, there is a level at which children may work unaided using only knowledge which is secure and well known. When working at this level, consolidation and practice of old material is the most which is likely to be achieved. This results in a quiet lesson, but no new learning, with the possible exception of a few particularly mindful children who reflect on their own work without external prompting and initiate their own development (Salomon and Globerson 1987). Second, there is the level of work which is so far beyond the children's current level that it goes completely over their heads resulting in off-task behaviour and no learning. Third, between these two extremes lies the learning zone, the ZPD, in which children can operate only with some form of help, either from a teacher, a pupil, a group of pupils, or a learning resource like a book or computer (Table 5.1). This is when working noise can be heard, teachers are kept busy, and maximum learning occurs.

Table 5.1 The learning zone or ZPD.

Out of range		
Activities are too hard	Off-task behaviour	No learning
Work goes over their heads	Poor discipline	
The learning zone or ZPD		
Activities can only be completed with help	Working noise	Maximum learning
	Teachers kept busy	
Current level		
Activities involve familiar and secure knowledge	Silent working	No learning or very little learning
	Teacher not needed	

When lessons are organized so that pupils work by themselves through an individualized scheme, whether it is commercial or a series of teacher-designed worksheets, the dynamics of classroom interaction demand that tasks are set at a level which is either at the pupil's current level of development or only very slightly beyond it. The authors of individualized tasks have to assume that the pupil will be supported largely by the diagrams and text on the page with very little input from fellow pupils or the teacher. Consequently, the level of challenge in such materials is often very restricted.

Unfortunately when classrooms are organized to achieve *completely* individualized learning, the social mechanisms for learning which we have been discussing above are lost. Pupils are unable to discuss their work with their peers effectively, teacher time is used inefficiently (an average of 2 min per pupil per hour lesson). The teacher often becomes a 'facilitator' rather than a teacher and sometimes spends the lesson pinned at the desk marking (a task which we think should occur outside of lessons in most cases), or even worse just checking books and equipment in and out. It is difficult to keep all thirty pupils alert and motivated. All too often 'their own rate' is dictated by pupils' inclinations rather than their cognitive capabilities.

USING EXERCISES AND SCHEMES

Some published schemes use materials which are mundane, having been written on the assumption that the pupil will have no substantial support or scaffolding beyond the text. However, other commercial schemes include excellent exercises and lesson ideas, having been written and edited by teams of experienced teachers. (SMP is an example of this.) Such resources can be used in an active and imaginative manner which allows time for whole-class teaching, group work, and efficient use of classroom time.

For example, in one school we know well the SMP (11–16) materials have been grouped by topic and combined with teacher-produced materials to provide a rich, organized resource base which can be used with a high degree of teacher autonomy. All the materials on, say, 'Decimals for year eight' are held in a large box which includes booklets, worksheets, homework sheets, and physical equipment graded on three or four levels of difficulty. Some of the resources are activities and games to play with the whole class. Teachers lead interactive whole-class lessons as they see fit and only use the text resources from the box when they want some small group or individualized work to occur. They then choose whether to set the same task to the whole mixed-ability class or to differentiate the work on a limited number of levels for a short exercise period, before calling the class back for a plenary at the end. Teachers add new ideas and materials to the resource box as they see fit. They make their own professional judgements about which elements to use and which to replace, within the guidelines provided by the school's planned scheme of work.

Making such professional judgements are critical for effective teaching. Many textbooks are written on the assumption that children will work through exercises without support. In such cases, exercises will often replicate very closely the example given at the start, demanding little progression or mathematical thinking. When evaluating even a single exercise from a textbook for possible use in your lesson you should contrast it with the advice we offered in Chapter 4 on the construction of worksheets. We think that before using any commercial scheme, or series of textbooks, you should ask yourself a series of questions about its use.

Task 5.3 Analysing a commercial scheme

Find a copy of a current scheme or series of textbooks in use in your school or from a college library. Consider how you might be able to use it with a class you know. What opportunities does it offer for:

>   interactive whole-class teaching?
>   small-group work?
>   practical activities?
>   mental work?
>   working on extended problems?
>   developing the problem-solving processes of AT1?
>   entry-level work for the least able?
>   extension work for the most able?
>   using ICT to support learning?

Even if a scheme was designed to be used in a completely individualized form you may be able to find a way to use it as an effective resource, adding your own ideas and activities to fill in any gaps from the list above. No matter how good a scheme may be we believe that the best educational experience results from active teaching which draws on resources chosen by the teacher rather than by mindless scheme following.

SPECIAL NEEDS

Although we have emphasized the social processes of learning, and particularly whole-class approaches, we feel it is appropriate to remind you here that your pupils are all individuals, and the best teachers cater for the individuals in their classes. Some of the individuals in your classes will have Special Educational Needs (SEN) which will demand your attention. Some pupils may be particularly gifted and deserve to be challenged appropriately through extension work and the use of longer problem-solving tasks which they can explore in more depth than the majority. Other pupils will have special needs as a result of their Specific Learning Difficulties (SpLD) (e.g. dyslexia), for which you must cater. Other pupils will be designated as having Moderate Learning Difficulties (MLD). In all such cases pupils are likely to have Individual Education Plans (IEPs) defining their learning needs, which the school is obliged to enact in accordance with the code of practice on identification and assessment of SEN (DFE/WO 1994).

Task 5.4 Special needs in mathematics

Arrange through your mentor to speak to the SEN coordinator in your school (known as the SENCO). Ask about the range of special needs within the mathematics classes you are teaching and within the school as a whole.

Discuss with the SENCO the specific individual needs of the pupils you will meet in lessons and how you should support them.

All children with special needs must be officially designated as such within the school. Discuss with the SENCO the incidence of children whose learning difficulties were not severe enough to warrant official designation, but which require consideration in the classroom.

If there are no children with statements of special needs in your classes, ask to observe some lessons with other teachers to see how children with SEN are catered for in the mainstream.

Although there is no room here to deal with the full range of specific learning difficulties you are likely to meet, there is one which we should mention because of its prevalence and characteristics – dyslexia. Dyslexia covers a range of problems associated with reading and writing. Its precise definition is a subject of contention and debate with consequently widely varying estimates of the number of children who might be affected. We will not enter the debate as to the definition or incidence rate other than to say that between 10 and 20 per cent of the school population have sufficiently serious difficulties with reading and writing to impact on their learning of other subjects. Dyslexic children and adults are not necessarily unintelligent. In fact, many dyslexic children are extremely good at mathematics. This means that it is particularly important that their difficulties with the written word do not hold back their performance in an area in which they can achieve highly.

Task 5.5 Signs of dyslexia

Ask your SENCO or mentor to identify a group of between four and six dyslexic pupils or pupils with reading difficulties. Work closely with this group during mathematics lessons for a week, supporting their learning during exercise sessions. See if you can notice any characteristic difficulties.

Peer (1996) provides an easy and concise introduction towards dealing with dyslexia. If you wish to learn more about dyslexia and mathematics, examine Miles and Miles (1992); for dyslexia in general try Reid (1998).

Not all dyslexic pupils exhibit the same characteristics and many are not officially statemented or recognized, but here are some indicators which you may notice:

- disorganization, untidy book, wrong book, etc.;
- poor handwriting;
- reversals for b and d, p and q, etc;
- left/right confused;
- indeterminate hand preference;
- ear trouble in infancy (or even now) resulting in confusion between m and n;
- dominant hand/eye crossed laterality (i.e. right hand and left eye);
- immaturity;
- poor standard of written work compared with oral ability;
- difficulties in note taking.

(Peer 1996; Reid 1998)

If you know a child is dyslexic:

- make allowances for disorganization and help them to organize their work – as a form tutor or a mathematics teacher, you should support their use of homework diaries, help them to list deadlines, colour-code books, plan a place to work quietly, etc.;
- give clear instructions about the layout of work;
- teach them how to organize their work (e.g. using coloured markers to highlight key points in notes);
- teach them how to organize a revision programme;
- teach them about examination technique;
- teach procedures for drafting and redrafting coursework tasks;
- use wordy written questions only when strictly necessary and communicate orally as well as in writing where possible;
- avoid humiliation through public labelling or demanding that they read aloud;
- correct some (not all) of their spelling but avoid criticism of their spelling – they are not doing it deliberately!
- help them to read each word of a problem carefully in a one-to-one situation;
- place paper or ruler under the line they are reading in a one-to-one situation.

But most of all, never dictate notes. There will be two or three pupils in each of your classes who, whether they are designated as such or not, exhibit some dyslexic tendencies. These pupils will copy down your dictated note in a form which is useless for revision purposes. It is not acceptable to consider only the majority in whole-class lessons. Every individual has the right to an appropriate form of teaching and the best teachers cater for the needs of individuals even when teaching a whole class.

CONCLUSION

Children are individuals with individual backgrounds, experiences, and needs. However, although children learn in unique ways they do not learn in isolation. The most effective teachers are active in the learning process and intervene to provoke learning. They manage the teaching of the whole class and the learning of individuals.

Although each pupil in your class will begin a new piece of work with a slightly different set of schemata and misconceptions, whole-class teaching is still possible if teachers are sufficiently aware of the misconceptions which commonly occur and plan to address them directly. It is to this which we must now turn.

Summary

Effective teachers:

- use a variety of teaching and learning approaches;
- lead lessons with clear objectives and maintain a good pace;
- make good use of questioning, particularly to scaffold pupils' learning and to continually assess and inform their teaching;
- use pupils' ideas to develop new concepts;
- require pupils to be actively involved in their learning, to reflect on their learning and to explain their ideas to their fellow pupils;
- evaluate resources critically and only use if appropriate;
- differentiate work to meet the needs of individuals;
- arc aware of the special needs of some pupils and seek advice from colleagues when necessary.

6   Misconceptions and planning how to deal with them

To multiply by 10, add a nought.

An important element of mathematics is the development of the ability to spot patterns and to make generalizations. Pupils frequently create their own explanations and rules to account for the patterns which they find but some of these, like the 'rule' quoted above, are inadequate or incorrect. Pupils' errors are often due to misconceptions rather than careless mistakes. Many of these misconceptions are widespread and thus an awareness of them can help you to plan more effective teaching and learning.

The national curriculum for initial teacher training requires that mathematics trainees are taught to recognize and to address common misconceptions (DfEE 1998). The misconceptions cited in the document include:

- reading 206 as 26 as a result of misunderstanding about the number system and place value;
- an expectation that the outcome of division always gives a smaller value (e.g. $4 \div \frac{1}{2} = 2$);
- the way addition applies to whole numbers can be extended to fractions (e.g. $\frac{1}{2} + \frac{1}{4} = \frac{2}{6}$);
- thinking that, when throwing a die, a 6 is harder to get than other numbers;
- stating that two identical angles are unequal because the length of the arms is different in each, as a result of thinking that an angle is the distance between the ends of the lines.

(DfEE 1998: 57 ff)

Which of these examples surprised you? Were any of them misconceptions which you remember having had yourself as a pupil? As we will see later in this chapter, such errors are frequent and widespread amongst pupils. Your pedagogical knowledge as a teacher should include an awareness of the common misconceptions and appropriate strategies for addressing them.

Objectives

By the end of this chapter you should:

- know some of the common misconceptions;
- know where to find reference to others;
- know how to teach to address misconceptions;
- begin to predict possible misconceptions.

The more aware you are of the possible misconceptions associated with a topic the more effective will be your teaching.

The prevalence of misconceptions in pupils' thinking, from primary-school age through to undergraduates (and beyond!), have been confirmed by several surveys and research projects.

STUDIES INTO PUPIL'S MISCONCEPTIONS

Two of the seminal research projects are outlined below. Dating back to the mid-1970s, they predate the widespread use of calculators in schools. As you read the findings, you may like to consider what effect the more recent availability of calculators might have had on pupils' scores (see Chapter 10 for further discussion).

The 'Concepts in Secondary Mathematics and Science' (CSMS) project (1974–9) investigated pupils' levels of understanding of ten common mathematical topics ranging from fractions to vectors (Hart 1981). The key mathematical ideas in a topic were set in a problem-solving format and used for written tests and interviews. A representative sample of about 10,000 pupils aged 11 to 15 years was drawn from schools across England and about 300 pupils were also interviewed.

The interviews probed the methods which pupils used to solve the problems and attempted to understand any errors which were made. The insights gained during the interviews were used to interpret the results of the written papers. For example, many questions which were successfully answered by large numbers of pupils on the written paper were solved during the interviews by informal or non-taught methods. For instance, how do you think pupils might answer this question?

> A gardener has 391 daffodils. These are to be planted in 23 flowerbeds. Each flowerbed is to have the same number of daffodils. How would you work out how many daffodils to plant in each flowerbed?
>
> (Brown 1981a: 25)

CSMS found that many pupils used informal methods involving repeated subtraction or addition of 23 rather than the expected division algorithm.

On the written tests it was found that identical incorrect responses were given by many of the pupils. For example, 51 per cent of 12-year-old pupils thought that dividing 16 by 20 was impossible (Hart 1988: 20). Such pupils would appear still to be restricted to thinking of numbers as integers and reasoning, therefore, that you could not divide a smaller number by a larger one. If such responses are taken as indicative of an erroneous mode of reasoning rather than coincidental carelessness then we can infer that such wide-scale misconceptions are held by large numbers of pupils (Johnson 1989: 2).

Similar results were found by the Assessment of Performance Unit (APU) in their annual surveys of pupils' mathematical development at ages 11 and 15 (Foxman 1985; APU 1991). Between 1978 and 1982, written tests of mathematical concepts and skills were given to approximately 13,000 pupils across England, Wales, and Northern Ireland, with a 10 per cent sample being interviewed. Their findings also identified the existence of common, widespread errors. They also concluded that the pupils attempted to make sense of their mathematics and often devised methods based on seemingly rational, although erroneous, explanations (Foxman 1985: 851).

Follow-up research studies have probed further into pupils' own strategies, the reasons why pupils fail to adopt the formal algorithms taught in schools, and have attempted to identify more effective teaching approaches (see Hart 1984; Kerslake 1986; Johnson 1989; Bell 1993a, b).

More recent surveys, both national and international (see, e.g. Jones and Tanner 1997; Keys *et al.* 1996; Williams and Ryan 2000) indicate that pupils continue to exhibit similar errors and difficulties.

Misconceptions may arise in a number of ways:

- through developing a conceptual structure which is flawed (as in the first bullet point at the start of this chapter);
- by the overgeneralization of a rule, principle, or concept (as in the third bullet point at the start of this chapter);
- through the systematic application of a flawed procedure (e.g. always subtracting the smaller digit from the larger within the subtraction algorithm);
- by misinterpreting notation;
- by misreading diagrams or tables (e.g. by assuming that angles which look equal in a sketch diagram are equal);
- by making careless, random errors which indicate occasional lapses in concentration (i.e. the pupil is just plain wrong!).

(See Greer and Mulhern 1989; Bell 1993a, b; DfEE 1998)

We will next explore the misconceptions associated with some common mathematical topics.

Pupils' understanding of place value and decimals

Task 6.1

The following questions are designed to expose particular misconceptions. What mistakes can you predict your pupils making? Try to identify exactly how a child would get each of the questions wrong. Talk to your mentor about what they think the difficulties might be. Finally, estimate what percentage of 11-year-olds would get each question correct.

Now, during a lesson, either work with a small group of about four pupils and discuss with them the methods they use to solve each question, or select two or three questions to ask a large number of pupils as you circulate around the class during the exercise phase of a lesson.

1   $6.25 - 4 =$

2   $5.07 - 1.3 =$

3   $6 \times 0.5 =$

4   Divide £6.70 equally between two children. How much will each child get?

5   $4.3 \div 2 =$

Commentary

The questions are similar to those used in previous surveys and the common misconceptions and success rates will be discussed as a comparison for your own findings.

The first three questions test pupils' understanding of decimal notation and the place value of each digit. Common errors include ignoring the meaning of the decimal point and aligning the digits with a left or right-hand margin. For example, question 1 would be set out as in Figure 6.1:

```
  6.25
-    4
  6.21
```

Figure 6.1 A vertical layout for a calculation.

APU found that only 28 per cent of 11-year-old pupils answered this question correctly with 44 per cent getting the answer 6.21 as shown above (Foxman 1985: 74).

Notice that if you had presented the question vertically then the pupil would not have had to decide how to align the figures and you would not have been alerted to the underlying misconception. When a similar question was presented vertically, 88 per cent of 11-year-olds answered it correctly compared with 46 per cent when the sum was set out horizontally as here (Foxman 1985: 68).

Question 2 probes for an additional misconception – that of interpreting the decimal point as a separator and performing two separate operations on either side of it. Two incorrect answers are possible here, depending on how pupils treat the nought. For example:

$$5.07 - 1.3 =$$

could be interpreted as

$$(5 - 1) \quad \text{and} \quad (07 - 3) = 4.04$$

or alternatively as

$$(5 - 1) \quad \text{and} \quad (7 - 3) = 4.4$$

Only one-third of 11-year-olds got this question correct compared with 20 per cent who obtained the incorrect answers of either 4.04 or 4.4 (Foxman 1985: 77).

About half of the 11-year-olds were able to answer question 3 correctly. A common error, however, was to misplace the decimal point giving answers of 30 or 0.3. This was done by 27 per cent of the pupils (Foxman 1985: 80).

Questions 4 and 5 compare the effect of context. Usually, setting the question as a problem makes it harder for pupils. However, if the context is money then pupils seem to use different strategies, based on their everyday knowledge, which lead to better performance. In comparable questions, 73 per cent of 11-year-olds answered the money problem correctly compared with only 21 per cent on the numeric question (Foxman 1985: 106).

In the numeric question, the remainder caused problems with 22 per cent of the pupils giving an answer of the form 2.1r1. No pupils gave this as an answer when the question was written as a money problem. This might be because the zero was provided in the money problem but it is more likely to be that pupils' everyday knowledge helped them, perhaps by dealing with the pounds and pence separately (i.e. following the misconception discussed in question 2).

How many of these difficulties were you able to predict? Which of the misconceptions would be exposed during a 'typical' exercise in a decimals lesson?

Many teachers begin their planning by choosing an exercise which they intend the pupils to be able to do by the end of the lesson. What features would you look for when selecting an exercise on decimals for your pupils?

Task 6.2

1   Look at the exercises on decimals in a school textbook. Analyse the questions against the misconceptions described above. Do the questions confront or avoid the probable errors?
2   Extracts from two worksheets revising pupils' knowledge of decimals are shown in Figures 6.2 and 6.3. Which do you think is the better? Why?

Worksheet A

For each question, add each set of numbers to find the 'odd answer out'

1a $0.2 + 0.6 + 0.5 =$
 b $0.6 + 0.1 + 0.8 =$
 c $0.3 + 0.2 + 0.8 =$
 d $0.7 + 0.3 + 0.3 =$

For each question, subtract each pair of numbers to find the 'odd answer out'

2a $4.8 - 1.5 =$
 b $7.6 - 4.3 =$
 c $6.5 - 3.2 =$
 d $9.7 - 6.6 =$

Work out the answers to the following:

3   $0.2 \times 4 =$
4   $0.3 \times 2 =$
5   $4.1 \times 7 =$
6   $8.4 \div 2 =$
7   $164.84 \div 4 =$
8   $11.4 \div 5 =$

Figure 6.2 Worksheet A.

Worksheet B

1. $5.07 + 1.3 + 27 =$

2. $12.6 - 3.81 =$

3.   Jo says that $5.23 - 3.7 = 5.14$. What should the answer be? What mistakes did Jo make?

4.   Add one-tenth to 7.9.

5.   13.5 m of string is cut in half. How long is each piece?

6.   Divide 4.6 by 100.

7. $6 \times 0.5 =$

8.   Which is bigger: $10 \div 0.2$ or 10×0.2? Explain your answer.

9.   Make up a problem to match this sum: $1.4 + 2.03 =$

10   Write the most difficult problem which you can solve which has an answer of 2.5.

Figure 6.3 Worksheet B.

Commentary

On the first worksheet, once you have shown the pupils how to do the first problem in the first two questions, the others can be solved in the same fashion. This should result in a quiet, orderly lesson with the pupils busily getting on with the task.

However, this worksheet requires little more of the pupils than their ability to follow algorithms. What significance would the teacher's instruction to 'line up the decimal points' have in questions 1 and 2? The pupils will obtain the correct answers even if they believe they have to align the digits with the right or left margins. Similarly, questions 3 to 7 avoid pupils having to 'carry' digits or to deal with remainders.

Such questions do not expose the main misconceptions and, therefore, pupils are likely to leave the lesson still not knowing that they misunderstand. Indeed, their misconceptions are being reinforced through use. The pupils are also likely to score high marks on this worksheet even if they have a limited, instrumental understanding of the topic. This is likely to result in confusion and disillusionment later on when they try to apply restricted rules to more testing contexts.

In worksheet B, there is less repetition. Pupils have to think about each question rather than unthinkingly following a routine. The questions attempt to target the common misconceptions and so to challenge the pupils' understanding of the concepts. Pupils are asked to think about their knowledge and to use it to identify errors or to solve problems (see questions 3, 8, 9, and 10). The disadvantage of this worksheet is that the pupils are less likely to be able to complete it without the teacher's help. If the pupils have not understood place value and decimals then the teacher will have a busy lesson!

A word of caution is necessary here – worksheet B is more problem based than worksheet A. If your class have been taught in a purely instrumental manner, they may exhibit *teacher dependence* and, being unable to think for themselves, not know how to cope when confronted with problems. If this is the case, you may have to wean them off their dependence gently at first. However, it remains your responsibility to teach them to think for themselves and the problem should be addressed rather than avoided.

Which worksheet, however, is more likely to develop pupils' understanding of decimals – the selection of 'straightforward' questions which yield the correct answer despite underlying misconceptions, or the confrontation of those possible errors through the use of probing questions? How can we best teach pupils to address their misconceptions?

TEACHING TO ADDRESS MISCONCEPTIONS

What would have been going on in the pupils' minds as they calculated the wrong answers indicated above? Have they been incorrectly taught? Or, do you think it is more likely that they have just forgotten the correct methods? It might seem, therefore, that careful reteaching would remedy the situation. However, as you will discover for yourself within days of starting to teach, a clear, logical exposition is not enough to ensure that pupils will understand a concept.

In Chapter 2 the theories of Piaget and Vygotsky were used to describe learning as a process of individual construction assisted by the social context of the classroom. Pupils try to make sense of the teaching, assimilating those aspects of the information which fit into their existing schemata and, occasionally, modifying their mental structures to accommodate new knowledge. Such restructuring is hard work as it requires deliberate mental effort and a recognition by the pupils that their existing concepts are inadequate in some way.

For learning to occur then:

- the pupils need to appreciate that something is not quite right – to have a sense of unease about their current understanding;
- the learning process needs to be important enough to the pupils for them to make the effort to change;
- just telling them is not enough – pupils need help to construct new knowledge and to connect it to their existing concepts.

Pupils develop their own versions of the concepts being taught. In order to learn, pupils then need to compare their ideas with the teacher's official version during classroom interactions. Unfortunately, pupils cannot volunteer the information that they have a misconception – by definition, if you have a misconception you do not know that you are wrong! It is up to the teacher to find pupils' misconceptions and challenge them.

However, teachers cannot know directly how good the match is between the pupils' constructed concepts and their own. They can only test, through questioning or discussion of key aspects, for the extent to which the pupil's concept appears to fit their own (von Glasersfeld 1991). The teacher has no information about the aspects which were not examined.

A useful metaphor is that of trying to sail a boat at night without navigational aids through a narrow channel. If you hit a rock then you know that you have made a mistake but a successful passage gives you little information about the topography of the channel or whether you had taken the best route (Watzlawick 1984, cited in Kilpatrick 1987).

Similarly, a pupil may achieve the correct answer to a problem through the use of a limited or inefficient strategy. The production of the answer alone will not alert the teacher to an underlying misconception; further interaction is necessary to elicit the pupil's thinking. Good teachers anticipate before the lesson exactly what their pupils are likely to misunderstand. Some misconceptions you will be able to predict yourself; reading the research studies and asking the advice of more experienced teachers will help you to identify others. Your teaching strategies should then address such misconceptions.

There are two aspects to be considered when planning your teaching:

1   your approach should avoid the use of metaphors or analogies which may lead to the pupils forming restricted concepts;
2   pupils will need to be convinced of the limitations of their current thinking before further learning can occur.

Now we can consider how these aspects translate into practice.

Developing sound metaphors for teaching

Poorly thought-through teaching strategies can result in pupils developing conceptual structures which cannot be generalized to more difficult mathematics. The rule 'to multiply by 10 add a nought' is one example. Such an approach can be somewhat harshly described as 'quick and dirty' teaching. It requires little effort on the part of the teacher and can result, in the short term, in the pupils achieving satisfactory performance on routine questions. It represents the worst type of instrumental understanding, however, as the pupils have to unlearn this strategy when they meet decimals or fractions. An explanation based on moving the digits across the columns so that each value becomes ten times larger is preferable as it is mathematically sound and thus can be extended without difficulty to decimals.

Another example of a restricted teaching metaphor can all too often be found in introductory algebra. Think back to when you first met expressions such as:

$$2a + 3b$$

How would you explain the meaning of such an expression to a pupil?

It may be tempting to introduce some 'fruit-salad algebra' here and interpret the expression as 2 apples and 3 bananas. This allows pupils to deal happily with simplifying expressions such as:

$$2a + 5b + a =$$

but makes less sense when applied to:

$$2a \times 3b =$$

Explaining algebra in this way distorts the meaning of the letter from that of a variable to that of an object. Six levels of algebraic understanding have been identified according to the way the letter is used (Küchemann 1981).

Letter evaluated   For example, in the equation $a + 5 = 8$, the answer, $a = 3$, can be obtained without having to perform any algebraic operations by counting on or by recalling the number bond.

Letter not used   Here the letters may be ignored; for example, '*If $a + b = 43$, then $a + b + 2 =$*' can be answered by 'matching' both sides of the equations.

Letter as object   As in the fruit-salad examples above, the letter is interpreted as an object.

A specific unknown   Each letter is understood to represent one number; for example '*If $e + f = 8$, $e + f + g = \ldots$?*'

A generalized number   Pupils appreciate that questions such as '*If $c + d = 10$ and c is less than d then what can be said about c?*' will yield a range of values.

A variable   Pupils are able to analyse a relationship between the variables; for example, '*Which is larger, 2n or $n + 2$?*'

(after Küchemann 1981: 104).

Children whose understanding is limited to that of *letter evaluated* will be successful in questions like the one given, in which all that is required is to evaluate the number which can stand in the place of the letter in the equation but will fail for the other questions. On the other hand, children who understand that letters represent *variables* will be successful in all the examples.

The first three categories do not require any concept of algebra as a generalization of arithmetic. Only when letters are interpreted as, at least, a specific unknown (categories 4–6) can the pupils be said to have an understanding of algebra. Küchemann found that only 17 per cent of 13-year-olds interpreted letters in such general ways.

Questions like:

$$a + 7 = 11$$

do not demand the use of algebra. They require no generalization and will generally be solved by *counting on* no matter what the teacher says. On the other hand, questions like:

$$a + 0.4356 = 17.65$$

if solved with a calculator, begin to require algebraic understanding as the pupil has to begin to apply a general rule, reversing an operation.

Introducing algebra by interpreting letters as objects leads to a mathematical dead end. It fails to offer pupils a basis for developing a true understanding of the mathematical concept. To progress to the higher categories, pupils would have to first unlearn the restricted fruit-salad metaphor. This is poor teaching.

$$2a + 3a = 5a$$

depends on the distributive law. This might be approached relationally by discussing a number of arithmetical examples before making the generalization to any number by introducing letters. For example:

$$2 \times 3 + 3 \times 3 \quad = \quad 15 \quad = \quad ? \times 3$$
$$2 \times 7 + 3 \times 7 \quad = \quad 35 \quad = \quad ? \times 7$$
$$2 \times \tfrac{1}{2} + 3 \times \tfrac{1}{2} \quad = \quad 2\tfrac{1}{2} \quad = \quad ? \times \tfrac{1}{2}$$
$$2 \times -3 + 3 \times -3 \quad = \quad -15 \quad = \quad ? \times -3$$

should be calculated mentally and then discussed as a class as an introduction to questions like $2a + 3a = 5a$.

Children should be encouraged to begin writing algebraic expressions from Y5 or Y6. They occur naturally as the general term in a number series. Alliteration should be banned from day 1.

Task 6.3 Avoiding alliteration

Consider this question:

Pens cost 12p each and rubbers cost 10p each. Write an expression which shows how many of each I can buy for £1?
One boy wrote $5p + 6r = 100p$
What do you think p stands for?

We think he means that one solution is that you can buy 5 pens and 6 rubbers, so p means pens rather than the number of pens (or even pence). You should, therefore, avoid using fruit-salad algebra, such as a = apples, and encouraging a misconception. It helps during the early stages if you avoid using the initial letter of an object as a variable associated with that object.

Alternative teaching strategies should, therefore, interpret letters as numbers and lead to an understanding of an expression as a generalized statement. Work on equations, such as $\Box + \bigcirc = 7$, can lead to an appreciation that the symbol may represent a range of values rather than just a single number. The values should not be restricted to integers – include fractions and decimals as appropriate.

Consider how the use of algebra would arise in the following task:

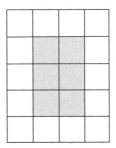

Figure 6.4 A tile investigation. The 6 grey tiles are surrounded by 14 white tiles. How many white tiles would be needed if the grey rectangle measured 5 tiles by 2 tiles? Find a general expression for the number of white tiles for any size of grey rectangle.

'Data–Pattern–Generalization' tasks, such as this, require pupils to find relationships between variables and encourages them to represent that relationship unambiguously and efficiently. Such relationships can often be written in different ways; for example, for this task pupils could have derived expressions for the number of white tiles in the form $2x + 2y + 4$, or $2(x + y) + 4$ where x and y represent the dimension of the inner tiles. Asking the pupils to compare the alternative expressions generated will require manipulation of the algebraic expressions and consideration of possible equivalences.

Practical activities such as timing balls rolling down slopes can also lead to pupils developing understanding of a variable. Plotting the data on a graph, perhaps using a graph-plotting package or a graphic calculator, can help pupils derive a relationship between the variables. It also provides an alternative representation of equations in pictorial form thus encouraging broader understanding of the concept. The graph can also be used to develop appreciation of intermediate values.

Teaching in this fashion will avoid introducing misconceptions into pupils' thinking. It will not, however, prevent pupils from constructing other misconceptions for themselves. We shall now look at how you can address these.

TEACHING FOR COGNITIVE CONFLICT

Pupils do try to generalize their learning and, as discussed earlier in this chapter, some of their generalizations will be limited or incorrect. A successful strategy for addressing these is to generate 'cognitive conflict'.

Having anticipated the most likely misconceptions, try to choose problems which will lead to clearly illogical outcomes when those misconceptions are present. The problems should result in 'cognitive conflict' as the pupils realize that their answers cannot be correct. For example, many pupils overgeneralize the addition of integers to that of fractions. The common strategy of 'add tops, add bottoms' will clearly fail if applied to $\frac{1}{2} + \frac{1}{4} =$ and then compared, in discussion, with their real-life knowledge of halves and quarters. This strategy requires that feedback is provided at frequent intervals within the lesson so that errors are challenged as they occur rather than being reinforced through practice.

Your role as a teacher is then to help to resolve the conflict through the use of questioning, discussion, visual aids, etc. as appropriate. Requiring pupils to talk about their work, perhaps by trying to justify their answer to a small group, is often sufficient to clarify a misconception.

Structuring the work in this way so that the pupils are confronted with the dilemmas and illogical outcomes which result from their misconceptions has been shown to be more effective than warning pupils in advance of the possible errors and thereby pre-empting cognitive conflict (Bell 1993a, b).

Cognitive conflict can be used with pupils across the age range as we will see in the two lessons described below.

Provoking cognitive conflict in KS2 and KS3

The ability to order a mixed set of numbers with up to three decimal places is one of the key outcomes specified for Year 6 in the National Numeracy Framework. The difficulties which pupils found with this topic were explored by the APU. Consider the following question taken from the APU study and predict what misconceptions it might expose.

Circle the smallest value:

0.375   0.25   0.5   0.125

The response rates of 11-year-olds to this question were:

34%   2%   43%   17%

(Foxman 1985: 56)

The first main error which the APU identified was a tendency to ignore the decimal point and consider the value of the significant digits as if they were integers. The 43 per cent of pupils who considered 0.5 to be the smallest value probably held this misconception.

The other common error is shown here by the pupils who chose 0.375. Their reasoning seemed to be that the more digits there are after the decimal point, the smaller the number becomes. Indeed, even some of the pupils who answered correctly might have held the misconception that the longer numbers are smaller.

Pupils will have to be convinced that their reasoning is incorrect if such misconceptions are to be overcome. Consider the following lesson outline. The lesson, suitably adapted, could be taught to pupils from Year 5 to 8, depending on ability.

A lesson to provoke conflict when ordering decimals

Lesson objective

For pupils to be able to order a mixed set of numbers with two or more decimal places.

Setting up the conflict

The following problem was written on the board.

My friend says

    375 is bigger than 137 which is bigger than 52

and therefore

    0.375 > 0.137 > 0.52

Is she right?

Allow the pupils a few minutes to think individually about the problem. They should then discuss their answers in small groups and agree on an answer and a justification. A brainstorm of the responses can then lead into the main teaching activity based on the number line.

Teaching the concept

Draw a number line from -1 to 2 on the board. Ask pupils out to mark in a range of familiar fractions, decimals, percentages (e.g. $\frac{1}{2}$, $\frac{1}{4}$, 50%, 0.1, 150%), etc. Remind pupils to convert the fractions and percentages to decimals, using a calculator if necessary.

Extend the range of the decimals and ask pupils to predict where on the number line they should be placed. Discuss the size of the numbers and link to their position on the line.

Extend the number of decimal places and use the idea of magnifying or zooming in on the line to help mark the numbers' positions.

Lead on to the idea that there are an infinite number of decimals between any two points on the line.

The 'sting'

Finally, refer back to the original question and ask pupils to use the number line to justify why the two main misconceptions must be incorrect.

Exercise

As we discussed earlier in this chapter, when comparing the worksheets, the questions should be chosen to test pupils' understanding of the concepts and to allow them to demonstrate any remaining misconceptions.

The first few questions in the exercise here could ask pupils to draw a number line and use it to order a range of percentages, fractions, and decimals. The numbers would be chosen to expose the two main misconceptions. Such questions should be similar enough to the main teaching activity to allow all the pupils to attempt them. The 'stopper question' for the final task could be:

> Which is bigger:
>
> $0.7 + \frac{1}{2} + 10\%$ or $\frac{1}{4} + 12\frac{1}{2}\% + 0.4$

Plenary

Discussion of the stopper question by calling on pupils to explain their methods would enable you to focus pupils' attention on the main points of the lesson.

Finally, hand out four cards with $\frac{1}{4}$, 50%, 0.7 and 0.8 written on them. The pupils holding the cards have to line themselves up, in order of size, at the front of the class. Then hand out three blank cards and ask the pupils to write a decimal number so that they can place themselves between two of the existing numbers. Ask the pupils to explain how they worked out which numbers they could be. Extend the number of decimal places, and the conversion between fractions, percentages, and decimals, according to the ability of the pupils.

Commentary

Starting the lesson by asking pupils questions, as suggested in Chapter 5, establishes a firm base for learning by reminding them of their prior knowledge. This phase provides you with information about the level of understanding of the class so that you may adjust the pitch of the lesson appropriately.

Once the conflict has been created it may then be resolved through analogy, metaphor, or physical references. Questioning and discussion play a crucial part here in focusing attention on the key concepts.

Incorporating percentages and fractions with decimals helps to reinforce the connections between the different representations of numbers. Such links are made explicit during the plenary when pupils have to reflect on what they have learned during the lesson, and how it relates to their previous knowledge.

A similar approach can be used with sixth-form students.

Provoking cognitive conflict through the use of concept questions

Many pupils seem able to hold two parallel sets of knowledge – one which applies to school mathematics and the other to real life. Although they may be able to complete an exercise correctly within a lesson, pupils often revert to naive, intuitive methods when confronted by a non-standard problem. Many sixth-form students hold misconceptions about fundamental concepts in mechanics which persist even after they have been formally taught those topics. For example, how would you answer the following question?

> Two balls are exactly the same size and shape but have masses of 1 kg and 3 kg. They are dropped at the same time from the same height. How does the time that they take to fall to the ground compare?
>
> (Graham and Berry 1993: 474)

Probably, you answered that both balls would hit the ground together. However, when over 200 sixth-form mathematics students were asked this question 31 per cent of them stated that the heavier ball would land first and a further 14 per cent argued that the 3-kg ball would land in one-third of the time (Graham and Berry 1993). Thus nearly half of the students were incorrect.

After analysing the students' incorrect responses, Graham and Berry identified three different arguments which had been used. The first approach assumed that the time taken for an object to fall is inversely proportional to its mass. Another possibly related approach reasoned that the force of gravity was greater on the 3-kg ball than on the 1-kg ball. Finally, those students who had suggested that the time difference between the balls landing would be small attributed this to the effects of air resistance.

Table 6.1 Results of pre- and posttesting.

	Before teaching (%)	After teaching (%)
Fall in same time	54	57
3 kg falls in $\frac{1}{3}$ time	16	19
3 kg lands first	26	20
Other	4	4

Berry and Graham (1991: 752; Taylor and Francis publishers http://www.tandf.co.uk/journals).

These students were questioned after they had started their A-level mathematics courses but before they had studied any mechanics. You might expect, therefore, that once they had been taught the topic their understanding would improve. Graham and Berry were able to retest about fifty of the students after they had studied the topics of force and Newton's laws. The results are given in Table 6.1.

Only a small proportion of the students changed their intuitive views as a result of the teaching. As we discussed earlier, students construct their own mathematical models from their experiences. Many of these models are limited and need to be refined. It would appear that the teaching these students received did not lead to a restructuring of their intuitive concepts.

Task 6.4

1   Think back to the way in which you were taught the mechanics concepts described above. Which aspects of the teaching and learning process led you to overcome the misconceptions held by so many of the sixth-formers?

2   Examine an A-level mechanics text used by your school. How does it approach the teaching of such concepts?

The traditional approach to mechanics teaching emphasized the application of algebraic techniques to standard problems (Berry and Graham 1991). The relationship between the mathematical models used in the questions and the real-world contexts which they represented was often not discussed explicitly. Contradictions with students' own mental models were not confronted.

Real life?

As an aside here, we should like to point out that the heavier ball does land first in real life, but only just! If you are unconvinced consider Newton's second law and air resistance.

When we have presented this question to mathematics PGCE (Post-Graduate Certificate of Education) students, they all 'know' that the balls land at the same time so fail to think about the mathematical model and the assumptions made

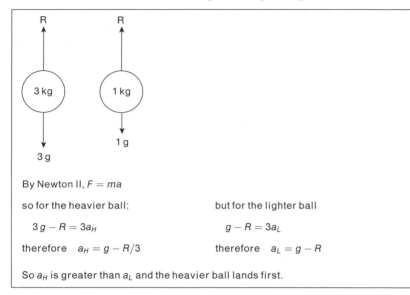

By Newton II, $F = ma$

so for the heavier ball: but for the lighter ball

$3g - R = 3a_H$ $g - R = 3a_L$

therefore $a_H = g - R/3$ therefore $a_L = g - R$

So a_H is greater than a_L and the heavier ball lands first.

Figure 6.5 A concept problem.

(usually zero air resistance!). The difference is small, but big enough to ensure that the makers of a famous short film, teaching A-level mathematics concepts, to resort to camera tricks to 'fake' the answer to be learned. We think this is a different sort of misconception but that it should not be hidden.

The nature of the misconceptions held by pupils remain a secret under traditional teaching approaches. However, a more effective teaching approach suggested by Graham and Berry (1993) mirrors the cognitive-conflict strategy discussed above by using such 'concept questions' to challenge students' misconceptions before teaching the topic. Concept questions, such as the one at the start of this section, are problems 'designed to test student understanding of a basic concept or principle upon which the models in mechanics are based' (Berry and Graham 1991: 754). For example, an introductory lesson on forces and gravity would be structured as follows.

Setting up the conflict

Set the students the concept question about dropping the 1-kg and 3-kg balls. After a few minutes for individual thought, ask them to discuss their answers in small groups and to try to arrive at a consensus. Then brainstorm the ideas onto the board.

The responses obtained by the survey suggest that there will be a wide range of opinions within the class allowing misconceptions to be exposed and setting up the need for their resolution.

Teaching the concept

Asking the students how they could find out which answer is correct is likely to result in the obvious but too often underused approach of 'doing it'! (There are obvious opportunities here for liaison with the physics department, but why let the scientists have all the fun? Practical mechanics kits are available commercially.)

The experimental approach is more likely to convince students who argued for an incorrect solution than just an explanation of the right answer from the teacher. However, the practical should be supplemented with a discussion, led by the teacher, to formalize the mechanics principles which underpin the result.

The 'sting'

Finally, check that the students have restructured their concepts effectively by testing with the original question or with structurally similar new tasks. We presume that our air-resistance issue would be openly debated at this point.

Plenary

As before, requiring students to reflect on the main points of the lesson helps them to identify what new knowledge they have learned and how it links to previous work.

Although the examples here are taken from mechanics, similar work has been undertaken in statistics and in pure mathematics (see Crawford 1997; Jolliffe 1988).

CONCLUSION

The extent and range of pupils' misconceptions have been considered together with a variety of approaches for overcoming them. The use of teaching strategies which involve cognitive conflict have been shown to be very effective. In particular, the use of practical work can provide valuable feedback to pupils about the limitations of their concepts and can assist pupils in learning to think mathematically.

Summary

Contrary, perhaps, to our own experiences, research suggests that mathematics is a very difficult subject for most children.

When preparing to teach a topic:

- identify the main mathematical concepts which underpin it;
- use the research findings to help you to predict the common misconceptions.

Choose problems which:

- challenge and involve the pupils;
- are not easily solved by informal methods;
- lead to illogical outcomes when misconceptions are present thereby provoking cognitive conflict;
- address different aspects of the mathematical concepts being taught rather than merely requiring repetition of an algorithm.

Choose teaching strategies which:

- use a variety of strategies (e.g. discussion, practical work, visual representations, etc.) to reinforce the mathematical concepts;
- bring misconceptions into open discussion;
- require pupils to explain their thinking to each other and to you;
- require pupils to listen to each other's methods and try to understand them;
- encourage pupils to reflect on their own strategies and to adopt more effective ones;
- encourage pupils to try to predict where errors might occur (e.g. by asking them to find and to correct deliberate mistakes);
- use errors as teaching points.

Plan ways of providing feedback to pupils so that:

- misconceptions are not reinforced through usage;
- your marking indicates why they have made an error, not just whether the answer is correct.

7 Learning to think mathematically

Using and applying mathematics

INTRODUCTION: WHAT DOES THINKING MATHEMATICALLY MEAN?

You have probably noticed that people who are particularly good at mathematics often seem to think about issues slightly differently to others. As a teacher of mathematics it will be your task to help pupils learn to think like mathematicians.

Thinking mathematically is not an end in itself; rather it is a process through which we make sense of the world around us (Mason *et al.* 1982). Learning to think mathematically is far more than just learning to use mathematical techniques, although developing a facility with the tools of the trade is clearly an element. Mathematical thinkers have a way of seeing, representing, and analysing their world, and a tendency to behave like mathematicians – that is, to use mathematics to explain situations and solve problems.

Learning to think mathematically has three major components:

1   developing competence with the tools of the trade: the facts, conventions, skills, routines, techniques, and results which comprise the content of mathematics;
2   using those tools for sense making, developing the conceptual structures of mathematics;
3   developing a mathematical point of view – valuing the processes of mathematics and having the predilection to apply them to problems within and outside of mathematics.

(developed from Schoenfeld 1994: 60)

What we are concerned about in this chapter is how children learn to use and apply their mathematics in the solution of problems. These problems may lie within mathematics itself, in the learning of new mathematics, or in the real world outside of the classroom. These are the aspects of mathematics which we referred to in Chapter 2 as 'the problem-solving processes of mathematics' which are assessed under Attainment Target 1 of the National Curriculum: using and applying mathematics.

Objectives

By the end of this chapter, you should have a greater understanding of:

- the importance of integrating a wide range of challenging tasks within your teaching including practical investigation and extended problem solving;
- the significance of metacognition for problem solving;
- how certain teaching approaches can help to develop metacognitive knowledge and problem-solving ability;
- the importance of techniques which encourage collective reflection in plenary sessions, such as peer assessment.

WHAT IS NEEDED FOR SUCCESSFUL PROBLEM SOLVING?

> Research on cognitive skills has taught us ... that there is no such thing as expertness without knowledge – extensive and accessible knowledge.
>
> (Simon 1980: 82)

Thus we wish to make it clear from the beginning that although we regard the problem-solving processes of mathematics to be vital for effective mathematical thinking, they cannot stand alone.

Although problem-solving strategies are vital when attempting to apply an old piece of mathematics to a new situation or when trying to learn a new piece of mathematics, they are not sufficient. Problem-solving strategies require an extensive and accessible knowledge base of mathematical facts and conventions, skills and routines, conceptual structures, techniques and results on which to operate.

This does not mean, however, that learning about problem solving can wait until that knowledge base is secure. Rather, we would claim that it is only when learning is based on the processes of mathematical problem solving that secure, accessible knowledge develops. The development of mathematical knowledge and understanding should proceed alongside problem-solving ability.

You should notice that to be of use in real problem solving, mathematical knowledge must be 'accessible', meaning that a person can recognize its potential for use at appropriate moments outside of the context in which it was learned. To access specific mathematical knowledge, you must (a) realize that you know it and (b) have some idea of its potential.

When you are in the early stages of learning a new technique, it is often easier to work through the process than to describe how it works. You may recall the comment by a teacher in Chapter 5: 'If you can explain it then you know you understand it.' This leads most researchers on problem solving to demand an emphasis on learners articulating their thinking – talking about their mathematical understandings and making their knowledge statable (e.g. Prawat 1989a, b; Cobb and Bauersfeld 1995). Talking about knowledge helps to structure it in your mind and explaining it helps to forge links with older knowledge. It is when new ideas become connected to older concepts and techniques that mere information becomes potentially accessible knowledge. In other words, knowledge must be both statable and connected before it is accessible in real problem-solving situations (Glaser 1995). You may wish to consider how this relates to our demand for relational understanding in Chapter 2.

Knowledge must not only be accessible, it must also be valid. We saw in the last chapter that children often have conceptual frameworks or models which are independent of the teaching to which they have been exposed. Furthermore these intuitive or naive structures can be both very different from 'official' models and very resistant to change (e.g. Berry and Graham 1991).

Research conducted on young Brazilian children who make their living selling on the streets shows that they have very well-developed mental-arithmetic skills which bear little relationship to school-taught methods. The children's methods are very effective in their context – the streets – but do not seem to be useful to them when they meet more formal approaches in school (Nunes *et al.* 1993). Unfortunately, schools sometimes fail to respect the informal, intuitive, or real-world knowledge which children bring to the classroom.

Of course, sometimes children bring misconceptions and misunderstandings to problem situations as their tools to work with, and teachers need access to these tools to adjust and refine them (Schoenfeld 1992: 349). Thus one of the first tasks for the teacher hoping to develop mathematical thinking in any domain must be to gain access to the learner's intuitive, naive knowledge.

Task 7.1 Why should we link mathematics with real life?

Consider any examples you have seen of teachers trying to link the mathematics they are teaching with real life.

Consider what purpose was served by the use of the real life context in each case you thought of.

Why do we wish to link mathematics to real life contexts? Is it because we consider mathematics to be a tool rather than a discipline?

Why use real-life examples?

We doubt that many mathematics teachers consider their subject to be a tool rather than a discipline, although this may be in the minds of some politicians. Here are a few possible reasons why we include practical and real-life contexts in our teaching:

- to add 'distracters' to hide the mathematics and make a harder problem;
- to make mathematics appear useful and therefore motivate pupils to learn;
- to provide 'applied contexts' within which we can develop mathematical thinking;
- to give pupils opportunities to practise applying what they know;
- to gain access to children's intuitive knowledge and thinking;
- to relate mathematics to pupils' interests and previous experiences thus building on real-world knowledge rather than creating a separate mathematical domain;

- because we think that by learning mathematics in a variety of situations they will learn mathematics in useable form;
- because the learning skills involved in applying mathematics across the curriculum are the same skills which are involved in learning new mathematics.

The reasons can largely be divided into two groups – first, to motivate pupils and second, to improve the quality of learning. Many teachers try to make their work appear relevant by placing their questions and tasks in real-life settings. However, Mason (1988: 202) warns against placing too much importance on relevance:

> When pupils ask
>   'Why are we doing this?'
> they are rarely satisfied by a reply of the form
>   'It is important in the steel industry.'
>
> (Mason 1988: 202)

The issue is more to do with engaging pupils' imaginations (Lave 1992: 87) and helping them to develop personal meaning rather than the relevance of the situation. This is associated more with the freedom for pupils to determine the direction which the activity will follow than the context in which it is set (Boaler 1993a, b; Silver 1994). It would seem likely that it is not the context which is important, but the processes with which the pupil engages while exploring the context (Boaler 1993a, b). Although real-world contexts may provide more opportunities for discussion and debate challenging pupil misconceptions and encouraging the development of process skills, this is highly dependent on teaching style.

Knowledge would be more authentic or believable if built on the valid intuitive everyday experiences of learners rather than attempting (and often failing) to replace them with formal ways of knowing. Apprenticeship or coaching is often suggested as a more natural model for learning which might overcome this. Pupils' activities would be made more like those of young mathematicians working alongside an expert on a shared task than receiving instruction (Lave 1988). In the end, the distinction is between the mere acquisition of inert concepts and useful, robust knowledge.

A significant degree of autonomy on the part of the learner is required if pupils are to behave as real mathematicians. Real-life problems may be generated by the pupils themselves if sufficiently open situations are provided (see Chapter 2).

Clearly the range of problems experienced must be wide and varied if children are to be offered opportunities to 'use and apply mathematics in practical tasks, in real-life problems, and in mathematics itself' as demanded by the National Curriculum (DFE/WO 1995: 1). However, more than opportunity is required, as even when pupils have valid and connected knowledge, which would be useful in the solution of a problem, they often fail to use it. They do not realize that the knowledge would be helpful and they lack strategies which help them to deal with being 'stuck'. Pupils often do not know how to start in an open problem-solving situation. The National Curriculum demands that pupils should be *taught* how to behave in such situations and specifically that they be taught to:

2   make and monitor decisions to solve problems;
3   communicate mathematically;
4   develop skills of mathematical reasoning.

(DFE/WO 1995)

Task 7.2 How can we teach the skills required for using and applying mathematics?

Before reading on, pause and think how you would attempt to *teach* pupils to make and monitor decisions, communicate mathematically and develop skills of reasoning.

THE USE AND PRACTICAL APPLICATIONS OF MATHEMATICS PROJECT (PAMP)

At the start of the 1990s, few teachers were comfortable about teaching the skills defined in Attainment Target 1 (Tanner 1992b). Between 1991 and 1994 we were funded by the Welsh Office to conduct school-based research on the use and practical application of mathematics in KS3 and KS4. In the first phase of the project we worked closely with a group of teacher-researchers to develop activities, materials, and teaching approaches to teach practical problem-solving skills (Tanner and Jones 1993, 1994a, b).

In the second phase of the project we developed a mathematical thinking-skills course based on the activities and approaches used in phase 1. The impact of the course was then evaluated in a quasi-experiment with 641 pupils using pretests, posttests, and delayed tests to compare control classes with those who had followed the course (Tanner and Jones 1995a, c, 2000; Tanner, 1997). The project involved the systematic observation of large numbers of lessons ($\sim$200) aimed at Attainment Target 1 and has led us to firm conclusions on teaching approaches.

THE TEACHING APPROACHES

The most successful teachers observed led activities with a clear sense of purpose. They allowed pupils to think for themselves, to plan, and to discuss the work, but they were not afraid to intervene to guide discovery and ensure success.

In the least successful lessons teachers taught didactically and did the thinking and planning for their pupils, removing much of the challenge. 'Cookbook investigation' where the pupils filled in a table laid out by the teacher failed to make children think and, although the lessons passed quietly, learning did not occur.

Equally unsuccessful were those lessons in which teachers failed to intervene in situations where pupils were failing to progress in the mistaken belief that Attainment Target 1 should not be 'taught'.

In the most successful lessons, teachers provided structure to encourage pupils to make plans, choose and evaluate strategies, and communicate results. The most successful strategies which were used to provide structure emphasized social processes, discussion, and teacher intervention. The project developed an approach known as 'start–stop–go' (named by the teacher who used it most) which included the strategies which follow:

Questioning using organizational prompts

A list of organizing questions was provided and supplemented with oral questions which were asked on a regular basis; for example,

> What variables are there? Could we measure any of them easily in the classroom today?
> Can you explain your plan to me?
> When you have found that, how will it help you?
> What are you going to do next?
> Do your results make sense? Do they help to test your ideas?
> Could you make a prediction and test it?
> Does that always happen?
> How could you convince someone else that it always happens?
> If you had more time to do this again, what would you do differently?

The aim was to encourage pupils to develop a framework of questions to organize their thoughts. An expectation developed that such questions would be asked and pupils seemed able to internalize them and began to ask such questions of themselves.

Internalization of scientific argument

Teachers circulated during the early stages of an investigation and selected a few groups of pupils to present interim approaches and findings. Presentations were followed up by questioning and constructive criticism. Questioning was led by the teacher at first, with a gradual increase in the amount of pupil-initiated questioning. Pupils began to copy the form of question used by the teacher when framing their own. It became clear that groups were anticipating the same form of question about their own presentation and preparing a suitable response. The pupils were learning how to conduct a scientific argument (Wheatley 1991).

Start, stop, go

This approach combined the internalization of organizational prompts and scientific argument with an emphasis on self-monitoring and reflection.

Tasks began with a few minutes of silent reading and planning. Small groups then discussed possible approaches. A whole-class brainstorm followed during which groups suggested approaches to the teacher who listed them on the board. The teacher then led a whole-class discussion in which the attention of the class was focused on key ideas and strategies which had been suggested. The groups returned to planning but with the suggestion that they should incorporate the ideas of other groups if necessary. This ensured that all pupils engaged with the task and began to plan but that a variety of perceptions and plans were examined, discussed, and evaluated. Strategies which were obviously misguided were usually rejected by pupils following an effective class discussion in which their weaknesses had been exposed.

At intervals the class was stopped for reporting back. Groups were encouraged to compare their plans and progress with that of others and to modify their plans if necessary. Teachers selected the groups for reporting back carefully to focus attention on key points and ensure that the class were gently nudged towards successful approaches. The questions which were asked by teachers and pupils in these feedback sessions were often in the form of organizational prompts.

Pupils began to anticipate not only the form of questioning which would be used, but also that reporting back would occur. Groups began to monitor their progress in anticipation, which restrained impulsive planning and encouraged self-monitoring. This approach led naturally into the use of assessment to encourage reflection.

Using peer and self-assessment to encourage reflection

Pupils were required to write up their final report individually, but selected groups also presented their work to the class for peer assessment. Reflecting on the work of others led pupils inevitably to reflect back on their own work. Through assessing the work of others, pupils learned to evaluate and regulate their own thinking. These plenary evaluation sessions were considered to be a critical element in the teaching approach.

Requiring groups of pupils to talk about their mathematics and justify their approaches to others gives teachers opportunities to emphasize that which is important. Pupils look to teachers for approval of their approaches and for guidance on how to improve. The best teachers used reporting situations as opportunities for offering such approval and guidance. Such occasions also act as an opportunity for collective reflection, during which teachers are able to question the class to focus their attention on the strategic learning which should have occurred during the lesson. Pupils talking about mathematical strategies helps them to formalize their learning and encourages the development of statable knowledge about problem-solving processes.

A knowledge of problem-solving processes is not sufficient for successful application of mathematics to problem situations: the pupil must also choose to use that knowledge, to monitor the progress being made, and to evaluate the solution gained (Schoenfeld 1985; Silver 1987; Gray 1991; Tanner and Jones 1994b). Phase 1 of the project led us to the conclusion that the effective use and application of mathematics demands higher order skills such as:

- recognizing when the use of a mathematical process might be appropriate or effective;
- planning how mathematical techniques and processes are to be used in a task;
- conjecturing, discussing, and testing the strategies and data to be used;

- monitoring the progress of problem-solving activities;
- making and testing hypotheses;
- evaluating the outcomes of using a specific strategy to solve a problem;
- reflecting on the learning which might have occurred during the task.

We refer to these skills as 'higher order' because they are associated with knowledge about knowledge and the control of mental processes. The literature refers to such knowledge and skills as *metacognitive* (meta = higher, cognition = thinking).

Metacognition

Metacognition refers to the knowledge and control which you have of your own thinking (Flavell 1976; Brown 1987).

There are two aspects to metacognition:

a metacognitive knowledge – knowing what you know; and
b metacognitive skill – your ability to monitor and regulate your thinking.

(see Flavell 1976: 232)

The first aspect refers to the knowledge and beliefs which you have about your own mental resources in a situation, how well you think you are likely to perform, the mathematical techniques and processes you might be able to use, and your beliefs about the nature of mathematics itself (Flavell 1987: 22–3). Such subjective self-knowledge, whether true or not, is an important influence on your behaviour and is heavily influenced by your previous experiences in that situation.

The issue is not always whether a pupil knows a mathematical technique or process, it is often whether they know that they know it and are thus able to decide to use it. Have you ever seen the solution to a problem and thought 'I knew how to do that, but I never thought it might be useful here'? A further aspect of metacognitive knowledge is how pupils feel about using a technique; if they feel positive or confident about it they are more likely to choose to use it.

The second aspect of metacognition refers to the active monitoring and regulation of thinking (Flavell 1976: 232). It has to do with 'when, why, and how' pupils explore, plan, monitor, regulate, and evaluate progress; and is influenced by pupils' metacognitive knowledge, including their attitudes and beliefs about themselves and mathematics (Lester and Kroll 1990).

Task 7.3 Calculating VAT

Work out the answer to this real-world problem before reading on:

A television costs £125 plus $17\frac{1}{2}$% VAT. What will the total cost including VAT be?

How would you deal with this problem if you were the customer in the shop?
How would you deal with it if you were the salesperson?
How would you deal with it if you were a pupil in school?

We guess that most customers would estimate, use a mental method, or even leave it to the shopkeeper. The shopkeeper will probably use a calculator or an automatic till. Pupils, however, are likely to behave very differently.

For many pupils, the problem will end before it begins as they think:

> I know percentages are hard and I already know that I can't do fractions so I certainly won't be able to do this. What was on TV last night?

Many other pupils, being well conditioned in the use of standard algorithms, will not think of any alternative methods but will begin automatically by writing:

$$17\tfrac{1}{2}\% \text{ of } \pounds125 \;=\; \frac{17\tfrac{1}{2}}{100} \;\times\; 125 \;=\; \frac{17\tfrac{1}{2}}{4} \;\times\; 5$$

and begin to get tangled up in dividing $17\tfrac{1}{2}$ by 4 (because BODMAS says divide before multiply doesn't it? And then you have to turn something upside down don't you?) before multiplying by 5.

A few will know a trick for dealing with such fractions and will continue the process by writing

$$=\; \frac{35}{200} \times 125 \;=\; \frac{35}{8} \times 5 \;=\; \frac{175}{8} \;=\; 21\tfrac{7}{8}$$

A few will then remember the context, change to money, and add on.

The best problem solvers in the class will begin by thinking 'I don't like the look of the fractions in the usual approach – there must be a better way! They will then begin a search for an alternative method. Some will think:

> I'm not going to do this in my head – I'll use a calculator and type in 0.175×125;

Some will use their knowledge of place value and write:

$$1\% = \pounds1.25$$
$$\text{so} \quad 17\tfrac{1}{2}\% = \pounds1.25 \times 17\tfrac{1}{2} \;=\; \pounds21.25 + 62\tfrac{1}{2}\text{p} \quad \text{and round to } \pounds21.88;$$

A few will know a quick mental method for working out $17\tfrac{1}{2}\%$ and will jot down:

$$10\% \text{ of } \pounds125 \;=\; \pounds12.50$$
$$5\% \text{ of } \pounds125 \;=\; \pounds6.25$$
$$2\tfrac{1}{2}\% \text{ of } \pounds125 \;=\; \pounds3.12\tfrac{1}{2}$$
$$17\tfrac{1}{2}\% \text{ of } \pounds125 \;=\; \pounds21.87\tfrac{1}{2}$$

and round up to $\pounds21.88$ before adding on to get $\pounds146.88$.

Our contention, which is supported by research (e.g. Schoenfeld 1985; Gray 1991; Tanner and Jones 1994b), is that the most able problem solvers do not rush into a possible approach to a problem, but consider alternatives before selecting one approach from many. They think ahead and monitor their progress while they are working. They use their knowledge of their own mental resources to select one method from many, avoiding their weaknesses and playing to their strengths. The most mindful pupils evaluate their success, comparing other pupils' methods with their own in a search for efficiency.

Unfortunately schools often fail to encourage the use of the metacognitive skills of selecting alternatives, planning an approach, monitoring progress, and evaluating the method used. All too often, the questions which pupils solve in class are based on the repetition and practice of an algorithm which has just been demonstrated. No choice is involved, no mathematical thinking is required and a pupil using an alternative method would be in the wrong. No wonder then that school-taught algorithms are rarely used in real life!

Developing metacognition

Conscious control of a technique or process usually appears quite late in its development, usually only after it has been practised unconsciously and spontaneously (Vygotsky 1962: 90). This suggests that unconscious self-regulation should precede conscious self-regulation. The stages involved in 'start–stop–go' do precisely this. They make pupils behave like expert problem solvers, examining a number of possible strategies, planning, monitoring, and evaluating their work at appropriate points in the lesson in an unconscious manner before focusing their attention on the processes.

The unconscious use of metacognitive skills is turned into conscious metacognitive knowledge through articulation and reflection during plenary evaluation sessions. The significance of articulation or verbalization in making processes explicitly available as objects of thought is confirmed by research. Several studies have included articulation by pupils as significant aspects of their approach (e.g. Schoenfeld 1985; Lester and Kroll 1990; Tanner and Jones 1994b, 1999b).

In fact, in the second phase of our project we discovered that pupils whose teachers made effective use of plenaries to evaluate approaches, summarize key issues, and encourage collective reflection were not only the most successful in practical problem-solving situations, but also showed the greatest improvement in the content areas of mathematics (Tanner 1997; Tanner and Jones 1999a).

We suggest then that teaching approaches focusing on the development of higher level skills and knowledge should emphasize:

- significant pupil autonomy in the selection of approaches;
- active participation by pupils in the process of planning and evaluating in problem situations;
- teacher intervention in the form of focusing questions to assist pupils in the formation of generalizations;
- demands that pupils articulate their thoughts about the opportunities and constraints offered by specific techniques, processes, and strategies which they have experienced;
- articulation might be verbal or written but should always be interactive allowing teachers or other pupils to provide support when necessary;

- teaching should develop pupils' enthusiasm and confidence with mathematics so problem solving should be associated with success rather than failure;
- that pupils be given opportunities and encouragement to reflect formally on their learning.

THE TASKS

Many of the problem-solving activities which we used in the project (PAMP) involved the use of practical equipment. Contexts were provided which were mathematically rich, and which were susceptible to a range of investigations or approaches, allowing pupils significant autonomy in the selection of both targets and approaches. Many of the activities involved the measurement of physical quantities such as height, weight, distance, angle, speed, time, etc. Pupils were required to hypothesize which variables might be related and to devise an approach which would test their hypothesis.

For example, Figure 7.1 shows one popular activity which we used, called 'Papercopters'.

Papercopters – a practical investigation in the real world

The question is presented in a deliberately open form, pushing pupils to decide which variables might be effectively measured and which should be controlled. We wanted pupils to have to choose their own strategies. The aims for the lesson often included developing the concept of a variable and learning about the need to control variables.

Task 7.4 Papercopters – investigating in the physical world

Consider the task 'Papercopters'. If you were doing this yourself, which variables would you suspect were related? Which will generate the most interesting mathematics? Which variables would you control?

Although the lesson aims to teach mathematical thinking associated with AT1, it may also have aims associated with the 'content' ATs. Make a list of the mathematical knowledge and skills which might be taught during this task.

When we have conducted this investigation in school we have found it helpful to set the task of producing an effective papercopter for homework to ensure most effective use of limited lesson time (A6 size paper gives good results). Make a papercopter and investigate!

Selecting variability

We have found that the following investigations of papercopters produce fairly clean data and interesting mathematics, although other investigations may also prove to be effective:

Papercopters

Siwan saw a film in which a helicopter ran out of fuel and crash-landed.

The next day in school she decided to investigate what affects the way helicopters fall by using a papercopter.

Make a papercopter from this plan:

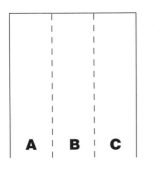

Fold flap **A** towards you.

Fold flap **C** away from you.

Put a paperclip on flap **B** – this represents the pilot!

Try to make a papercopter which flies well.

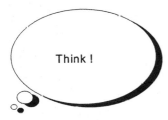

Think !

What could you measure and vary in this situation?

Do you think that any of the variables might be related?

What would you like to Investigate?

Make a list of all the important variables.

Decide which variable would be the most interesting to investigate in the classroom today.

Discuss !

Discuss how to make your measurements accurate.

Decide on a plan which you would all like to follow before you begin your investigation

Figure 7.1 Papercopters.

comparing time of descent with the height of drop; or

comparing the time of descent with the number of paperclips (passengers) hanging on the 'copter.

In discussion, pupils often suggest speed of descent as a variable, but this is not easily measured. Pupils may sometimes use 'speed' and 'time' interchangeably so accuracy in language should be demanded. The role of the teacher is critical in ensuring that all pupils arrive at a practical strategy and yet leave the pupils the perception that they are following their own plans. This is where the strategy of 'start–stop–go' is particularly effective.

Pupils are asked to think about possible variables in silence for a minute or so before being allowed to discuss it within small groups, ideas are then brainstormed onto the board. During the brainstorming session, teachers are able to focus the attention of the class on important features. For example, some genuine variables – such as wind speed – are impractical to measure and should be controlled rather than investigated. It is important to discuss the inaccuracy of real data and to devise strategies for dealing with it. Effective teacher intervention leaves pupils in a position to choose their own strategy from several which have been considered, but with a sense of the potential problems which might arise. Thus, the teacher effectively coaches the class, making them behave as expert problem solvers through the sharing of expertise.

Monitoring

During the interventions which follow during the remainder of the start–stop–go process, when the class are stopped at intervals to compare progress, further coaching opportunities are available to the skilled teacher. With encouragement, computer graph-plotting software may be used to plot results. Quite young pupils can use trial-and-improvement methods to find a formula to fit a curve to empirical data. We have found year 7 and 8 pupils quite able to do this when given sufficient support. Only a small amount of guidance from the teacher about the likely form of the equation is needed. For example, telling a class that the equation of a straight line is of the form *something x plus something else* is usually enough to get them started. This allows predicting and testing of results using a formula.

One of the major advantages of such practical investigations, apart from the obvious and significant motivational factors, is the way that the abstract concept of a variable is linked closely to a physical quantity which varies continuously. Algebra becomes real and believable. When formulae are checked, immediate physical feedback is available to check predictions.

Plenary

Significant intuitive and practical knowledge about variables and formulae may be developed by this task. However, we would wish to emphasize that our results suggest that this is not used to best effect unless teachers ensure that the knowledge is formalized through plenaries and periods of collective reflection about the knowledge which has been learned.

The lesson which we have just described probably sounds quite unusual to most of our readers. The results of the quasi-experiment conducted in the second phase of the project indicate, however, that time spent on such practical activities is far from wasted and that the depth of understanding and habits of mathematical thinking which were developed led to significantly increased performance in standard mathematical tasks (Tanner and Jones 1999a).

Although we would encourage you to use practical approaches to using and applying mathematics when possible, we should also like to remind you that AT1 is as much about solving problems within mathematics as it is about solving real-world problems with mathematics. We consider the skills of problem solving pay for themselves many times over, both in the application of known mathematics and the learning of new mathematics. The next example we offer you is chosen to indicate how the teaching approaches apply equally to problem solving within mathematics itself.

Terminator: investigating within mathematics itself

The following case study attempts to provide a flavour of the teaching approaches used. It also illustrates how the skills of using and applying mathematics can be developed whilst reinforcing basic number work.

The lesson develops the concepts of ratio and variables through equivalent fractions and addresses the concept of infinity through the conversion of fractions to recurring decimals. The strategies developed by the task include working systematically, working exhaustively, trying simple cases first, searching for patterns, and generalizing.

The lesson started with a scene-setting introduction by the teacher:

T: My children watched *The Terminator* last week. Have you seen it? What sort of things did he like to do? What other word could we use instead of 'terminate'?

Pupils' responses included killing things, finishing things off, ending things.

T: Let me tell you a little story about Arnie. Even when he was still in school he liked terminating things (pencils, rulers, calculators and so on).

Laughter.

T: One day he had to convert a fraction into a decimal like this (teacher goes through the conversion of $\frac{3}{5}$ on the board). He liked this fraction because its decimal terminates. He tried another fraction (teacher writes $\frac{2}{3}$ on the board). Do you think this fraction will convert to a terminating decimal as well? Let's have a look at what Arnie did:

$$0.6666\ldots$$
$$3\overline{)2.00000000}$$

T: Why did he write all these dots?
P: It's a recurring number.

T: What do you mean by recurring?
P: It goes on and on for ever.
T: OK. Now, Arnie wants you to investigate fractions and decimals. Look at the sheet and think quietly:

What would be an interesting question to investigate?
What data would you collect?
Could you work systematically?

After a minute or so of silent reading the teacher continued:

T: Now discuss your ideas in your groups of three. I want to see the team spirit please. Agree on a plan for your group.

After a few minutes for group discussion the pupils are asked to report back on their plans:

T: Now, I am going to ask volunteers to tell us what their plan is. Jayne's group, are you going to tell us your plan? Listen everybody.
P1:   We are going to investigate all the fractions from one-half up to one-tenth. One-half, one-third, two-thirds, one-quarter, two-quarters, three-quarters, etc. . . .
T: What do you think will happen?
P1:   Perhaps some groups of fractions will give the same answer . . .
P2:   We are going to investigate the effect of changing the denominator, but keeping the numerator 1 all the time. One-half, one-third, one-quarter and so on . . .
T: Are you making any guesses about what might come out?
P2:   Perhaps all the even numbers will be one sort of decimal or something like that . . .
P3:   First of all we are going to investigate the denominators up to one-tenth. We will start with one-half, then one-third and go up to one-tenth. Then we will do two-thirds, and so on, until we see a pattern. We will display our results in a table.
T: What sort of pattern do you expect?
P3:   Perhaps the same denominator will give the same type of decimal, like one-third will be the same type as two-thirds.

The other groups were invited to comment on the plans – What do you think of that plan? What did you like about it? Pupils were encouraged to modify or change their plans in the light of comments. During the discussion it became apparent that some form of systematic working was to be expected, but that more than one approach was acceptable. It was also clear that patterns were anticipated. However, the task remained open and strategy selection was under the control of the pupils.

Before the pupils started work the inevitable question was asked – can we use a calculator? The teacher referred the class back to the two examples and asked what answers would be displayed on a calculator? Pupils agreed that the recurring decimal would be truncated and that it would not be possible to differentiate between decimals that terminated at the maximum number of displayed digits and a recurring decimal. Calculators were in use in the classroom, but their use was supposed to be restricted to checking. Most pupils used them in this way, and when the teacher saw misuse she discussed the dangers involved with the pupils concerned.

The class then started work: the more efficient groups distributed sets of fractions amongst themselves. There were long periods of silent working whilst lists of examples were generated. The silence was broken by discussion whilst the pupils checked on values, looked for patterns and made and tested hypotheses:

P: One-third, one-sixth and one-ninth are recurring fractions and one-seventh is a repeating fraction. Will two-thirds recur and two-sevenths repeat?

P: We thought we had a hypothesis but it's wrong. We thought all the odd numbers (denominators) would recur and all the even denominators would terminate.

Monitoring

After about 10 minutes the teacher stopped the class and asked a few groups to describe their progress. This forced the pupils to monitor their progress against their plan and also against the progress of others. It also gave the teacher the opportunity to stress the strategies she had targeted such as the need to work systematically, the need to organize results, etc. Groups were encouraged to adopt strategies described by others to improve their progress.

During the course of the lesson, several pupils discovered with amazement and excitement that some sets of fractions gave the same decimal.

P: Miss! Miss! One-half, two-quarters and three-sixths all give the same answer!

The class were all perfectly capable of writing down sets of equivalent fractions when asked to do so in a textbook exercise. However, this was known rather than believed. It was information, not connected to decimal or percentage notation. For many pupils, it was only during the course of the investigation that mere information became connected, statable, accessible knowledge.

The plenary

The pupils continued to work enthusiastically on the task until they were stopped 10 minutes before the end of the lesson and asked to report any interesting findings:

P: We have found that all the ninths are recurring, all the sevenths are repeating. All the tenths terminate. All the sixths (apart from one-half) are recurring.

P: All the sevenths have the same six numbers (digits) repeated.

The realization that it was the end of the lesson was accompanied by expressions of surprise and one pupil exclaiming 'Oh Miss, I was flying then!'. This is not a reaction that normally accompanies lessons on fractions! However, the pupils were working with a purpose on tasks which they had set for themselves, so intrinsic motivation was high.

The pupils continued with the task for homework and examined the data for relationships. The connection between fractions with the same denominator was discovered as were the patterns in the 'remainders' of repeating decimals. In the next lesson the pupils were asked to report back on what they had discovered.

Reporting back

During the reporting back session, the teacher focused pupils' attention on the ways in which they had worked systematically, how some pupils had controlled variables, holding the numerator constant and changing the denominator, and how the results had been tabulated. She also pointed out the value of looking at more than one plan before starting and the need to stop and reflect every now and again to evaluate progress.

When pupils were reporting back on the results of their investigations, she often helped the process by repeating key phrases which pupils had used, drawing attention to them and ensuring that everyone had heard. She used organizing questions to draw the maximum mathematics out of the task:

> Why do you think those fractions are the same?
>
> Are you sure that will always happen?
>
> How do you know there are no other possible remainders?
>
> Can you explain why the pattern repeats every seventh digit?
>
> Do you think that there are any decimal answers we could NOT get from fractions?'
>
> What would they look like?

Self-evaluation was encouraged as pupils reflected on their approaches to the task and attempted to answer the question 'If you were to do this investigation again, what would you do differently?'. The pupils wrote up their reports for homework.

An example of a pupil's work (Tom) is shown in Figure 7.2.

Assessing Tom's work

Task 7.5 Assessing Tom's work

Consult the National Curriculum and assess Tom's work in Figure 7.2 against Attainment Target 1.

Also assess Tom's work against AT2 – number and algebra.

Our investigation is based on finding a relationship between different types of fractions. When you work out the fractions into numbers you can put the numbers under different categories:

* **Repeat** – a sequence of figures which continually repeat themselves:

$$\frac{1}{21} = 1 \div 21 = 21\overline{)1.000000000000}^{\,0.047619047619} \text{ etc.}$$

* **Recur** – the same number continually repeating itself:

$$\frac{1}{6} = 1 \div 6 = 6\overline{)1.00000}^{\,0.16666}$$

(Note – a recurring number is shown with a dot above it – e.g. $0.1\dot{6}$)

* **Terminate** – the number stops and does neither repeat nor recur:

$$\frac{1}{10} = 1 \div 10 = 10\overline{)1.000}^{\,0.1}$$

NOTE – the amount of noughts after the whole number is endless.

   1.0 is equal to 1.00000 etc.

* **The plan**

The plan is to work out the fraction sums into decimal form (as shown in the previous examples), classify them, and to try and find relationships between our results. By this we can hopefully find a rule and test it on other fractions. We are going to change fractions with a denominator from 1 to 20. We will work systematically, starting with 1, then 2, and 3, etc.

$$\frac{1}{1} \quad \frac{1}{2} \quad \frac{1}{3} \quad \frac{1}{4} \text{ etc.}$$

* **The Workings**

1   $1\overline{)1.000}^{\,1.000} = \text{Terminate} \left(\frac{1}{1} = 1 \div 1 \right)$

2   $2\overline{)1.000}^{\,0.500} = \text{Terminate} \left(\frac{1}{2} = 1 \div 2 \right)$

3   $3\overline{)1.0000}^{\,0.333} = \text{Recur} \left(\frac{1}{3} = 1 \div 3 \right)$

4   $4\overline{)1.000}^{\,0.500} = \text{Terminate} \left(\frac{1}{4} = 1 \div 4 \right)$

   (Tom continued in this way up to $1 \div 20$)

19   $19\overline{)1.00000000000000000000}^{\,0.05263157894736842105} \text{ Repeat}$

20   $20\overline{)1.00}^{\,0.05} \text{ Terminate}$

Figure 7.2 Tom's investigation into the terminator.

* Results

Showing the categories that the denominator falls into:

Terminate	Repeat	Recur
1	7	3
2	11	6
4	13	9
5	14	12
8	17	15
10	19	18
16	21	
20	22	

* By studying these results I have noticed that:

1   The numbers in the terminate column are all halves of a different number in the column (i.e. if 8 is there 16 is there, if 4 is there 8 is there). Also they are all even numbers apart from 5 (which is prime).

2   The numbers in the repeat column follow a similar pattern to the terminating numbers as the half numbers are there, though the majority are prime.

3   Lastly are the recurring numbers, these are all numbers in the three times table, as long as one of the factors is not in the repeat section. If a number is in the three times table, but has a factor in the repeat column it will go in the repeat column.

* Using these rules I could predict that:

1   In the terminate column you would see the numbers: 32, 40, 64, 80, 128, etc.

2   In the repeat column you would see the numbers: 34, 38, 42, 44, 68, etc.

3   And in the recurring column the numbers: 24, 27, 30, 36, etc. (33 = 3 × 11 and 11 is in the repeat column).

* Testing our numbers

$$\frac{1}{32} = 32\overline{)1.00000000}\;^{0.03125} \quad \text{Terminate} = \text{Correct}$$

$$\frac{1}{40} = 40\overline{)1.00000}\;^{0.025} \quad \text{Terminate} = \text{Correct}$$

(Tom tested all his remaining predictions and found them to be correct except for 1/27)

$$\frac{1}{27} = 27\overline{)1.00000}\;^{0.03703} \quad \text{Repeat} = \text{Incorrect}$$

* Conclusion

By my results I have found that my set of rules are correct as far as 27 (1/27) which I predicted to recur, when it actually repeated. For this, I can find no reason! The predictions for the repeating and terminating fractions are all correct as far as my investigation has taken, I am very interested in what has gone wrong with that particular fraction, maybe there is no pattern on/after certain numbers.

* Evaluation

This investigation takes great amounts of planning, working out and perseverance. As far as this is concerned, I think I have shown all this at some point. I am very pleased to find a rule as it gives me great satisfaction of being able to decipher such problems where others have failed. I am disappointed though, as I have not managed to find a recurring rule, which is universal to all numbers and not restricted. Through this investigation I have learned how to correctly work out fractions and class them, also that you need to be very careful when working out and checking, as a mistake can knock you back tremendously.

Figure 7.2 (cont.)

It is inappropriate to make a summative judgement of a pupil's performance on just one piece of work. Our assessment of this report suggests, however, that Tom is working on the level 5/6 boundary in AT1. Similarly he was working at about level 6 in AT2 in this activity although level 6 in AT2 includes far more material than could be seen in any one lesson. Formative guidance from the teacher should indicate to Tom that he needs to provide mathematical justifications for his generalizations.

If the task is being used formatively then the first write-up should be considered as a draft. It might even form the basis of a class presentation by Tom's group rather than an assessed piece of work. The teacher should indicate what should be improved either on individual scripts or by helping the class to identify key points during the reporting-back session. Pupils should then complete their reports, amending them in the light of the comments.

All too often mathematical investigations end at this point – the pupils have discovered some patterns but remain unaware of their mathematical significance. The investigation should be rounded off by the teacher drawing out the mathematical structures underpinning the relationships discovered by the pupils.

Underlying the terminator are two interesting pieces of mathematics:

> Fractions will only terminate if the denominator is a power of 2 or 5, or a multiple of these.

> Fractions will either terminate or recur. The maximum length of the pattern in a repeating decimal is $(n - 1)$ digits, where n is the denominator. Any decimal which does not recur must therefore be an irrational number.

Both the task and a routine exercise will develop fluency and automaticity in the conversion of fraction to decimals. The task, however, required the pupils to analyse their findings and predict relationships. They were forced to look for the underlying mathematical structure rather than focusing on individual instances. The emphasis was on the deduction of a generality, not the unthinking application of an algorithm. The teaching approach increased the pupils' understanding of their own mathematical knowledge and strategies. Reporting back enabled pupils to learn from the work of others and also stressed the mathematical value of the task.

We hope that you realize, from the case study above, that the role of the teacher is critical in the development of mathematical thinking. Once a mathematically rich open-ended task has been selected, the opportunity exists for mathematical development; however, we do not believe that such development occurs unaided.

CONCLUSION: REFLECTIONS ON THE ROLE OF THE TEACHER IN DEVELOPING MATHEMATICAL THINKING

We began this chapter by emphasizing the importance of integrating a wide range of challenging tasks within your teaching including practical investigations and extended problem solving. We have emphasized the need for the learner to be given significant autonomy if they are to learn to think mathematically and to behave like mathematicians.

We would describe our approach as essentially constructivist, as we believe that only knowledge which individual learners have constructed for themselves is really believed or available for problem solving. However, we also hope that we have convinced you that, although knowledge must be constructed by individuals, that process should not occur in solitude!

Our research indicates that the most effective teachers are able to coach children and support their learning through focused questioning in such a manner which shares expertise and encourages novices to act as experts. Through the use of plenaries for collective reflection and evaluation, effective teachers are able to aid children in their attempts to make personal mathematical meaning. Although we seem to have travelled a long way from what some might refer to as basic skills, we hope that you will come to see in the next chapter that the teaching approaches to which we have referred are also at the heart of effective numeracy teaching.

Summary

To teach children to think mathematically you should:

- use a wide range of challenging tasks and contexts;
- include both practical and theoretical investigations;
- emphasize the metacognitive aspects of learning – make sure that they know that they know it!
- encourage self-evaluation and plan for periods of collective reflection;
- incorporate the start–stop–go approach into your teaching.

The start–stop–go approach:

- read and think alone in silence for a few minutes;
- discuss with a partner or a small group;
- the teacher brainstorms ideas on to the board for discussion;
- pupils select one approach from several possible ideas and begin the task;
- progress is formally monitored by the teacher after 5 to 10 minutes;
- pupils self-monitor and change plans if necessary;
- groups report back in a plenary session;
- groups assess their own work and the work of other groups;
- teacher invites the class to reflect on the learning which has occurred.

Now think back over your reading of this chapter. What is the most important idea from the chapter that you are going to use to develop your teaching?

8 Mathematics in the primary school

Although this chapter is contextualized mainly within primary schools, with the proposed extension of the National Numeracy Strategy (DfEE 2000) into secondary schools, it should also provide a useful background for teachers of older pupils.

INTRODUCTION: THE CHARACTERISTICS OF THE NUMERATE CHILD

Mathematics in English primary schools is now largely taught in line with the National Numeracy Strategy (NNS) (DfEE 1999a) and, although its use is optional in Scotland and Wales, its influence is great. Very similar advice is offered to teachers in Wales on most issues of substance. The advice given in the NNS framework will guide much of the discussion which follows. However, we shall also enrich our analysis with data gained in the Raising Standards in Numeracy (RSN) project (Tanner *et al*. 1999).

The RSN project

In 1999 we were part of a collaborative research project involving five Welsh local-education authorities (LEAs) which was funded by the National Assembly for Wales. The project was built around earlier work by the Vale of Glamorgan LEA involving the development of value-added analyses linking National Curriculum data to prior attainment scores, and the development of an approach to target setting, based on pupil-level data.

As part of the project, we used value-added analyses to identify schools where pupils obtained significantly higher-than-expected scores in statutory tests (fuller details may be found in Tanner *et al*. 1999). We then identified two primary and two secondary schools in each LEA whose results were far higher than would have been expected for their intake. On visits to the schools, we then interviewed head teachers, subject leaders, and teachers and asked them to describe the factors to which they attributed their success. Lessons were then observed to examine these classroom processes in practice.

On the basis of the observations made during the RSN project (Tanner *et al*. 1999), we have identified a number of features, which are under the control of the school and the teacher, which we feel represent good practice in the teaching of numeracy. In this chapter we will focus on the interactions between teachers and pupils which contribute to high standards of numeracy in the primary school. Chapter 9 discusses issues within the secondary school and international contexts.

During the RSN project we were privileged to meet large numbers of pupils who were highly numerate. In primary schools we observed lessons with pupils from reception to Y6. Clearly the older pupils knew more facts about the number system than their younger peers, but we felt that the vast majority of the pupils we observed were numerate on the basis of their attitude and behaviour towards the mathematics which was appropriate for their ages.

Task 8.1 What are the characteristics of a numerate child?

Think of a numerate child you have met. The age of the child does not matter.

Try to list the characteristics of attitude and behaviour which make that child numerate.

We are not looking for a list of techniques and processes which the child knows.

We think that there are many characteristics which are common to numerate children. We list a number below. Some are mentioned in official publications such as the *National Numeracy Strategy* (DfEE 1999a) or *Teaching Numeracy in the Primary School* (Griffiths 1999) but several are taken directly from our own observations. Many of these features were common to primary and secondary schools.

Numerate children at any age:

- are willing to have a go at questions involving number;
- have confident knowledge of some basic number facts and are willing to use them to derive new facts, about which they are then equally confident;
- have a sense of the size of the numbers they know and how they fit together;
- often know how to perform calculations or solve problems in more than one way, perhaps having a range of different written, mental, or calculator strategies to choose from;
- sometimes check answers by performing a calculation by another valid method;
- are able to estimate the answers to simple calculations;
- sometimes check through the use of inverse operations;
- often have their own personal ways of working things out mentally or in writing;
- sometimes have their own ways of recording their mathematics;
- are able to explain and justify the methods they have used orally;
- make effective use of a calculator when it is appropriate; but
- prefer to use mental calculations as their first resort;
- enjoy doing and talking about mathematics.

If you examine the list above, you might notice that numerate children have made and are making connections between elements of their mathematical knowledge with confidence and are willing and able to try things out for themselves. They are seeking relational rather than instrumental understanding. The guidance from the National Assembly for Wales takes this a stage further:

> They will not engage in the game of 'I'm trying to guess what the teacher wants me to say' because they will be confident that their own contribution will be valued and accepted as a piece of work worthy of further discussion with the teacher or their peers.
>
> (Griffiths 1999: 2)

We would suggest that this is as much a description of the classroom culture which the teacher has developed as it is a characteristic of the numerate pupil. Reflecting on its content also indicates how poor teaching could suppress the development of numeracy through stifling children's natural mathematical curiosity and imagination. The guidance goes on to say:

> Does this sound too good to be true? If it does then it confirms the concerns of many educationalists that our expectations of pupils are frequently too low
>
> (Griffiths 1999: 2)

We agree with this wholeheartedly. During the RSN project we regularly saw pupils from a wide range of ages, abilities, and social backgrounds exhibiting all of the characteristics above. It is the aim of this chapter to examine the teacher behaviours which encourage the development of this happy state of affairs.

Objectives

By the end of this chapter you should:

- be aware of the suggested structure of a typical numeracy lesson as recommended by the NNS framework;
- understand the nature and purposes of mental and oral work in a typical numeracy lesson including the use of both quick-fire questions and those demanding more extended responses;
- be aware of the demands for 'direct teaching' made in the framework and the forms which such teaching might take;
- understand how the successful teachers in the RSN project made use of interactive teaching to support learning;
- understand how children can benefit from whole-class interactive approaches in a mixed-ability situation;
- understand how different forms of classroom organization can contribute to effective learning, including group and individual work;
- understand how effective plenary sessions, particularly those involving collective reflection, can lead to improved learning.

THE PRINCIPLES UNDERPINNING THE NUMERACY 'HOUR'

The final report of the Numeracy Task Force (Reynolds 1998b) recommends that all primary and special schools review their practices to include teaching a daily 45–60-minute mathematics lesson and that the lesson should involve teaching mathematics to the whole class at the same time – that is to say, *not* through a form of integrated day. Furthermore, the lesson should include 'teaching mathematics to the whole class or to groups for a high proportion of the lesson', including oral and mental work every day, and providing homework (Reynolds 1998b: 16).

The NNS lays down an approach to teaching based on four principles:

- dedicated mathematics lessons every day;
- direct teaching and interactive oral work with the whole class and groups;
- an emphasis on mental calculation;
- controlled differentiation, with all pupils engaged in mathematics relating to a common theme.

The nature of direct teaching requires clarification, however, as we feel that the term might be thought to suggest a teaching approach which is very *directive*, whereas the elaboration which follows makes it clear that this is far from the intention of the framework.

> High quality direct teaching is oral, interactive and lively. It is not achieved by adopting a simplistic formula of 'drill and practice' and lecturing the class, or by expecting pupils to teach themselves from books. It is a two-way process in which pupils are expected to play an active part, by answering questions, contributing points to discussions and explaining and demonstrating their methods to the class.
>
> (DfEE 1999a: 1.11)

This is akin to what we referred to as 'interactive whole-class teaching' in Chapter 5, but the framework makes it clear that 'direct teaching' can also occur with groups, pairs, and individuals. However, it is clear that if teachers are to maximize the opportunities for 'direct teaching', the organization of the classroom should not be based purely on individualized learning. (See also Chapter 5.)

When children are working individually, it is sometimes difficult for teachers to judge the effort which is made. Is that pupil's slow progression because of lack of intellectual ability or laziness? We suspect that many poorly motivated children have found a place to hide and drift along in lessons based on individualized schemes.

In contrast, the work rate in teacher-driven whole-class or large-group activities is very high. This is due in part to not having to write down answers, but there is also a social pressure, created by the teacher, to stay with the class and stay on task. As a rough rule of thumb we would suggest that a class can perform between ten and twenty mental calculations in a minute of mental/oral interaction. During individual or pair working this might have taken half an hour or more. The gains made through the use of oral/mental activity are immense. Some individual written work is necessary, but we suggest that it should be for short periods only, limited to a maximum of say 15–20 minutes without teacher intervention.

Expectations

In contrast to individualized schemes, the teachers in the RSN schools had very high expectations of their pupils. Whole-class lessons or sequences were 'pitched at the upper quartile' with many of the teachers expressing the beliefs that 'the less able pupils benefited from listening to the explanations of the more able' and that 'a good way to develop your understanding was to try to explain your work to others'.

Several teachers professed that they were continually surprised by how much pupils were able to 'pick up' from others, even on topics which the teachers would have considered to be too hard for them. Although classes seemed to be operating at a higher level than might usually be expected, we saw no evidence of children being 'lost' or of work 'going over their heads'. Through effective use of the techniques of mixed-ability questioning – targeting pupils at an appropriate level – the pupils were engaged on tasks at all times and teachers received continuous feedback. Teachers used this feedback to adapt their pace and approaches while they were in action. More than one of the RSN teachers used the phrase *bouncing off the kids* to describe the process.

> *During whole class teaching you bounce off the kids. You listen to what they say and you react instantly with a new question, diagram, illustration or whatever in reaction. Its fast and furious and sometimes you misunderstand and get it wrong, but it's good fun and very effective.*
>
> (Y6 teacher)

The RSN teachers were able to support children who were working in their 'learning zone' by offering help to individuals through guiding questions and the use of illuminating diagrams and physical materials. The RSN teachers were able to offer sufficient support during whole-class and group activities to set up a learning zone which was wide enough to cater for the full range of pupils. This form of direct teaching was not directive – far from it. Although teachers knew the essential mathematical concepts to be learned in the lesson, the routes to developing those concepts were many and varied. Furthermore, when the aim of the lesson was to develop techniques or algorithms, pupils were expected to have their own ideas and suggestions which were valued and respected.

APPROACHES TO DEVELOPING NUMERACY

The Numeracy Task Force (Reynolds 1998b) recommends a common format for lessons to follow from Y1 onwards (Table 8.1). This has been largely accepted

Table 8.1 A typical lesson in the numeracy hour.

Clear start to lesson		
Whole class	Mental and oral work to rehearse and sharpen skills	About 5–10 minutes
Main teaching and pupil activities		
Whole class/groups/ pairs/individuals	Clear objectives shared with pupils	About 30–40 minutes
	Interactive/direct teaching input	
	Pupils clear about what to do next	
	Practical and/or written work on same theme for all the class	
	If group work, usually at no more than three levels of difficulty, with focused teaching of one or two groups for part of the time	
	Continued interaction and intervention	
	Misconception identified	
Plenary		
Whole class	Feedback from children to identify progress and sort misconceptions	About 10–15 minutes
	Summary of key ideas, what to remember	
	Links made to other work, next steps discussed	
	Work set to do at home	

From Reynolds (1998b: 18).

and versions of it appear in both the primary and secondary NNS framework documents (DfEE 1999a, 2000).

It is suggested in the NNS that this overall pattern of lessons should generally be the same for all classes, providing teachers with 'a common structure for developing ideas and sharing planning and teaching with colleagues' (DfEE 1999a: 1.13).

Many of the features of this 'typical lesson' were also to be found in the lessons we observed being taught in the particularly successful schools identified in the RSN project. However, they did not operate to a standard format. Rather, the teaching approaches varied according to the age and ability of pupils, the topic being taught, the constraints of the physical environment, and the pedagogical preferences of the teacher. Teachers in the most successful schools were not afraid to make their own professional decisions.

The practices described in the NNS were clearly impacting on primary schools. However, the teachers in our study were not new converts to such techniques, having developed their own comparable strategies and approaches during the period 1995 to 1998. The lessons we observed exhibited clear learning objectives, an obvious overall structure, and a variety of learning activities.

Mental and oral work formed a significant part of their lesson plans. Although mental work was used as a warm-up activity at the start of the lesson in most primary classrooms it was also used naturally during other periods of teaching and learning. It was clear that both teachers and pupils expected to be able to engage with simple mathematical situations mentally and that there were many situations when it was considered inappropriate to reach for pencil and paper or a calculator.

Not all teachers placed their period of mental practice at the start of every lesson. On occasions, teachers had decided to begin directly with the main focus of the lesson rather than following a specified format slavishly. They were not driven by commercial schemes or by external frameworks. However, in all the RSN primary schools, the teacher provided the focus for activity in the classroom.

In nearly all schools there was detailed collaborative planning, both of the overall scheme of work and of individual lessons. Teachers worked collaboratively in teams within their schools and devised their own teaching approaches within a clear set of guidelines for each year. They provided leadership and pace for the lessons and enjoyed their central role. Nearly all the teachers planned to end their lessons with plenaries and noted possible assessment opportunities in their planning.

We shall now examine each phase of the recommended numeracy lesson in greater detail.

Mental and oral work

In all the lessons we observed during the RSN project, there was a strong emphasis on both mental and oral mathematics. It should be noted that much of the mental activity seen was not of the traditional mental-test form (although this was also used very occasionally). If the lesson began with an oral/mental warm-up, the emphasis of the initial activity was often on participation and quick response.

There were several aims for such activities:

- to set a mathematical frame of mind, warming the class up for the lesson to come;
- to reassert a culture of collaborative oral participation from all pupils which would continue throughout the lesson;
- to revise and practise mathematical facts, conventions, and techniques which had been learned in previous lessons;
- to establish new mathematical facts, conventions, and techniques from older known material;
- to improve speed of mental calculation.

Most teachers would agree with the first four aims, although there would be some debate about the last one. The NNS appears to regard speed of mental calculation as a condition for numeracy, along with a demand that children know large numbers of mathematical facts off by heart and have them available for instantaneous recall.

The NNS lists the key objectives and the teaching programme for each year. This distinguishes between facts which should be 'known by heart' and those which pupils should 'derive quickly'.

For example, in Y3, children are required to: 'know by heart all addition and subtraction facts for each number to 20' and 'all pairs of multiples of 100 with a total of 1,000 (e.g. $300 + 700$)' (DfEE 1999a: 2.3), but 'derive quickly all pairs of multiples of 5 with a total of 100' (DfEE 1999a: 3.14).

Task 8.2 Key mathematical facts

Consider our comments on the numerate child above. Clearly some mathematical facts must be known off by heart so that other mathematical facts may be derived from them. What mathematical facts would you include as key objectives for learning by the end of Y3 and Y6?

Read the NNS, section 2, pages 3 and 5, for the key objectives for the 2 years. Also read section 3, pages 14–15 and pages 26–27, for the teaching programmes and focus on those facts which should be 'known by heart'. Compare the NNS demands with your own.

Similarly, by Y5, children are required to 'know by heart all multiplication facts up to 10×10' and by Y6 are required to 'derive quickly division facts corresponding to multiplication tables up to 10×10' (DfEE 1999a: 2.4–2.5). The teaching programme for Y6 further demands that pupils derive quickly:

> squares of multiples of 10 to 100 (e.g. 60×60);
> doubles of two-digit numbers (e.g. 3.6×2; 0.76×2);
> doubles of multiples of 10 to 1,000 (e.g. 670×2);
> doubles of multiples of 100 to 10,000 (e.g. $6,500 \times 2$);
> and the corresponding halves.
>
> (DfEE 1999a: 3.26)

We believe that these are ambitious, though achievable objectives although we are concerned that an overemphasis on speed of recall could lead to a return to the bad old days of rote learning to achieve short-term objectives. We are aware of a number of professional mathematicians who fail to meet some of these targets. In fact although we are able to calculate very quickly all addition and subtraction facts for each number to 20 we do not know them all 'off by heart', preferring instead to resort to quick and accurate strategies such as $17 - 8 = 7 + 2 = 9$.

In fact we have never regarded *speed* of mental calculation as a particularly highly placed objective for mathematics teaching. We have always been more concerned with *accuracy, confidence in results, the understanding of mathematical processes*, and the consequent *ability to check results in case memory fails*. Our mental image of the mathematician at work emphasizes characteristics such as systematic and methodical approaches rather than a good memory. Although the learning of some key number facts is necessary, rote learning or learning by heart without understanding could be damaging to the longer term development of true numeracy.

An overemphasis on speed of calculation in a whole-class situation may alienate many pupils from mathematics if not handled sensitively. In a recent meeting of a teacher-inquiry group, which included a number of special-education teachers, grave concern was expressed about the position of the least able pupils in a whole-class situation. During the meeting we played a common game for improving speed of calculation. One teacher turned pink almost immediately and confessed:

I've got all hot and flustered already, I won't be able to do this. I always hated this kind of thing at school. I always promised myself that I'd never show kids up like this.

Many of the children you teach will already have learned to fail rather than succeed, and you should think very carefully before using a game which places children at risk of public humiliation. However, it is often possible to cater for all pupils by grading questions using your own code and ensuring that they are allocated in such a way as to set an appropriate challenge (i.e. achievable) for all pupils.

Task 8.3 Making and using a set of mental-arithmetic game cards

Make a set of cards as shown in Table 8.2.

Table 8.2 Mental-arithmetic game.

Give me 40 more	It is 15	Give me double	It is 55
Give me half	It is 100	Give me 10 less	It is 110
Give me three times as much	It is 40	Give me thirty less	It is 120
Give me 20 less	It is 50	Give me 10 less	It is 30
Give me double	It is 20	Give me one-sixth	It is 90

Each card has an instruction on the left-hand side. If the answer to the previous question is the number on the right-hand side, then the instruction should be read out.

Examine the cards and decide which are the hardest. Put red dots on the back of the very hard cards and green dots on the very easy cards.

Find five friends to play with and give them two cards each. Give the red-dot cards to the most able and the green-dot cards to the least able.

Say 'It is 15' and see how quickly your friends can read out all the cards.

Shuffle the cards and deal them out again. Say 'It is 55' and see if they are quicker this time.

Continue like this until they all know the instructions instantly. Try them out with a suitable group of pupils in school.

Make a set of thirty such cards which are suitable for a class you know. Make sure that each card has a different 'It is' number and a range of levels of difficulty. Try them out in school.

The teachers in our RSN project had all considered the plight of the least able in such situations and had taken steps to ensure that they should not be exposed as weak in front of the class. They ensured that their questions to individuals were differentiated to ensure that all pupils were offered an achievable challenge

Figure 8.1 'Show-me' cards showing 7/9.

which was appropriate to their ability. The card game above lends itself to this by helping the teacher to plan the quick-fire mental questions by level in advance. Many of our RSN teachers had several sets of such cards which they had made. They are also available commercially. Even when quick-fire questions were oral and apparently random, the RSN teachers had generally planned them out in writing prior to the lesson to ensure that they had differentiated appropriately.

A number of different techniques were used to facilitate the use of whole-class mental sessions in mixed-ability and mixed-age sessions in order to avoid public humiliation and to encourage whole-class participation. Questions were asked and then targeted differentially to ensure participation and yet facilitate success by less able pupils.

The RSN schools used 'show-me' cards in many of their oral/mental sessions (Figure 8.1). Each pupil has a set of cards. Each card has a digit or symbol. Each set of cards includes the digits from 0 to 9 and perhaps a % sign, fraction sign, and decimal point. Most teachers had laminated sets of these cards. Some had made them in the form of a fan held at the bottom by a paper fastener to prevent loss (see Figure 8.2). Others used square cards which the pupils laid out on the desk in front of them.

When the teacher set a mental challenge, the pupils were given a few seconds to calculate their answer and find their cards. The teacher then said: 'One, two, three, show!'and the class all held the cards up for the teacher to see. All the pupils had to work out an answer. All the class said 'Yes!' when the teacher gave the correct answer – including those who had it wrong. The teacher had been able to scan the class and knew who had the wrong answer, but no one else did, so no pupils lost face.

These cards allowed teachers to set demanding mental challenges to the whole class and gain immediate and accurate feedback from each individual pupil without damaging anyone's self esteem. Not only did teachers gain feedback on

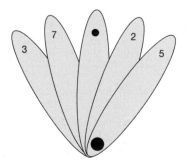

Figure 8.2 A number fan showing 37.25.

who had been successful, they were also able to see patterns of wrong answers and gain insight to the misconceptions which some children held. We think that all teachers of mathematics, at whatever level, should have a set of cards like this, adapted for their own purposes. The cards can just as easily hold algebraic symbols or language such as acute, obtuse, parallel, alternate as they can digits.

Many lessons began with counting on as a whole class in steps of different sizes from different starting points. This often moved on in difficulty quite quickly, for example, by introducing reverse counting and larger numbers. Individual contributions were sometimes required and carefully targeted. For example, we saw a mixed age and ability Y1/Y2 class begin by counting as a class in threes from 0, then threes from 4, then threes from 7, threes from 20, 50. A challenge was then thrown open.

> Who thinks they can count on in threes from 100?

A boy was chosen to answer from several pupils who had offered. All the class listened attentively to the answer.

> Excellent, John, really well done! Who thinks they can count on in threes from 200?

Lots of hands went up, and a girl was selected to answer, which she did correctly.

> Oh well done! We are doing well today!
> Now let's all try it together, counting on from 103 ... go, 103, 106, 109 ...'

We were impressed at how easily she had led all of her class to count using such large numbers. When we questioned her about it after the lesson she explained:

> *Only about a dozen of the class have a solid grasp of the meaning of 103 at this stage, and for them I am practising work with the concept of place value and I hope also pushing them a little further. I know that for the youngest children, they are just following a language pattern when they say 'one hundred and three, one hundred and six, and so on, but we've come to the conclusion that it doesn't really matter. When they eventually reach the stage at which I'll introduce them to the concept of hundred place value, that linguistic pattern will be there for me to work with.*
>
> *I really care about getting them to understand their mathematics and not just learning it by rote, but hearing some of the patterns in advance does not hurt them. They have always heard them outside of school anyway. Don't forget there is always the chance that some of the more thoughtful ones will work out the concepts for themselves. The important thing is for me to make sure that I help them to understand why the pattern works when we reach that point.*

Not all mental/oral sessions involved whole-class chanting. Very often after only a short period of quick-response, closed questions, teachers began to ask more open questions demanding greater thoughtfulness and explanation. Even quite simple arithmetical questions such as '225 − 177 = ?' were used as opportunities for pupils to explain their approaches to others and form a starting point for discussion. We often saw such an example lead to explanations of approaches from several different pupils. Depending on the layout of the room, we saw at least two different approaches taken to this. In crowded classrooms, pupils who were sat on the carpet or in their seats explained their reasoning while the teacher tried to illustrate their method in figures on the board or flip chart. When there was less pressure on space, children were invited to show their methods on the board or flip chart themselves. For example:

$$177 + 3 = 180, \quad 180 + 20 = 200, \quad 200 + 25 = 225, \quad 3 + 20 + 25 = 48$$
$$225 − 175 = 50, \quad 175 + 2 = 177, \quad 50, 2 = 48$$
$$77 + 23 = 100, \quad 25 + 23 = 48$$

With older pupils, placing the numbers under each other on the board often led the pupils to try to reproduce a standard algorithm instead of a mental method. Algorithmic approaches were accepted when offered and a number of valid approaches compared, but the RSN teachers preferred to delay the use of formal algorithms until mental methods had been securely established. In order to keep the children focused on mental rather than written approaches, mental questions were usually presented horizontally, leading one school to use the aphorism:

Primary teachers do it horizontally.

Traditionally, British children have been introduced to the formal algorithms for arithmetic far earlier than pupils in Europe and Asia (Graham *et al*. 1999). We suspect that one consequence of this early introduction is instrumental learning. Building on such shallow understanding is like building on sand. The RSN schools deliberately delayed the introduction of formal algorithms until after the development of effective mental processes which could be used as solid foundations for the construction of techniques and processes.

The questions we have considered so far have been closed. Numeracy is far more than fast recall, however, and more extended open-ended questions are needed if pupils are to gain a sense of mathematical structure and strategy. Happily such questions can easily be incorporated into a mental/oral session to a whole class without problems of differentiation. In fact, the RSN teachers frequently used open questions as one of their oral/mental strategies. Open questions were used very effectively by the RSN teachers to allow pupils to self-differentiate work and set their own targets.

In order to gain whole-class participation and task differentiation, teachers often created open questions which could be answered at a number of levels of difficulty. One simple technique for creating such questions is to give an answer and ask for a question which would produce it. This is easily extended into setting the task of getting an answer in a target range. For example, we observed a mixed class of reception and Y1 who had just read the story of 101 Dalmatians and who had produced a wall display of dogs with exactly 101 spots each. The teacher asked:

Who can tell me a sum with the answer 101?

Answers began with a simple $100 + 1$, and quickly moved on to examples like $65 + 36$. When a pupil suggested $102 - 1$, the teacher said:

> Very good – a new operation, who else can think of other operations?

The class quickly moved on to suggestions like $601 - 500$, or $710 - 600 - 9$. The pupils listened to the patterns of answers which the brighter pupils were calling out and adopted them as their own.

Other examples of this type of target question we have seen include:

> The answer is 20, what is the question?
> The answer to a fractions question was $1\frac{1}{2}$ what was the question?
> The answer to a decimals question was 0.5 what was the question?

> Give me two decimals that add to 1.
> Give me two fractions that add to 1.
> Give me two fractions which add to more than 1.
> Give me two fractions that add to 3.
> Give me three fractions that add to 3.

> Tell me a number between 20 and 30.
> Tell me a number between 2 and 3.

Questions like these allow pupils to choose an operation or mathematical fact with which they feel secure in order to set themselves a task at their own level. The teacher can then modify the question to challenge pupils, who are underestimating themselves, by demanding a particular operation from a particular individual. We observed teachers structuring the order in which they asked such questions in order to make a mathematical point which often led on into the next phase of the lesson. Several of the RSN teachers used their mental/oral session to set the scene for the main teaching activity in the lesson.

All shall have prizes

The journalist Melanie Phillips once wrote a book entitled *All Shall Have Prizes* (Phillips, 1996) criticising child-centred attitudes to education in which all pupils were valued. Our observations in the RSN schools showed us that skilled teachers were able to achieve high academic standards and teach dynamic, whole-class lessons precisely because they maintained an approach in which the needs and feelings of individual children were central. The RSN teachers *managed the success* of the individuals in their care, ensuring that all pupils were appropriately challenged and that all experienced success and reward for their various achievements. In mental arithmetic, all pupils must experience success if they are to develop the self-confidence to stay in the game.

The main teaching input and pupil activities

According to the NNS (DfEE 1999a: 1.14) the main part of the lesson provides time for introducing a new topic, consolidating previous work or extending it, developing vocabulary and notation, and using and applying concepts and skills.

The framework discusses this part of the lesson as possibly involving work with the whole class, groups, individuals, or pairs. It is left to the teacher's professional judgement to determine how the class should be organized for a particular teaching topic. However, it is made clear that the teacher should spend as much time as possible in the 'direct teaching' of the whole class, a group of pupils, or individuals, and although direct teaching and good interaction are important in all forms of classroom organization, whole-class and large-group teaching maximizes pupils' experience of this approach (DfEE 1999a: 1.11–1.12).

Many of the RSN teachers began this phase of the lesson with a teaching input to the whole class about a topic which would be studied by every pupil in the class. This phase was sometimes of quite short duration prior to the class breaking down into a number of ability groups with differentiated tasks based on the same theme. The framework recommends a maximum of four groups (DfEE 1999a: 1.14). The Numeracy Task Force (Reynolds, 1998b) recommends a maximum of three groups. The RSN teachers varied. Teachers would sometimes use two groups, sometimes three, and sometimes four according to the topic and the range of prior knowledge in the class. When a topic was new to all the pupils in a class, the work might not be differentiated by task, but by outcome.

All the RSN lessons were characterized by thorough planning of the teaching input to be made. Planning was usually over a period of a week or more to ensure that all groups received sufficient direct teaching. Typically the first lesson on a topic would have a greater degree of whole-class teaching than later lessons. Some schools referred to these as 'Monday lessons' no matter which day they occurred on. Pupil activities were sometimes undifferentiated following 'Monday lessons'. In succeeding lessons, say 'Tuesday' or 'Wednesday' lessons the whole-class input was sometimes shorter and the class moved fairly quickly to working on differentiated tasks in their groups. During such sessions, teachers were still involved in interactive teaching of groups. In fact they usually planned the teaching input which different groups were going to receive on each day. They did not spread their teaching thinly, but planned to make a significant input to no more than two groups on any one day. 'Friday' lessons often included a large plenary element as the work of the 'week' was summarized and discussed. Thus plans might include these elements in the main-activity section (see Table 8.3).

In order to prevent interruption during significant teaching inputs, a few teachers used a red-card system. Pupils knew that if the red card was on their group's table, they were not allowed to ask the teacher for help during the exercise, although they were allowed to ask for help from other group members. Red-card periods usually lasted a maximum of 10–15 minutes.

Teaching techniques

Questioning was used with a range of styles and purposes by the RSN teachers. Effective use was made of open questions, questions which required an extended response, and probing questions which demanded further explanation and justification, in addition to more traditional forms of short question for the purposes of recall, feedback, and accountability. Interactive whole-class teaching techniques were used in every lesson we observed and although these varied somewhat in

Table 8.3 Planning a series of lessons.

Monday

Whole-class teaching	Teacher input on place value using the magnetic number line (20 min)
Whole-class activity	All class work on naming and ordering decimals to two places (15 min)

Tuesday

Whole-class teaching	Short discussion on place value on number line, extended to multiplication by 10 and 100 (10 min)
Group work	(20 min)
Red group	Continue working on naming and ordering to two places with teacher support
Blue group	Working without support on exercise to consolidate multiplication by 10 and 100
Green group	Begin calculator investigation to discover how scientific calculators deal with large numbers. Teacher support towards beginning and end

Wednesday

Whole-class	Short discussion on place value, then extending to division by 10, 100, 1,000, etc. (10 min)
Group work	(20 min)
Red group	Working without support to consolidate multiplication by 10, 100
Blue group	Mixed exercises to consolidate multiplication by 10, 100 and extend to division by 10, 100, 1,000, teacher support at the start
Green group	Mixed exercises on multiplication and division by 10, 100, 1,000. Later questions involve an extension to the calculator task on standard form with teacher support

Friday

Group work	Plenary session in which each group writes a note about the most important thing they have learned this week, what they will try to remember in particular and any personal targets they are setting themselves
Whole class	Groups and individuals report back to the whole class and key points are discussed.

character, they were always more like interactive explanations rather than clearly explained lectures. At the very least, questions asked by the teacher were used to develop an interactive mathematical argument with the pupils. In the majority of lessons we observed, the interaction demanded far more from pupils than a simple response to a question.

Mathematics Attainment Target 1 (AT1) was not forgotten by the RSN teachers. Rather it was integrated into all their working. The knowledge and understanding aimed for in their lessons was relational rather than instrumental and opportunities for making links with real life were actively sought. Furthermore, their whole approach was based on pupils articulating their ideas and strategies emphasizing the processes and thinking skills of mathematics. Most lessons were characterized by significant participation by pupils and often this involved 'getting pupils out to the front' to explain and justify their work to other pupils (see Chapter 5).

We would have preferred to describe the teaching approaches employed by the RSN teachers as indirect rather than direct, but it is clear that the framework's use of the phrase 'direct teaching' includes approaches based on pupil exploration, investigation, and explanation in addition to more traditional approaches.

What does the framework mean by direct teaching?

The framework claims that good direct teaching is achieved by creating a balance between the following teacher behaviours with examples:

directing   sharing teaching objectives with the class, ensuring that pupils know what to do;

instructing   giving information and structuring it well;

demonstrating   showing, describing, and modelling mathematics;

explaining and illustrating   explaining a method of calculation and discussing why it works;

questioning and discussing   using open and closed questions which are framed, adjusted, and targeted so that all pupils take part, teachers listen carefully and respond to take learning forwards;

consolidating   reinforcing and developing what has been taught through class or homework, asking pupils either with a partner or a group to reflect on and talk through a process, getting them to think of different approaches to a problem;

evaluating pupils' responses   identifying mistakes, using them as positive teaching points by talking about them, discussing misconceptions, pupils' justifications, evaluating presentations, and giving oral feedback;

summarizing   reviewing what has been taught and learned, correcting misunderstandings, making links to other work, giving pupils an insight into the next stage of their learning.

(summarized from DfEE 1999a: 1.11–1.12)

The first three behaviours *directing, instructing, and demonstrating* illustrate the intention of the framework to make the teacher far more than a facilitator of an individualized scheme. It is clear that direct teaching places teachers at the focus of the activity. However, far more than lecturing followed by drill and practice is implied. It is clear that *explaining and illustrating,* and *questioning and discussing* require far more from pupils than simply to receive information from the teacher and absorb it like sponges – a far more active role is envisaged in which pupils are expected to be very active participants in the learning process, offering their own views and discussing alternatives. Finally, *consolidating, evaluating pupils' responses*, and *summarizing* again indicate a very active role for pupils towards the end of the lesson in a period of reflection during which teachers will try to encourage the construction of connected knowledge through processes which should lead to the development of metacognitive knowledge.

Plenaries

Although much of the discussion about the framework in the UK has focused on mental work and direct teaching, one of its most significant, and we think misunderstood and underestimated, aspects is the plenary. The timings suggested for a typical lesson by the Numeracy Task Force (Reynolds 1998b) allocate 10–15 minutes for this part of the lesson. This represents about 25 per cent of the time allocated for mathematics each day and we would suggest that to allocate this much time to a plenary session is a radical departure from traditional classroom practices in either primary or secondary schools.

The framework suggests that this part of the lesson can be used to help pupils 'to assess their developing knowledge and skills' and relate their mathematics to other subjects (DfEE 1999a: 1.14). A number of different activities are suggested for this part of the lesson, including:

- ask pupils to present or explain their work . . .;
- discuss and compare the efficiency of pupils' different methods . . .;
- help pupils to generalize a rule . . .;
- draw together what has been learned, reflect on what was important;
- summarize key facts, ideas and vocabulary, and what needs to be remembered . . .;
- make links to other work . . .;
- remind pupils about their personal targets . . .;
- provide tasks for pupils to do at home . . ..

(DfEE 1999a: 1.15)

In the RSN schools, we saw all of these activities used in a variety of lessons. Plenaries were planned in advance in most cases and offered opportunities for pupils to report back on findings and to reflect on their progress and learning.

The best plenaries we saw in the RSN project were driven by focusing questions from the teacher, and in many lessons the class had obviously come to anticipate such a session. Pupils expected to articulate and defend their own approaches in discussion with the rest of the class. When pupils attempt to explain their methods to others in this way, the explanation itself becomes the focus of their thinking and they are forced to bring it to a new level of understanding. Many psychologists consider that the objectification of thought through speech is associated with bringing the subconscious into the conscious and hence the development of reflective awareness and conscious control (e.g. Vygotsky 1978; Prawat 1989a).

Further research is needed on the value of the plenary for learning, but the results of phase 2 of the Practical Applications of Mathematics Project (Tanner 1997; Tanner and Jones 1999b) show that teachers who were successful in organizing periods of whole-class reflection in plenary sessions were most successful in developing mathematical thinking skills.

Awareness of one's own mathematical knowledge is a prerequisite for its application to problems or, indeed, for its use in the learning of new mathematics. Good plenary sessions helped pupils to develop such metacognitive awareness as they reflected back on what they had learned. Several of the RSN teachers specifically asked pupils to identify what they had learned during the lesson and what they thought would be most important to remember. We believe that if teachers introduce such strategies into their practice, improved learning will result.

CONCLUSION

The teaching and learning practices observed in the RSN project were based on high expectations of pupils. Lessons had clear objectives and were planned to ensure progression and continuity of learning. The classroom culture was disciplined, supportive, and required pupils to take an active part in their learning.

Pupils were expected to articulate and discuss their own methods and tentative conjectures; however, the teacher's role was the most significant in the classroom discourse. The teacher was in control at all times, leading and driving the lesson forwards, challenging the pupils, supporting, probing, encouraging, and, perhaps most important of all, focusing the attention of the class on what was significant in the activity and what they were learning through their participation in the lesson in an effective plenary.

Many of suggestions of the NNS were exemplified within the RSN schools and appeared to have contributed to their success. It is important, however, that the superficial, structural aspects do not overshadow the more important issues of the quality of the teaching and classroom interactions.

Interestingly the findings of the RSN project in primary schools do not differ in any significant manner from our findings for secondary schools. It is our contention that the practices which constitute good mathematics teaching and learning are consistent across the age phases. It is only the content which changes. We shall next look at how secondary schools may adapt their practices in the light of the NNS.

Summary

- The key to the effective teaching of mathematics is not the lesson organization but the quality of interaction between teacher and pupil;
- interaction may occur in a number of formats – oral work, direct teaching, reflection on learning;
- mental mathematics means more than just the recall of number facts;
- direct teaching does not equal telling;
- effective teaching often involves more asking than telling;
- effective differentiation is needed to ensure participation and avoid humiliation;
- the most effective plenary sessions support pupils' learning by encouraging articulation, reflection, and the development of metacognitive knowledge.

9 Numeracy in the secondary school

Although this chapter is contextualized mainly within secondary schools, it should also provide a useful background for teachers in the primary phase.

INTRODUCTION

According to the National Curriculum (DfEE/QCA 1999b), numeracy is a key skill, ranked alongside literacy and ICT, underpinning all other school learning. In recent years it has become a topic of great interest to the media, who regularly delight in offering sensation-seeking headlines proving that standards of numeracy are poor.

> English children lag even further behind their counterparts in other countries than recent international surveys suggest ... Although English children fared well in science, they were among the lowest scorers for literacy and numeracy.
>
> (*The Times*, 14 January 2000)

Although we are far from complacent about standards of numeracy in the UK, we contend that the reporting and interpretation placed on these results is grossly distorted by the political aspirations of the authors. The Third International Mathematics and Science Study (TIMSS) study, apparently reported above, actually shows English Y9 pupils to be performing at the international average; for example: at the same level as Sweden, Norway, Germany, and the USA; better than Spain, Iceland, Portugal, and Iran; but worse than Singapore, Korea, Japan, Hong Kong, France, and Hungary (Beaton *et al.* 1996: 23). However, although it is possible to argue with both the validity of and the interpretation placed on such international comparisons, it is impossible to ignore them. Numeracy and its teaching are at the centre of the political agenda and it is generally accepted that standards of numeracy should be improved.

Hard on the heels of the National Numeracy Strategy (NNS) for primary schools (DfEE 1999a), there is now a draft NNS framework for teaching mathematics in year 7 (DfEE 2000) which is intended to act as a bridge between the KS2 and KS3 PoS. In this chapter we focus on the nature of numeracy, the conclusions which might be drawn from international comparisons, and the impact of the NNS. We try to identify those teaching approaches which have been associated with high attainment in research studies. Our objectives are as follows.

Objectives

By the end of Chapter 9 you should:

- understand the wide-ranging nature of numeracy as a concept;
- be aware of some of the issues arising from international comparisons;
- understand the approaches advocated by influential projects such as NNP and MEP;
- be particularly aware of the evidence arising from the TIMSS videotape study into Japanese approaches;
- understand some of the approaches which made the RSN schools so effective.

WHAT IS NUMERACY?

Even with the current focus on numeracy, there remains some confusion as to the exact meaning of the term, which has changed considerably since its early use as 'mathematical literacy' in the Crowther report (1959) to the more recent emphasis on arithmetical calculation (e.g. Reynolds 1998b). It is ill defined in terms of knowledge, being highly dependent on context. For example, when a professor of engineering demands that students are numerate, it is usually knowledge of algebra and calculus which is sought rather than skill with multiplication tables. Perhaps a better question than 'What is numeracy?' might be 'Numerate for what purpose?'. However, as a starting point, we consider that to be numerate suggests both an ability to cope with the practical mathematical demands of everyday life and also an 'at-homeness' with number (Cockcroft 1982). Does this mean more than a knowledge of basic number bonds such as multiplication tables? Yes, indeed, and we think such simplistic solutions fail to grasp the real issue.

For example, consider the case of a graduate mathematician friend of ours who is a published author of textbooks and a successful teacher of mathematics but does not know his multiplication tables. His explanation to us is that when presented with a question like '$7 \times 8 = ?$', he is able to calculate in sequence:

$$10 \times 7 = 70, \quad 2 \times 7 = 14, \quad 70 - 14 = 56$$

in less than 2 seconds. He sees no reason to change. He is able to do this quickly and accurately for most multiplications less than 100.

Similarly, for '$23 \times 18 = ?$', a question for which would lead many towards paper-and-pencil methods, he responds:

$$23 \times 20 = 460, \quad 2 \times 23 = 46, \quad 460 - 46 = 414$$

It is not necessarily how we would have chosen to perform these calculations, but it would seem unreasonable to describe him as innumerate. He clearly knows suffi-cient number bonds and mathematical processes to allow him to perform swift and apparently effortless mental arithmetic. He is sufficiently numerate for his own purposes.

Task 9.1 What is numeracy?

Try to write your own definition of numeracy.

At a recent meeting of a teacher-inquiry group we asked a group of primary and secondary teachers to describe what they thought numeracy implied. Their answers encompass a far wider set of knowledge and processes than simply a facility with a few basic number bonds. Numeracy is:

a   . . . knowing enough mathematical structure to be able to use what they know, to be able to work out what they don't know . . .

b   . . . being fluent with number, being at ease with it, so that you can play around with it to get what you need . . .

c   . . . knowing the language, grammar, and symbolism of mathematics . . .

d   . . . being able to solve problems with number and language and knowing when your answer is reasonable . . .

e   . . . coping with the demands of everyday life and knowing how to choose an efficient process in any situation which will lead to a reliable answer . . .

f   . . . knowing when it is appropriate to use a calculator.

The role of the calculator with respect to numeracy is contentious. Girling (1977) equated numeracy with the ability to use a calculator sensibly but the Numeracy Task Force suggests that 'numerate primary pupils should: . . . recognise when it is *not* appropriate to use a calculator;' (Reynolds 1998a: 7, our italics). We do not wish to see pupils exhibiting dependence on calculators when simple mental methods should be easily available. However, neither do we subscribe to the view that to labour over pages of arithmetical calculations is intrinsically good, an integral part of mathematical character building! We regard the use of a calcula-tor as one strategy among many, to be chosen or not as considered appropriate for the task. We will discuss the appropriate use of calculators in Chapter 10.

We suggest that a numerate person has 'the ability to solve simple everyday problems involving number, by using effectively the knowledge and skills that they possess' and that this effective use should include being able to choose and to devise their own appropriate strategies (Mathematical Association 1992: 71).

The choice of an effective strategy for a problem is dependent not only on the knowledge which has been learned but also on one's awareness of that knowledge and the realization that its use would be appropriate to the problem. It should include also a judgement as to one's personal accuracy in recall of the facts and processes used. To devise a personal strategy requires confidence, an at-homeness with number maybe, and a classroom culture which encourages pupils to view mathematics as a subject in which they are allowed, even expected, to create their own strategies and approaches.

To be numerate then is not merely to know numerical facts and processes, numeracy also includes the capability and disposition to construct personal approaches to the solution of problems which are appropriate to the context you are in and are based on your knowledge of your own strengths and weaknesses. To be numerate is to be able to apply mathematical techniques and processes which you are confident will lead to a secure answer. Numeracy therefore involves an interaction between mathematical facts, mathematical processes, metacognitive self-knowledge and affective aspects including self-confidence and enjoyment of number work.

The National Numeracy Strategy for primary schools makes it clear that a broadly based practical skill is intended:

> Numeracy is a proficiency which involves confidence and competence with numbers and measures. It requires an understanding of the number system, a repertoire of computational skills and an inclination and ability to solve number problems in a variety of contexts. Numeracy also demands practical understanding of the ways in which information is gathered by counting and measuring, and is presented in graphs, diagrams, charts and tables.
>
> (DfEE 1999a: 4)

In fact, although the document refers to a numeracy strategy, what is offered is a framework for raising standards by teaching *mathematics* in a manner which makes it both accessible and practical. The NNS extension emphasizes that it is a framework for teaching *mathematics* in Y7 (DfEE 2000). It demands that number facts learned in Y6 are consolidated and that mental methods are extended to include decimals, fractions and percentages (with suitable jottings) (DfEE 2000: 28). However, it also places great emphasis on laying the foundations for algebra, as well as setting clear objectives for problem solving, shape space and measures, and handling data.

STANDARDS

As we suggested above, there is no room for complacency about the standards of numeracy achieved by pupils in the UK. Large-scale studies conducted in the 1970s and 1980s by Concepts in Secondary Mathematics and Science CSMS (e.g. Hart 1981) and Assessment of Performance Unit APU (Foxman 1985) reveal that a large proportion of the school population failed to understand what might be referred to as basic arithmetic more than a quarter of a century ago (see also Chapter 6). You should notice that these large-scale surveys were conducted before the use of calculators had become widespread in schools.

In order to study how standards of numeracy had changed over the quarter century, we devised a numeracy test which included a number of items which had been used in the CSMS and APU studies (Jones and Tanner 1997) and arranged for it to be taken in a carefully selected stratified (representative) sample of schools. The test did not allow the use of calculators.

A questionnaire was sent to all secondary schools in Wales to identify how calculators were used. We found that secondary schools were split between allowing calculators to be freely available, restricting their use, and discouraging their use, in the ratio 4 : 3 : 4. We then arranged for the test to be taken by all the year-8 pupils in a sample of schools which represented the national range of calculator use and had GCSE league-table positions for all subjects at the median and quartile positions to ensure general academic comparability.

Interestingly we found no significant differences between the mean scores for the three forms of calculator use. However, when we analysed the results according to how pupils reported that they used calculators in mathematics lessons, the pupils who agreed with the statement 'I use a calculator in most of my maths lessons' gained significantly higher scores on average than those who disagreed (significance level < 0.001, Jones and Tanner 1998).

There were three sections in our test: number, decimals, and fractions. Overall the success rates in number and decimals were comparable with those reported a quarter of a century ago. Only in fractions were standards lower and our questionnaires indicated that, in line with National Curriculum demands, schools no longer taught fractions extensively at this age. However, although standards had not generally fallen, they were not impressive.

Task 9.2 What are your expectations for pupils' numeracy in year 8?

Consider the following questions selected from the tests and estimate the proportion of Y8 pupils you would expect to answer correctly. Consider also the proportion you think should be able to answer correctly if schools are teaching numeracy well.

1   Write the number two hundred thousand and sixty eight in figures.
2   The mile counter on Mrs Smith's car says 55,499. What will it say after one more mile?
3   Add one-tenth to 6.9.
4   Divide 2.8 by 100.
5   Put these three decimals in order of smallest first: 0.06 0.24 0.1.
6   $2/3 = ?/15$.

You may be surprised and disappointed at how many children have failed to grasp basic arithmetical concepts by year 8. Table 9.1 shows the percentage of year-8 pupils who answered each question correctly with the CSMS (Hart 1981) or APU (Foxman 1985) data for comparison. Thus although standards may not generally have fallen, they have not improved either and there is certainly no room for complacency!

Table 9.1 Comparing performance in 1996 with earlier studies.

Question number		Percentage correct in 1996	CSMS (or APU) equivalent
1	200,068	43%	51% (42%)
2	55,499 + 1	71%	77% (68%)
3	1/10 + 6.9	48%	44%
4	2.8 ÷ 100	13%	27%
5	0.06, 0.24, 0.1	33%	(23%)
6	2/3 = ?/15	27%	58%

The Third International Mathematics and Science Study

Forty-five countries and over half a million pupils were involved in the Third International Mathematics and Science Study (TIMSS) (Beaton *et al.* 1996). England and Scotland participated. Wales and Northern Ireland did not. The study included tests of pupils aged 9, 13, and in the final year of secondary school. The study also included pupil and teacher questionnaires and the analysis of videotaped lessons. You will find further information and detailed results at http://www.ed.gov/NCES/timss

International comparisons reveal a similar sorry state for basic numeracy in England and many other Western-bloc countries. As we indicated above, although the mean score for English year-9 pupils was in line with the international average pupils, some other countries performed far better. In particular, comparisons have been drawn between teaching approaches in England and those in Hungary and Japan who both scored significantly higher than England in Y9. Again we offer you a selection of questions used in the study for you to use for purposes of comparison.

Task 9.3 Sample TIMSS questions

Here are a few questions selected from the TIMSS eighth-grade (Y9) paper. Many of the questions were originally presented in multiple-choice format, but we have not reproduced that here. Examine Figure 9.1 and estimate the proportion of English pupils who would be able to answer the following questions successfully.

For the purposes of comparison we list in Table 9.2 the results for England, Hungary, Japan, and the international average for Year 9.

Although the results of Y9 pupils of Japan and Hungary are better than those of England on this test, they are not universally so. The questions which correspond most closely to formal school-taught algorithms are the ones in which English pupils seem to be weak in comparison with others, whereas the questions which require insight and problem solving are those in which we sometimes excel. We seem to show a relative weakness in number and algebra.

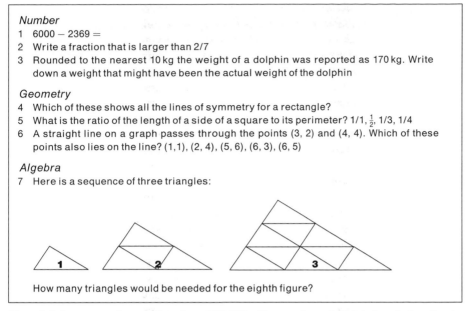

Number

1 6000 − 2369 =

2 Write a fraction that is larger than 2/7

3 Rounded to the nearest 10 kg the weight of a dolphin was reported as 170 kg. Write down a weight that might have been the actual weight of the dolphin

Geometry

4 Which of these shows all the lines of symmetry for a rectangle?

5 What is the ratio of the length of a side of a square to its perimeter? 1/1, $\frac{1}{2}$, 1/3, 1/4

6 A straight line on a graph passes through the points (3, 2) and (4, 4). Which of these points also lies on the line? (1,1), (2, 4), (5, 6), (6, 3), (6, 5)

Algebra

7 Here is a sequence of three triangles:

How many triangles would be needed for the eighth figure?

Figure 9.1 Some sample questions from TIMSS. (Source: International Association for the Evaluation of Education Achievement (IEA), *Third International Mathematics of Science Study (TIMSS)*, Beaton *et al.* 1996.)

Although the algebra question (7), which has some similarities with an investigation, is well answered by English pupils, some more formal algebra questions were badly answered.

Similarly for the 9-year-old pupils, the median score for English pupils is only one percentage point behind that of Hungary. Although we score relatively badly in number, we were joint top in geometry. Some of the differences may be attributed to curriculum decisions rather than other features.

The top four countries in the Y8 and Y9 mathematics tests were Singapore, Korea, Japan, and Hong Kong.

Table 9.2 Results of sample questions for England, Hungary, and Japan. (Source: International Association for the Evaluation of Education Achievement (IEA), *Third International Mathematics of Science Study (TIMSS)*, Beaton *et al.* 1996.'

Question		England	Hungary	Japan	International average Y9
1	6,000–2,369	65%	96%	93%	86%
2	Larger than 2/7	79%	87%	87%	75%
3	Rounded weight	72%	67%	76%	53%
4	Lines of symmetry	82%	82%	77%	66%
5	Square: perimeter	52%	55%	80%	56%
6	Points on a line	55%	51%	47%	41%
7	Triangle sequence	42%	34%	52%	26%

Task 9.4 International comparisons

Consider what you know about the top four countries in the TIMSS mathematics tests. What features would you suspect contributed to their success?

Even a few moments' thought will probably have led you to the conclusion that the number of variables which might have contributed towards success or failure in these tests is extremely large. The cultural differences between the participants are so great that it is impossible to ascribe success or failure to one issue alone.

Data were collected on several measurable variables with mixed results. Unsurprisingly, home factors were strongly related to achievement in mathematics and science in every country. Strong positive relationships were found between achievement and study aids in the home, including a dictionary, computer, personal study desk, number of books, and parental education. Beyond this, however, the findings suggest diverse routes to success with no single solution, no single form of classroom organization, or teaching approach, leading to educational achievement (Beaton *et al.*, 1996). As you might expect, there are no simple answers to complex questions.

The precise message taken from the survey varies from country to country. In the USA, for example, the results are seen to favour the reform movement. In the UK, on the other hand, they are used to support a move towards direct whole-class teaching. Neither case is sustainable purely on the basis of international comparisons, but in both cases the *Zeitgeist*, the spirit of the times, has its own momentum.

Although it is not possible to prove the effectiveness of particular forms of teaching approach or classroom organization on the basis of such comparisons, as a result of the interference of significant uncontrolled social and cultural variables, it is valid to consider and compare case-study reports to illuminate how classroom processes operate within their own contexts.

TEACHING APPROACHES ADVOCATED BY PROJECTS

A number of different projects have explored the impact of different teaching strategies on pupils' learning. We shall compare the key features advocated by a range of projects and consider in what ways they support the development of mathematical thinking.

The National Numeracy Project (NNP)

The National Numeracy Project was set up in October 1996 with a budget of £2.8 million under the direction of Anita Straker. They conducted developmental work in 520 primary schools from fourteen LEAs. The project worked with 5,460 children from reception to Y6.

NNP schools use the framework for numeracy to help them plan lessons and develop a scheme of work. In lessons, work is sometimes differentiated on to at most three levels from a common topic. The preliminary results showed 'statistically significant progress' on the mental and written tests given, and that the overall improvement was better than the National average in both KS1 and KS2. These limited results are perhaps unsurprising given that the schools were a select group working on a special project.

Prior to the changes set in motion by the NNP and the NNS, Reynolds (1998a: 19) claims that evidence from OFSTED and TIMSS showed that teachers 'usually deploy only a narrow range of teaching strategies' and that they 'rely too heavily on published schemes, which pupils work through individually'. Pupils were 'fundamentally left to "teach" themselves'. Our own observations lead us to believe that this was probably the case in some of the least successful primary schools and a minority of secondary schools.

The preliminary report of the Numeracy Task Force (Reynolds 1998a: 10) admitted that there was no 'wonder drug' to improve mathematics teaching and rejected the need for a root-and-branch change which would throw out the good along with the bad. Although they admitted that their proposed changes had not been fully evaluated, their proposals hardened to produce a high level of prescription in the final report (Reynolds 1998b: 18) in which a 'typical lesson in the numeracy strategy' was quite closely prescribed (see Chapter 8).

The extension to the NNS for Y7 offers the same model for a typical lesson in key stages 1–3. It is a three-stage lesson based on:

> oral work and mental calculation (about 5–10 minutes);
> the main teaching activity (about 25–40 minutes);
> a plenary to round off the lesson (about 5–15 minutes).
>
> (DfEE 2000: 1.10)

However, the guidance advising on the content of each of the three stages is so wide ranging and open to interpretation and variation under professional judgement, that we think most secondary teachers will already consider themselves to be following the prescribed format. In fact, we consider the three-stage lesson format to be only a superficial feature of the changes in approach which should be encouraged, which are more associated with interactive teaching than lesson structure.

Direct teaching of the whole class in mixed-ability primary schools is now being accepted almost uncritically although the research evidence to support it is thin at best. Although a number of studies have shown that teachers who question the entire class on a regular basis achieve positive results on average (e.g. Galton *et al.* 1980; Askew *et al.* 1997), closer analysis reveals a number of teachers who act against the trend achieving good results from an individualized organization or poor results from direct whole-class teaching (Brown 1999). International studies tend to show no difference or a slight advantage on average for whole-class over individualized approaches; however, there are many exceptions to this trend in which whole-class teaching achieves poor results (Brown 1999).

Although initial results from the NNS appear to be very positive, it seems likely that direct whole-class teaching will not prove to be a 'wonder drug' any more than any other form of classroom organization. It is more likely to be the quality of the interactions between pupils and teachers which is important rather than the organization in which such interactions occur (Brown 1999). One possible explanation for the slight advantage seen on average for whole-class approaches may well be that good teachers are able to use interactive whole-class teaching to set up challenging problem-solving situations in which they are able to encourage and support children to think at a higher level.

Whilst the National Numeracy Project has been highly influential in shaping practices in primary schools, it has had less impact on practices in secondary schools so far. However, some aspects of interactive whole-class teaching approaches have been encouraged by the Mathematics Enhancement Project and the influence of both these projects may be seen in the new NNS framework for Y7 (DfEE 2000).

The Mathematics Enhancement Project (MEP)

The Mathematics Enhancement Project (MEP) (CIMT 1997) has been very influential politically in England and has made recommendations with respect to teaching methods, the curriculum, and assessment in mathematics. The project was strongly influenced by the way mathematics is taught in other countries and in particular by observations of Hungarian mathematics lessons (Graham *et al.* 1999: 50).

MEP focuses on whole-class teaching approaches, and identifies several differences between British and Hungarian teaching approaches (Graham *et al.* 1999: 51). Hungarian children are taught to learn through participating in whole-class activities from an early age. Moreover, Graham *et al.* (1999: 51–2) claim that it is not just pupils, but also teachers who have been 'trained to manage classes and teach their students in a consistent way'. This is contrasted with British teachers who 'are encouraged to use a variety of different approaches'. Rather than applauding the flexibility and professionalism of British teachers, this range of approaches is criticised as a potential source of confusion. We disagree vehemently with any suggestion that teaching would be improved by turning teachers into the equivalent of machine minders in the education industry rather than professionals making their own judgements.

Some of the approaches and forms of classroom organization suggested by MEP would allow teachers to engage in the forms of interaction which other research has suggested might be effective. However, they will only do so if teachers understand what it is they are trying to achieve and MEP's recipe is not the only approach to effective interactive teaching. As we suggested above, we believe that it is necessary to convince professional teachers of the need to develop opportunities to support and encourage mathematical thinking rather than order them to change more superficial aspects of their classroom organization.

> Almost all educational changes of value require new (i) skills; (ii) behaviour; (iii) beliefs or understanding ... changes, to be productive, require skills, capacity, commitment, motivation, beliefs and insight, and discretionary judgement on the spot. If there is one cardinal rule of change in human con-

dition, it is that you cannot make people change. You cannot force them to think differently or compel them to develop new skills.

(Fullan 1993: 22–3)

MEP suggests claims that a typical Hungarian lesson is structured as follows:

- the teacher summarizes the homework, pupils mark their own work;
- the teacher takes the whole class forwards together;
- the class only moves on to the next phase when everybody has understood the last phase;
- the teacher concentrates on oral and mental work;
- there is a balance between whole-class teaching and individual work;
- individual work occurs in short intermittent breaks;
- pupils' mistakes are used as teaching points;
- pupils demonstrate their work at the blackboard;
- the teacher insists on precision in mathematical expression;
- progress is monitored continuously, every mistake is checked by the teacher before the class moves on;
- summarizing is a key feature and main points are summarized at the end;
- homework is set at the end to help prepare for the next session.

(summarized from Graham *et al.* 1999: 55–6)

Task 9.5 Analysing the format of MEP lessons

Consider each of the MEP bullet points in turn. Does it sound unusual or unfamiliar in comparison with your experiences in school so far?

Make a list of positive features and negative features associated with any of the points you think are unusual or problematical.

Several of the points made above about Hungarian teaching approaches strike us as mundane or even superficial descriptions of everyday practice in Britain. MEP argues in favour of whole-class teaching led by the teacher; however, in our experience, most mathematics classes in secondary schools now are teacher led. Individualized schemes are not as common as they were in the 1980s and few schools now use them exclusively. For example, in an LEA of sixteen schools, which we surveyed in 1999, only one school was using an individualized scheme to any significant extent.

We would be concerned if lessons were always to begin with teachers reading out answers to homework questions for pupils to self-mark. Even when such sessions are based on pupils offering answers when requested by the teacher, our experience leads us to believe that, if books are not collected in and marked on a regular basis, homework will not be completed and work will not be laid out correctly. We will discuss this further in Chapter 12.

MEP's insistence that the whole class moves on together only after all pupils have understood causes some practical difficulties. MEP suggest that quicker pupils sit and reflect whilst waiting for their slower peers to catch up. We know of very few classrooms where such advice would not cause discipline problems. It also strikes us as unfair to clever children. In the small sample of MEP schools we have visited, this rule is ignored and extension work is provided when necessary, or *stopper questions* are included to occupy quick workers (see Chapter 4).

The increased emphasis on oral and mental work suggested by MEP strikes us as long overdue, as does the emphasis on summaries at the ends of lessons, but, as we suggested in the last chapter, we believe that the success or failure of such approaches depends significantly on the quality and aims of the pupil–teacher interactions involved. We believe that whole-class teaching can be extremely *ineffective*, or even damaging, when it loses sight of the development of higher order knowledge and skills because of an overemphasis on instruction in instrumental techniques and routines. In such circumstances it can become directive, dogmatic, stifling of imagination, and lacking in real intellectual challenge.

In fact, Szalontai (1995: 151) reports that weaker Hungarian teachers sometimes engage in less-than-positive teacher–pupil interactions, emphasizing an instructivist approach with frequent incidental questioning. This is supported by Andrews (1997) who claims that:

> Weaker teachers are more didactic, have difficulty managing pupils' responses, and adhere too rigidly to their lesson plans
>
> (Andrews 1997: 16)

He also suggests that few Hungarian teachers are skilled at using open questions. On the other hand, Graham *et al.* (1999: 54) offer a description of a teacher in an MEP school making good use of *interactive* whole-class approaches to support learning. In this lesson, the teacher began by posing a non-trivial, multi-step problem on the board. The problem left room for strategic thinking and did not invite an instantaneous response.

> Rather than expecting instant responses to her question, the teacher asked the students to think about it, and they were encouraged to discuss with each other. After a few minutes, the class were invited to contribute their ideas and decide on a way forward. The class then set out to take a first step towards the solution to the problem. They worked for a short time and then contributed their responses. After discussion of these with the class, one was selected as a way forward to solve the next stage of the problem. This process was repeated a number of times in the lesson.
>
> (Graham *et al.* 1999: 54)

Graham *et al.* (1999: 55) talk about the class working in the *collective* Zone of Proximal Development (or collective ZPD) which we referred to in the last chapter as 'the learning zone'. This is defined as what the class, taken as a whole, cannot understand unless aided by the teacher. The function of the teacher when working in the ZPD is to provide a form of support for learning. The term 'scaffolding' was coined by Wood *et al.* (1976) to describe a form of temporary support which a teacher could offer to support development but which would be later withdrawn allowing the pupil to work alone at a higher level. The metaphor is useful to a point, but it tends to imply:

> an unresponsive activity, the scaffolding erected and the building put up according to a predetermined plan. Scaffolding in the classroom must be much more dynamic, and ways must be found for the teacher and pupils to work jointly on activities.
>
> (Askew *et al.* 1995: 216).

Graham *et al.* (1999: 54) claim that the role of the teacher in this process is to bring together pupil suggestions, to guide the class forward and to ensure that all the pupils were working from a common base. We would not wish to be as didactic as this.

The Practical Application of Mathematics Project (PAMP)

The details of this project can be found in Chapter 7.

In the second phase of the PAMP project, when we evaluated the effectiveness of differing teaching styles in a quasi-experiment, we found that teachers who used such discussions to ensure that the class were all working towards the teacher's plan were far less successful than teachers who helped pupils to clarify their thoughts in discussion and either negotiated a class plan or encouraged the development of a number of different but viable plans (Tanner 1997; Tanner and Jones 2000). The difference may seem to be quite a subtle one, but our experience is that all pupils understand it. It is the difference between following someone else's plan and having some degree of ownership of a class or group plan. We characterized the difference as between three forms of scaffolding support provided by teachers during discussion:

Rigid scaffolders   aimed to develop the teachers' preferred approach rather than helping pupils to develop their own plans. The discussion was superficial as the scaffolding support provided by the teachers' questioning constrained pupils' thinking, funnelling them down a predetermined path. When questioned about their plan, pupils said 'He wants us to ...'. The explanation and instructions had been clear. They knew what to do in the lesson, but it was the teachers' plan.

Dynamic scaffolders   organized their lessons around 'start–stop–go'. Their scaffolding was dynamic in character and was based on participation in a genuine discussion in which differences in perspective were welcomed and encouraged. The most significant participant in the discourse was the teacher, who validated conjectures and used focusing questions to control its general direction ensuring that an acceptable whole-class plan was generated. Although a whole-class plan was developed, the negotiation and participation was sufficient to ensure that students referred to 'our plan' in terms which indicated a sense of ownership.

Reflective scaffolders   also used 'start–stop–go' and a form of dynamic scaffolding. They granted their pupils more autonomy, however, encouraging several approaches to the problems rather than forcing the discussion to produce a class plan. Pupils thus had to evaluate their own plans in comparison with the plans of other groups in the posing, planning, and monitoring phases of the lessons. However, the characteristic feature of the *reflective scaffolders* was their focus on evaluation and reflection. During interim and final reporting-back sessions, scientific argument was encouraged to make pupils' explanations an object for discussion. Peer and self-assessment were encouraged through group presentations of draft reports before redrafting for final assessment. Teachers deliberately generated a reflective discourse (Cobb *et al.* 1997) after activities to encourage self-evaluation and reflection on mathematical processes.

Rigid scaffolders made only marginal gains over their control groups. The dynamic and reflective scaffolders made significant gains in modelling questions over their controls with good-effect sizes. Only the reflective scaffolders made significant gains in cognitive development in advance of their controls. The reflective scaffolders taught mathematical thinking (Tanner 1997; Tanner and Jones 2000).

The aim of the teacher and the nature of the interaction during whole-class interactions is crucial. This is further supported by the TIMSS videotape study (Stigler *et al.* 1999).

The TIMSS videotape study

This study examined mathematics teaching in a representative sample of 231 eighth-grade classrooms from Germany (100), Japan (50), and the USA (81). The three countries make an interesting set for comparative research as they sample a range of performance. All three countries include significant amounts of whole-class teaching in their approaches. In all three countries chalkboards and overhead projectors were used regularly in lessons. In all three countries pupils were invited to use the board or OHP on a regular basis. However, on average, Japanese students scored amongst the highest in mathematics whereas the USA scored significantly below the international average. There was no statistically significant difference between the USA and German students' average scores, although the German mean was close to the international average.

The findings reveal a number of differences in practice between the three countries in terms of the kind of mathematics which is taught, the teachers' goals for the lessons, the way lessons are structured and delivered, and the kind of thinking students engage in during lessons. British schools did not feature in the videotape study, so it is left for you to judge which country is most similar to your usual classroom experience.

The lesson content observed in the three countries was graded against international standards. The USA sample of lessons was working at a level significantly below those of Germany and Japan, with the USA lessons assessed as seventh grade whilst the others were assessed as at eighth or ninth grade (Table 9.3).

However, Japanese teachers were also more inclined to introduce new work. One-quarter of all USA and German lessons were all review or mostly review of

Table 9.3 Level of work in Germany, Japan, and USA.

Country	Mean grade
USA	7.4
Germany	8.7
Japan	9.1

Stigler *et al.* (1999: 44).

previous work. Only 3 per cent of Japanese lessons were mostly review, 53 per cent were half and half and 35 per cent mostly new work (Stigler *et al.* 1999: 44).

Japanese teachers' goals for their lessons were also significantly different from USA and German teachers. When teachers from the USA and Germany were asked what they most wanted students to learn from their lessons, their most common response was mathematical skills to solve specific problems using standard formulae (61 per cent and 55 per cent respectively contrasting with 25 per cent for Japanese lessons). Japanese teachers were far more likely to aim to develop mathematical thinking – emphasizing student explanation, concept development, or the discovery of multiple solutions to a problem (73 per cent compared with 21 per cent in the USA and 31 per cent in Germany). Japanese lessons focused on being able to *understand* something whereas lessons in Germany and the USA focused on being able to *do* something (e.g. to perform a procedure or algorithm, Stigler *et al.* 1999: 46).

The kind of mathematics which was taught differed in consequence. Teachers are often faced with a choice – do I develop or prove a concept or theorem or do I just state it and use it? Pythagoras' theorem, for example, might be simply stated as $a^2 + b^2 = c^2$ and then practised, or it might be developed and derived over the course of a lesson. More than three-quarters of German and Japanese teachers (77%, 83%) develop such concepts or theorems during the lesson compared with only one-fifth (22%) of USA teachers. None of the USA lessons in the study included proof, compared with the 10 per cent of German and 53 per cent of Japanese lessons which included proofs (Stigler *et al.* 1999: 52).

Japanese lessons included significantly more multi-step problems than in Germany or the USA (77%, 52%, 53%). Furthermore, the locus of control was far more in the hands of the pupils in Japan and Germany than in the USA. In 83 per cent of USA lessons, the tasks set for pupils required them to apply a technique which a teacher had just demonstrated to a similar problem, leaving no room for pupils to make strategic decisions about how to approach the problem. This applied in only 48 per cent of German and 17 per cent of Japanese lessons. On the other hand, in some lessons pupils had complete freedom to choose one of several approaches in order to solve a task. Pupils were sometimes asked if they could find a different method to their teacher's. This occurred to some degree in 83 per cent of Japanese lessons, 52 per cent of German lessons, and only 17 per cent of USA lessons (Stigler *et al.* 1999: 68–9).

In spite of the apparent similarities between the three countries in their use of whole-class teaching and pupil use of the board, typical lessons ran to different 'scripts'. Stigler *et al.* (1999: 135–6) describe the lessons in Germany and the USA

Table 9.4 Patterns of lesson flow: Japan, USA, and Germany.

Japan	USA and Germany
• Teacher poses a complex thought-provoking problem.	• Teacher instructs students with a concept or skill.
• Students struggle with the problem individually or in groups.	• Teacher solves example problems with the class.
• A range of students present their ideas or solutions to the class.	• (In Germany, some pupils work through problems at the board.)
• The teacher summarizes the class's conclusions.	
• Students practise similar problems.	• Students practise individually while teacher helps.

Adapted from Stigler *et al.* (1999: 135–6).

as running to 'an acquisition/application script' in which the role of the teacher is to show pupils how to do an example, which the pupils then practise during a period of individualized or pair working. In German lessons pupils are often asked to work through demonstration examples on the board, prior to practising the routine in an exercise. In contrast, however, lessons in Japan are very different – they follow a 'problematizing script' in which 'problem solving becomes the context in which competencies are simultaneously developed and utilised' (Stigler *et al.* 1999: 135). Problem solutions are not the goal of the lesson – rather problems are the means through which pupils come to understand the principles of mathematics. Japanese children are learning to think mathematically.

The pattern of lessons flow differs across the three countries as summarized in Table 9.4.

We offer below a short summary of a Japanese lesson on area, to give you a flavour of the processes involved. Fuller descriptions of this lesson and a few other videotaped lessons are available at: http://nces.ed.gov/timss/video/

A Japanese area lesson

A detailed analysis and coding of this lesson is given in Stigler *et al.* (1999: 26–8).

The teacher began by spending a minute linking today's lesson with yesterday's by reminding the class about triangles between parallel lines having the same area. He then drew a figure on the board (see Figure 9.2) and described the problem – which was to adjust the boundary between two plots of land, A and B to make the boundary straight without changing the area.

There was then a brief question-and-answer session during which the question was clarified and some pupils made predictions. He then asked the class to work on the problem individually for 3 minutes. While they were doing this he circulated offering support where appropriate.

After 3 minutes he suggested that they could work by themselves, with friends, or with the assistant teacher. They then worked busily together on the problem.

After about 10 minutes, the teacher asked two groups of pupils to draw their

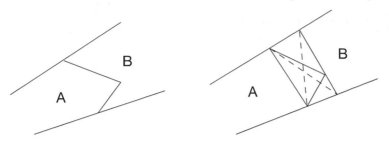

Figure 9.2 A Japanese area lesson.   *Figure 9.3* A Japanese area lesson – possible solutions.

solution on the board while the others finished off. The two groups of pupils then explained their solutions to the class, who asked questions and requested clarifications. A series of different solutions from other groups were then discussed by the class. (Solutions involve drawing a line to join the boundary end points along with a parallel-line segment through the vertex of the triangle formed by the first line. By moving the vertex of the triangle along the parallel-line segment, a new straight boundary can now be formed that retains the same areas – see Figure 9.3.)

The teacher then reviewed and clarified the pupils' approaches before setting a follow-up problem based on changing a quadrilateral into a triangle of equal area. The process then repeated itself, with individual working for 3 minutes followed by group work followed by whole-class discussion of a range of different solutions, in which the teacher draws the attention of the class to the general principles involved.

All the solutions involve dividing the quadrilateral into two triangles and using the same general principle as before. The teacher ends the lesson by suggesting that the pupils attempt to do the same with other polygons for homework.

Task 9.6 Reflect on the processes described in Chapter 7

Compare the description of the Japanese lesson on area with the process of 'start–stop–go' which we described in Chapter 7.

You may wish to examine further details in Stigler *et al.* (1999: 26–8) or http://nces.ed.gov/timss/video

How many of the processes which we suggested as necessary for the development of higher level thinking could be incorporated into such a structure?

We consider that the structure described for 'typical' Japanese lessons in the videotape study parallels 'start–stop–go' quite closely. The structure could quite easily accommodate the processes which we suggested would be necessary for the development of higher level thinking (see Chapter 7). This is unsurprising given the aims stated by the Japanese teachers in the TIMSS questionnaires (Stigler *et al.* 1999: 46).

In fact, the TIMSS study notes that, when judged by their teaching approaches, in many respects Japanese teachers appear to share more of the ideals of the USA reform movement than do USA teachers (Stigler *et al.* 1999: 6). This is a concern for those who wish to modify teaching approaches within any system. It is always easier to modify organizational structures than underpinning beliefs and philosophies about education (Fullan 1991). The NNS may succeed in increasing the quantity of whole-class teaching fairly easily, but changing hearts and minds to produce the style of teaching and learning interactions which international comparisons suggest are necessary may be far more problematical. TIMSS reports that Japanese teachers spend a considerable amount of their non-teaching time working collaboratively with colleagues developing teaching ideas (Wiliam 1999a: 17). A distinctive feature of the high-performing schools in the RSN project was that they collaborated effectively as teams.

The RSN approaches

Secondary heads of department often began interviews with the claim 'We're very traditional in our teaching here . . .'. However, our lesson observations revealed that their practices were far from Victorian. For example, in one lesson we observed, pupils were investigating the impact of varying a in curves such as: $\sin ax$, $a \cos x$, $\tan(x + a)$, etc. using a computer graph plotter. The teacher had prepared a worksheet which used trigonometric functions to provide curves which the pupils then had to duplicate by trial and improvement using their developing knowledge about the effect of the constant in the trigonometric function.

Towards the end of the lesson the teacher had set aside a period of time for class discussion about the effect of varying the constant a in different positions. At this point the knowledge which had been gained informally through investigation was formalized through teacher-led discussion. (You should note that the teacher had planned the concrete experience to precede the abstract generalization and notes as we suggested in Chapter 2.) 'Traditional' clearly means something quite novel when applied to a computer-based investigation and it would be unhelpful to use the term to describe the rich and varied range of activities and strategies which we observed.

From our observations, 'traditional' seemed to mean teachers *leading* lessons with *clear objectives* and *good pace*, maintaining a balance between periods of individual work, small-group work and interactive whole-class teaching with a high level of pupil involvement. It seemed to be distinguishing *active teaching* from a situation in which a commercial scheme was used for individualized learning with the teacher as facilitator. These characteristics were common to both primary and secondary phases. There were, however, a number of other significant elements of their teaching strategies which were common to the successful teachers.

Expectations

Expectations in the RSN schools were very high. Lessons were typically pitched at the upper quartile and teachers assumed that children would understand rather than merely repeat work. Multi-step problems were a regular feature of lessons and it was assumed that, with appropriate support, all pupils would be able to

attain the highest levels. Difficult issues were not avoided. When teachers anticipated that a particular misconception might develop, they aimed directly for it,
in order to challenge and develop the pupil's understanding.

Classroom ethos

Classroom discipline was strong; however, it was not based on fear but on agreed
and shared norms. The lessons observed were characterized by a sense of rapport
between the teacher and the pupils. There was a shared expectation that pupils
would be expected to contribute to the lesson, to hypothesize, and to explain,
that errors were to be expected as an integral part of learning and the identification of such errors would help the learning process for all pupils. In such a
culture, the pupils felt secure and able to offer tentative hypotheses, or to identify
a lack of understanding, without fear of ridicule.

Mental and oral work

Mental and oral work formed a significant and planned part of the mathematics
curriculum. This contrasts with the findings of a recent all-Wales survey of mathematical practices in secondary schools where only half of the heads of
mathematics departments reported mental-arithmetic practice to be a regular
feature in their Y7 classes with the frequency of such practice declining sharply
after Y8 (Jones and Tanner 1998).

   Although mental work was occasionally used as a warm-up activity at the start
of the lesson, in secondary classrooms it tended to be used more naturally during
other periods of teaching and learning and it was clear that both teachers and
pupils expected to be able to engage with simple mathematical situations
mentally and there were situations when it was considered inappropriate to
reach for pencil and paper or a calculator. Mental mathematics was required by
teachers, not just mental arithmetic.

   A number of different techniques were used to facilitate the use of whole-class
mental sessions in mixed-ability and mixed-age sessions in order to avoid public
humiliation and to encourage whole-class participation. Questions were asked
and then targeted differentially to ensure participation and yet facilitate success
by less able pupils. The 'show-me' cards which were used so often and so effectively in primary schools were also used in some secondary schools. One teacher
had adapted the idea by giving each pupil a small sheet (A5) of white plastic and
an OHP pen to write answers. The usual think/write/show pattern was then used
effectively with algebra questions. In KS3, open questions were used very effectively to allow pupils to self-differentiate work and set their own highest targets.
For example, 'Give me two numbers and an operation to make 2.25' proved to
be quite challenging for many pupils in year 8, revealing several misconceptions
and yet allowed one pupil to shine with $(1.5)^2$.

Questioning and pupil involvement

Questioning was used with a range of styles and purposes but we regularly
observed open questions, questions which required an extended response, and

probing questions which demanded further explanation and justification. Interactive whole-class teaching techniques were used in every lesson we observed and although these varied somewhat in character, they were always more like interactive explanations rather than clearly explained lectures. Most lessons were characterized by significant participation by pupils.

Pupils were frequently required to explain and justify their work to each other. Problems were often set to incorporate a number of different valid approaches. Typically such problems could not be solved instantaneously and pupils had to think by themselves, plan in small groups, and then report back. We saw several versions of 'start–stop–go' in use. When teachers called pupils to the board to explain potential approaches, the teacher's role was to provide just enough support through the use of questions and hints to allow the solution to progress without 'stealing the problem' by taking over. The scaffolding provided in such circumstances was certainly 'dynamic' and required teachers to think quickly on their feet listening carefully to pupils' half-formed ideas, repeating them back, and adding just enough help to move on. One teacher said:

> *You bounce off the kids. You have to be a good listener and a quick thinker. The trick is that no matter how much help you end up giving to make it work, they must still think that they would have done that by themselves. It has to be their plan and not just yours.*

You may recall that in Chapter 5 we distinguished between two types of questioning used to provide such scaffolding support: funnelling and focusing. Although both forms were used by the RSN teachers, focusing predominated.

Ma1 and teachers' views of mathematics

The majority of the lessons observed were underpinned by an investigative approach to mathematics. Mathematics was viewed as essentially a problem-solving activity. Pupils were required to focus on the mathematical structure being taught (e.g. by listening to another pupil explain a different approach to a task), and to choose an appropriate strategy for the problem. They were expected to apply their knowledge of mathematics in new contexts with teachers emphasizing the use of 'twists' and 'variations' in the questions set rather than requiring merely the repetition of an algorithm or technique.

Plenaries

Plenaries were planned in advance in most cases and offered opportunities for pupils to report back on progress and to reflect on their progress and learning. Unfortunately, plenaries did not always occur as planned and several teachers talked about the plenary they had intended to have if only the bell had not rung. The majority of the lessons did end in some form of plenary, however, and in the best cases we considered the plenary session to have contributed significantly to learning.

Some of the teachers had formalized the plenary session and demanded that pupils write a summary of their learning experiences at the end of each lesson.

These pupil commentaries included points which had been found difficult, mistakes which had been made, and key points to be remembered. These commentaries were shared towards the ends of lessons providing the teacher with valuable feedback on the lesson.

CONCLUSION

If the early successes of the National Numeracy Project (Straker 1997) are repeated when they are developed on a larger scale, it is possible that secondary schools will soon have to cope with more self-confident and numerate pupils who will not only expect to devise their own approaches to problem situations, but will also expect to understand the new mathematics they meet in a relational manner. Furthermore, evidence suggests that once children have learned to think for themselves in this way, they do not give up the capability easily (Cobb *et al.* 1992; Tanner 1997). We hope that more secondary-school teachers develop the confidence to support them in this aim.

Summary

- Numeracy should be interpreted as more than a knowledge of number bonds;
- numeracy is to do with the pupils' willingness to use the mathematics which they know to solve problems;
- national and international studies into the teaching of mathematics confirm that there is no simple recipe for success;
- it is the quality of interactive teaching which is important rather than superficial aspects of lesson organization;
- effective teaching strategies focus on the development of higher order thinking skills;
- lessons should be based on complex problems with an emphasis on mathematical thinking and proof;
- teaching should emphasize pupil articulation of multiple approaches;
- scaffolding should be dynamic, respecting pupils' articulations and focusing attention on key points;
- strategies such as start–stop–go help to develop planning and monitoring skills;
- peer and self-assessment helps to develop metacognitive knowledge;
- plenary sessions should be used to encourage pupils to summarize and reflect on their learning.

10 Role of the calculator in learning mathematics

Seldom can so fierce a controversy have been provoked by so cheap a piece of technology as the calculator. New technologies form an ever larger part of everyday life and pupils and teachers are required to develop their ICT skills as part of the school curriculum. However, the use of calculators in mathematics is viewed with suspicion.

The indiscriminate use of calculators has been blamed for a decline in students' arithmetic skills and their failure to develop elementary mathematical thinking (Bierhoff 1996; Gardiner 1995). There have been calls for the use of calculators to be discouraged until the start of secondary education (Reynolds 1998a: 25). The National Tests as well as GCSE and A-level examinations now place more severe restrictions on when and which type of calculators may be used.

The underlying assumption here appears to be that the use of calculators leads inevitably to a lack of mental fluency and a decline in basic arithmetic skills. However, as we shall discuss later, the research evidence suggests that this is not the case. Many research studies point to the opportunities provided by calculators to enhance the teaching and learning of mathematics. They also argue that new technologies require a reappraisal of the mathematics curriculum.

In this chapter we shall examine the potential of calculators for enhancing the learning of mathematics and discuss when and how calculators should be used in the classroom.

Objectives

By the end of this chapter you should:

- know the main research findings on the impact of calculators on the learning of mathematics;
- be able to identify ways in which calculators can enhance the learning of mathematics;
- be aware of the pitfalls of inappropriate calculator use;
- know how to decide if the use of a calculator is appropriate;
- understand the importance of teaching pupils to use a calculator efficiently.

THE IMPACT OF CALCULATOR USE ON MATHEMATICAL DEVELOPMENT

Two large-scale, longitudinal projects have explored the potential of calculator use at primary level.

The Calculator-Aware Number (CAN) project (Shuard *et al.* 1991) explored the impact of calculator use on primary-school pupils' understanding of number. The project started in 1986 with twenty schools from one Welsh and four English local-education authorities (LEAs). Four other LEAs subsequently joined the project.

CAN investigated the effect of allowing primary-school pupils unrestricted access to calculators. The traditional vertical paper-and-pencil methods for the four rules of number were not taught as the pupils could use calculators for any calculation which they could not do mentally. The project required the children to explore 'how numbers work', to develop their mathematical language, and their confidence in talking about numbers. The project also emphasized the importance of mental calculation and the children were encouraged to share their methods with others.

The evaluation of the project was largely based on case studies of the classrooms drawn from the reports of two external evaluators. Although the use of calculators was encouraged, the evaluators found that the CAN children competed amongst themselves to develop a wide range of strategies for performing computations without a calculator. These strategies often drew on an intuitive use of basic mathematical principles. The CAN children were considered to show far greater mathematical understanding. Discussion in the classroom emerged as a crucial mechanism through which children shared, extended, and elaborated their ideas. Instead of replacing mathematical thinking, the calculator came to be used as a source of ideas and starting points.

Although no overall, statistical evaluation of the effects of the project was conducted one local-education authority was able to use standardized tests to compare the performance of the CAN pupils with their non-CAN peers. The tests evaluated general mathematical performance, not just number work. The results of a group of 116 CAN pupils were compared with a random group of non-CAN pupils. The CAN pupils outperformed the others on twenty-eight of the thirty-six test questions. The results also suggested that the CAN pupils were more willing to attempt questions and to work independently.

The Calculators in Primary Mathematics (CPM) project (Groves 1994) aimed to use calculators to provide a rich learning environment for mathematics. Over 1,000 pupils and sixty teachers from six Australian schools were involved from 1990 to 1993. Each pupil was given a calculator to use when they chose. Professional support was provided for the teachers who also met regularly in school and project meetings to plan and to share their teaching activities.

The pupils were found to use the calculators in four main ways:

- as an object for discovery – to explore number, as well as exploring the calculator itself;
- as a counting device – to explore patterns and relationships;

- as a 'number cruncher' – to allow the use of larger numbers and more realistic problems;
- as a device for recording and manipulating numbers.

(Groves 1994: 2)

The evaluation of the project included a range of written tests and interviews with pupils, lesson observations, and interviews with teachers. As in the CAN project, the teachers considered that their teaching practices had changed to make more extensive use of discussion, and that they now encouraged the sharing of children's ideas in mathematics lessons. The project children did not become reliant on calculators, rather they outperformed their comparison groups of pupils without long-term experience of calculators on a range of estimation and computation tasks, and displayed a better knowledge of number, especially place value, decimals, and negative numbers (Groves 1994: 12).

Thus, in these research studies of primary-age pupils, when the use of calculators was accompanied by an emphasis on mental strategies, there was a positive impact on pupils' mathematical development.

Such results are supported by a meta-review of research into the effects of calculator use (Hembree and Dessart 1992). Nearly ninety research studies were analysed, each of which had compared the progress of pupils who were allowed use of calculators in mathematics lessons with matched control groups who did not. The pupils' performance was compared in three mathematical aspects – computation skills, conceptual knowledge, and problem solving. In most of the tests, the use of calculators was not permitted.

No effect was found on pupils' conceptual knowledge. However, with the exception of pupils aged 8 and 9, the pupils who had used calculators either matched or outperformed their peers on measures of computational skill and problem solving. The students who had used calculators also had more positive attitudes to mathematics. The review concluded that calculators could be used to enhance the teaching and learning of mathematics and that future research should focus on ways to integrate the calculator into the mathematics curriculum.

In our study of calculator use in Welsh secondary schools (Jones and Tanner 1997), the degree of availability of calculators in mathematics lessons, as identified by the heads of departments, had no significant impact on the students' performance on tests of basic skills (see Chapter 9 for further details). However, those students who reported free and frequent use of calculators in mathematics did significantly better in the test.

In our Welsh study, no variation was found between the different modes of calculator use and the practice of mental arithmetic. In contrast, a common feature of the research and development projects which allowed unrestricted use of calculators, such as CAN and CPM, was the emphasis on the development of students' mental strategies and 'number sense' alongside the availability of the calculator.

Similar findings emerged from an analysis of the TIMSS survey (Kitchen 1998). Consideration of the mean achievement of pupils in the mathematics test against the frequency of calculator use in mathematics lessons reported by the teachers revealed no overall correlations. Further analysis of the distribution of scores within each country, however, revealed that students with the highest mean scores tended to use calculators more frequently than those with the lowest mean scores. Such findings do not indicate for what purpose calculators were used, merely that the impact of calculators is more complex than that of frequency of use.

It would appear then that research does not support claims such as that made by Bierhoff (1996: 41) that the use of a calculator 'risks retarding the mental development of calculating-strategies' but it does emphasize the need for calculators to be used effectively.

> Only a very small proportion of schools submitted detailed policies that offered teachers clear guidance about the principles, purposes and practice of calculators use . . .
>
> (SCAA 1997b: 10)

The issue then is not whether to allow the use of calculators but how best to use them in combination with other strategies to improve the teaching and learning of mathematics.

Task 10.1 Calculator policies

Obtain a copy of your department's policy on the use of calculators. To what extent does it offer the guidance suggested above by SCAA (School Curriculum and Assessment Authority)?

Does your school have an overall policy on calculator use?

The National Numeracy Strategy describes the calculator as 'a powerful and efficient tool' but states that children 'need to learn when it is and when it is not appropriate to use a calculator' (DfEE 1999a: 8). It argues that a child's first approach to a problem should involve mental calculations wherever possible and thus 'schools should not normally use the calculator as part of Key Stage 1 mathematics' (*ibid.*: 8). Accordingly, there is no mention of the use of calculators in KS1 in the latest version of the National Curriculum for Mathematics in England (DfEE/QCA 1999b).

In Wales, however, the use of the calculator as a tool is seen as appropriate even in KS1; for example, 'for numerical problems where the numbers involve several digits' (ACCAC 2000: 11). Such different requirements indicate continuing tensions between those who consider the calculator as a tool with potential for enhancing teaching and learning, and those who fear that its use will adversely affect the development of mathematical skills.

ROLE OF THE CALCULATOR

The calculator is just one of the latest in a series of calculating devices to be used in mathematics – the abacus, Napier's bones, the slide rule, and four-figure tables of logarithms might be familiar to some of you. Interestingly, the introduction of some of these into mathematical practice met with similar opposition to that currently surrounding the use of calculators (see Butt 1999; Johnston-Wilder and Pimm 1999). In this section we shall examine how the calculator can contribute to (or hinder) the learning of mathematics.

Task 10.2 Categories of calculator use

Make a list of five occasions when you have used a calculator (or seen calculators being used) as part of a mathematics lesson. Try to identify the prime purpose for the use of the calculator in each case. Why was a calculator used rather than mental methods, or paper-and-pencil algorithms, or four-figure tables?

Pupils are often allowed to use calculators to check answers to problems which they have calculated by other means. The calculator provides instant, private feedback so that the pupils may carry on reassured that their methods work or, alternatively, they are alerted to an error which needs correcting before they can continue.

Sometimes the use of calculators is permitted for the 'harder' questions with more difficult numbers such as decimals. Use of the calculator here permits more realistic data to be used; for example, when calculating the areas of circles the diameters no longer need to be exact multiples of seven so that they can be cancelled! Such exercises may then be completed in a shorter time than if all the calculations had to be done 'by hand'.

Another purpose is to provide information such as powers or roots of numbers, or trigonometric ratios, which would be laborious to calculate by hand. The calculator here replaces the logarithm tables which were used until the mid-1980s.

Occasionally, calculators may be used to play games. Whilst the motivational effect may be valuable, the games should also contribute to the learning of mathematics. 'Decimal Space Invaders' (Graham 1982), for example, can assist in developing pupils' understanding of place value. In this game a number, say 12.34, is entered into the calculator. Each digit then has to be 'shot down' in turn by reducing it to zero by, for example, subtracting the appropriate number. The game can be constrained in various ways; for example, by ruling that only the digit in the units column can be shot down so that pupils have to multiply or divide by powers of 10 first to set up the digits.

We suggest that the use of a calculator may be categorized in the following ways:

- as a crutch to avoid learning;
- as scaffolding to assist learning;
- as a window into mathematics;
- as a tool for thinking.

These categories are not distinct but serve to illustrate the main ways in which a calculator may be used within the teaching and learning process. We shall now consider a range of examples in each category.

A crutch to avoid learning

In this guise, a calculator may be used to perform the calculation, but the process contributes nothing to the pupil's mathematical development. The calculator is being misused as a crutch if the pupils depend upon it instead of developing their mathematical expertise.

For example, Y6 pupils are expected to calculate questions such as 15×6, or 0.7×8, using prior knowledge and a variety of mental or written strategies (DfEE 1999a). If pupils reach for a calculator to answer such questions then they avoid practising their mental strategies and their basic number bonds.

If this is as far as the question goes, we might class this as misuse of the calculator as it inhibits the development of conceptual connections and mental fluency. In such situations the pupils need further teaching and other activities to develop their number concepts and procedures for calculation.

However, the decision as to whether the use of a calculator for a task is appropriate or not is rarely clear cut. It depends partly on the individual pupil and partly on the purpose of the task. Whilst we would agree that pupils should know 'basic' number facts and have a range of calculation strategies available to them, these can take time to acquire. This should not mean that pupils (and, in particular, lower ability pupils) should be denied access to other mathematical ideas purely because their arithmetic fluency is not fully developed. On such occasions the use of a calculator to perform the more routine operations may allow the pupil to comprehend the mathematical concepts being taught. So if the use of a calculator to evaluate 15×6 or 0.7×8 allowed a low-ability pupil to attempt an otherwise inaccessible activity on similar triangles we would consider the use appropriate.

Scaffolding to assist learning

In such situations, which might be superficially similar, we would class the role of the calculator as assisting learning. The distinction lies in whether the calculator is being used to promote mathematical thinking or to avoid any thinking! Suppose that you wished to teach the formula for calculating the area of a rectangle. Your lesson objectives would probably include the following:

By the end of the lesson the pupils should:

- *understand the connection between the number of squares within the rectangle and the formula;*
- *be able to apply the formula to calculate the areas of composite shapes.*

The pupils' attention, therefore, needs to be focused on the underpinning concept of area and the similar structure of the problems. One approach is to restrict the lengths of the sides to integers to facilitate easy calculations. Alternatively, you could use a variety of numbers, perhaps even some 'real measurements' and use the calculator to perform the more difficult calculations. The use of the calculator in this context avoids the pupils becoming 'bogged down' in the detail of the arithmetic and thus losing sight of the main concept being taught. Pupils whose multiplication skills are poor would still be able to understand the concept even though they would have had difficulty in performing the calculations unaided.

Once the concept has been established, however, then the scaffolding provided by the calculator may be removed. The connections between the concept of area and the pupil's other mathematical knowledge should have been created. The pupil no longer has to concentrate so hard on understanding what 'area' means and which strategies should be used to calculate it. The pupil is now able to think about the mechanics of performing the calculations, and thus practise these skills, without losing sight of the main purpose of the task.

For learning to occur, there must be a gap between what the pupil can already do unaided and what the teacher is trying to teach. Just as the teacher can scaffold the pupil across the gap by provoking new ideas through questioning, demonstrating, or explaining, the calculator can support the learning process by doing the routine operations whilst the pupil focuses on understanding the new concept. As with all true scaffolding, the support provided by the calculator may be removed once the concept has been understood.

Similarly, when introducing trigonometric ratios by scale drawing of triangles, the ratio of the lengths of the sides can be calculated easily on the calculator. The pupils can focus on the connections between the ratios and the size of the angles rather than on the arithmetic.

The use of the calculator to perform the mundane operations whilst the pupil maintains a more complex line of mathematical thinking is often subsumed within the next two categories.

A window into mathematics

Using a calculator may provide impromptu opportunities for pupils to explore areas of mathematics which might not normally have been addressed at their stage. For example, in the CAN and CPM projects, primary pupils discovered negative numbers whilst learning subtraction. They also encountered much larger numbers, decimals, etc. than they would have met if their calculations were to have been done mentally or by pencil-and-paper methods. As an illustration, consider how pupils might respond if they incorrectly entered the subtraction $14 - 17 =$ on their calculators and hence obtained -3.

> Why does the 3 have a subtraction sign in front of it?
> The answer should be 3 because, um, . . . start at 14, then 15, 16, 17, makes 3.
> We've put it in the wrong way round, it should be $17 - 14$.

If the pupils query their answer with you, you might briefly demonstrate that the number line may be extended beyond zero to include negative numbers. You could connect this to real-life knowledge about temperatures. You might also suggest that they try some other subtractions the 'wrong way round' and see what they notice about the answers. Other pupils may note the conflict between the negative numbers and the standard algorithm chant of '4 take away 7 you can't . . .'!

Such an incident then, whilst not digressing into an unplanned lesson on negative numbers, could provide pupils with an insight into the way that the number line extends, and an understanding that the operation of subtraction is not commutative.

Many pupils are naturally curious (even about mathematics) and may explore the keys on their calculators to try to find out what they do. Exploration of the square or square-root keys can lead to an informal introduction to these concepts and symbols. Other pupils may set themselves challenges such as finding the biggest number they can make, and thus meet numbers displayed using scientific notation. The calculator affords pupils opportunities to gain insights into mathematical structure.

A tool for thinking

The use of calculators also enables pupils to extend their mathematical concepts. In this category the calculator may be used in three main ways, for:

- abstraction and generalization;
- graphical representation;
- programming.

Abstraction and generalization

Many problem-solving tasks are approached by collecting data, searching for patterns, and then abstracting the underlying principles and generalizing from them. The calculator can often be used to generate the data quickly and easily.

A Y5 class was set this question:

> Choose a number between 1 and 10, multiply it by 3 then by 37. Now try this with different numbers. What do you notice? Will this always happen? Why does it happen? Can you predict what $40 \times 3 \times 37$ will be?

The role of the calculator here was to provide data quickly whilst the pupils focused on the structure of the problem. Notice that although the calculator provided the multiplication facts it did not answer the problem. The pupils had to abstract that from the patterns noticed in the data together with their prior knowledge of multiplication.

The pupils could have undertaken this task without the calculator but it would have taken longer and they would probably have restricted themselves to simpler numbers. They would also have been denied the instant feedback which supported or refuted their conjectures.

Another example of a situation where calculators can be used as a tool for thinking is when teaching standard deviation. Questions, such as those below, probe the pupils' understanding of the concept rather than just their ability to substitute numbers into a formula. Advanced scientific and graphical calculators enable pupils to generate lists of numbers quickly and to test how closely they meet the criteria. Pupils who understand the meaning of standard deviation should be able to explain why one of the questions is impossible!

Create a set of 10 marks that have:

1   A mean of 5 and a standard deviation of 0. Are there any other sets of marks that would also have the same mean and standard deviation?
2   A mean of 5 and a standard deviation of 1. What is the median for your set? What is the mode? Are there any other sets of marks that would also have the same mean and standard deviation?
3   A mean of 5 and a standard deviation of 2.
4   A mean of 5 and a standard deviation of -1.

The calculator may be used in other open-ended questions to support the extension of concepts to different areas of mathematics.

Graphical representation

Many powerful examples of this lie in the use of graphic calculators in algebra. Pupils need to be able to plot simple functions by hand, constructing tables of values, drawing axes, making an appropriate choice of scales, and plotting the co-ordinates. They also, however, need to understand how the equation relates to each of the points, how the equation determines the shape of the graph, and how the constants in the equation transform its basic shape. Pupils should be able to use such knowledge to sketch and to identify functions. For example, in KS3 pupils are expected to appreciate of the meaning of m and c in the equation of a straight line. How would you teach this topic?

Graphic calculators can display graphs very quickly and pupils can explore the effect of changing m and c without having to spend considerable time plotting each line by hand. Our favourite approach is to give the pupils the information contained in Figure 10.1. We then ask pupils to work in pairs to explore the question using graphic calculators. Their findings are then formalized through a whole-class discussion.

A straight line always has an equation of the form

$y = mx + c$

where m and c can be any numbers you like.

Find out what happens to the position of the line as you vary m and c.
Remember to work systematically.
Sketch some of your graphs to help you to record your findings.

Figure 10.1 Exploring straight-line graphs.

Figure 10.2 Graphic-calculator display projected onto a whiteboard.

For the whole-class feedback we would connect a graphic calculator to an OHP display unit and project it onto a whiteboard. Initially just the axes can be shown. Pupils can then draw on the board where they predict a given line will lie (Figure 10.2). The accuracy of their prediction can then be checked by projecting the graph from the calculator.

The feedback session is very effective when structured as a challenge. Divide the class into two or three teams. Pupils from each team take turns to try to sketch a line given its equation, before the line is projected onto the axes. One point is awarded for a correct intercept, another for a correct gradient.

Teacher: So, I'll start with an easy one. Group A, who thinks they can sketch in the line $y = x + 2$?

A volunteer comes out to the board and draws the line on the projected axes.

Teacher   (*addressing the class*): Who thinks that's right? Why?
Class: Because it goes through 2 on the y axis.
Teacher: OK, let's see. (*Teacher types in equation and projects line.*) Well done! Now, it goes through $y = 2$ but it's a bit too flat. Just one point for that I think. (*Groans from Group A.*) Now, you can choose the equation, just keep your numbers less than 10 to fit on the scale.
Pupil A: We challenge Group B to sketch $y = 2x + 3$.

A volunteer from Group B comes out, marks $y = 3$ then draws the line making its slope steeper than the previous graph. The teacher invites comments from the class and then pupil A projects the equation onto the board. It is then pupil B's turn to set the next equation.

The challenge continues with the teacher focusing the pupils' attention on the significance of the intercept, the gradient, parallel lines, and the connections with the equations.

Finally, the teacher asks each pupil to write down what they have learned about plotting a line given its equation. A number of pupils are asked to read out their ideas. The key points from these are discussed and summarized on the board. This summary is then copied into the pupils' notebooks.

A similar approach can be used to consider the transformations of quadratics and other functions. The speed at which the calculator draws the graphs allows consideration of far more examples than time would allow if the graphs had to be drawn by hand.

Far too often pupils do not associate algebraic functions with their graphical representations, partly because these are taught as separate topics. The solution of simultaneous equations, for example, can be taught as the application of an algebraic routine. The pupils' conceptual understanding, however, is likely to be enhanced if the equations are drawn on a graphic calculator and the connections made between the point(s) of intersection and the solution to the equations. Of course, these graphs could be drawn by hand (time permitting!), but the use of the calculator allows pupils to focus on the underlying concept rather than being distracted by the incidental issues of choosing scales, plotting points, tables of values, etc.

Programming

The distinction between the capabilities of computers and calculators is becoming increasingly blurred. Just as the graph-plotting activities described above could originally only be done on a computer with a graph-plotting package, many graphic calculators now also enable you to write programs. Although there is a syntax or programming language to be learned, the use of menus, etc. reduces the level of difficulty of this.

As a teacher you may wish to write short programs to use the calculator as a 'black box', perhaps as an input/output machine. The pupils choose the input number, the calculator then generates the output according to the programmed function, and the pupils try to work out what the function is. This variation on the usual teacher-led 'think of a number' game has two advantages. First, the calculator is seen as non-judgemental by the pupils and second, once individual pupils have worked out the formula they may be encouraged to 'beat the calculator' in their speed of substitution.

Asking pupils to write their own programs requires them to know their mathematics sufficiently well to be able to 'teach it to the calculator'. Programming requires pupils to think logically through the stages in a mathematical process and then to write a series of commands in precise and unambiguous language. This could represent the final stage in an investigation when, having understood the mathematical concept, it is then formalized and used as the basis of a program to generate a series of examples.

For example, pupils could be asked to write a program to:

- generate prime numbers between 100 and 1,000;
- calculate the ratio of successive terms in a Fibonacci sequence for different starting numbers;
- draw a family of curves (e.g. $y = x^2 + a$) for varying values of a.

Task 10.3 Programming your calculator

Write a program to generate prime numbers between 100 and 1,000 on your graphic calculator. What did you discover about prime numbers in the process?

Programming, in particular, requires a significant level of knowledge about the calculator's facilities. However, any use of a calculator requires some knowledge of its functions and we shall now look at how such knowledge can be taught.

LEARNING TO USE A CALCULATOR EFFICIENTLY

The focus of the discussion so far has been on how mathematics may be learned with the calculator. The calculator is a tool, however, just like protractors or compasses, and pupils should be taught how to use the calculator efficiently.

Task 10.4 Efficient use of a calculator

When do you think pupils should know the following about their calculators:

- whether it uses arithmetic or algebraic logic;
- how to use the 'constant' facility;
- how to use the memory;
- how to use brackets;
- the use of the second function keys;
- how to use reciprocals, powers, roots;
- trigonometric functions;
- graphical facilities?

Compare your answers with the National Curriculum, the National Numeracy Strategy and your department's scheme of work.

At Key Stage 2, pupils are expected to understand how the calculator displays remainders and rounds numbers. They are also expected to be able to plan a sequence of operations to answer a problem, including, at Key Stage 3, the use of the memory and brackets. Many of the cheaper calculators still do not follow algebraic logic and asking pupils to carry out carefully chosen arithmetic calculations

Table 10.1 Using a calculator efficiently.

Problem	Teacher prompts
$2 + 3 \times 4 =$	What should the answer be? How many people got 20? How should the question be written so that 20 is correct?
$\dfrac{3 \times 4}{6}$	What should the answer be? Would it make a difference if you entered $3 \div 6 \times 4$? Why?
$\dfrac{5 \times 6}{5 \times 6}$	Does the calculator give you the answer you expected? Why? What do you have to alter to obtain the correct answer?
$1 + 3/4, \quad \dfrac{1+3}{4}$	Do these two questions give the same answer? Should they?

on their calculators can demonstrate the need for thinking about the order of operations, the correct use of brackets, etc. For examples, see Table 10.1.

Discussion of such questions with the pupils not only leads to a greater understanding of how to use the calculator but also of the mathematical notation and conventions.

Whether pupils are using calculators or employing other methods of calculation, it is important that they learn the value of checking that their answers are sensible. Many pupils, when told to check their answers, redo the calculation they have just completed and probably repeat the same errors. How would you check your answer to $923 \div 36$?

You could draw on your knowledge of place value to approximate the question to $1,000 \div 40$, and then possibly to $100 \div 4$. Alternatively, you could multiply the answer to the division by 36 and check that it equals 923. This second method requires and develops an understanding of the inverse relationship between the operations.

As a result of such teaching, pupils should appreciate the capabilities and limitations of the calculator. However, the decision as to whether the use of the calculator is appropriate for a particular task still has to be made.

DECIDING WHEN TO USE A CALCULATOR

The National Curriculum requires that pupils are taught to select methods of computation, including the use of a calculator, which are appropriate to the problem (see e.g. ACCAC 2000: 19). In a survey of English schools, however, only about 70 per cent of respondents in Key Stages 2 and 3 reported that their pupils were specifically taught how to decide when to use calculator methods, written methods, or mental strategies (SCAA 1997b: 26).

The National Numeracy Strategy suggests that pupils' 'first-line strategy should involve mental calculations wherever possible' (DfEE 1999a: 8). This surely depends on the problem and on the capabilities of the individual pupil. Whilst we would wish to avoid pupils depending on the calculator as a crutch

Each pupil in the class has to write down three questions:

  one which is quite hard but can be done mentally;
  one which would probably need to written down; and
  one which would probably need to be done on a calculator.

All the questions are placed in a hat and drawn at random.
  Points are given as follows:

  10 points if correct by a mental method;
  6 points if correct by a written method;
  4 points if correct by a calculator method;
  lose 10 points for a wrong answer.

The pupils are placed in four teams who take turns to answer.
  The teacher reads the question out and pupils put their hands up if they want to try to answer.
  The chosen pupil has to nominate whether they will answer by a mental, written, or calculator method.
  The teacher takes care to direct the easier questions at the weaker pupils.
  The scoring system is designed to encourage the pupils to choose a mental method if they are confident that they will be accurate.

Figure 10.3 'Who wants to be a mental calculator?'

they should also learn to recognize when a failure to utilize the calculator is likely to lead to inaccuracies or inefficient strategies.

For pupils to make an appropriate choice of strategy they need to be aware of:

- the nature of the problem;
- the capabilities and limitations of the calculator;
- their own proficiency in the relevant skills and techniques.

The calculator can be useful for generating lots of examples quickly but many problems are then better solved by studying the examples and working more analytically. For example, a Y8 class was set the question 'Is it possible for the perimeter of a shape to be numerically equal to its area? The easy calculations could be done mentally, harder ones on the calculator, but the pupils then needed to generalize their findings to the meaning of area and perimeter in order to be able to reach a firm conclusion.

SCAA (1997b: 27) suggest using games like 'beat the calculator' to help pupils to identify their own capabilities and limitations. We prefer our own game shown in Figure 10.3.

CONCLUSION

Calculators can be a valuable tool in the teaching of mathematics. They can perform routine calculations quickly and accurately thereby allowing pupils to concentrate on the appropriate strategies and the underlying mathematical structure.

Similar advantages are also afforded by the use of computer technologies and we shall consider their role in the teaching and learning of mathematics in the next chapter.

Summary

- Research indicates that calculators can contribute to the effective learning of mathematics if used appropriately;
- calculator use can be categorized:

  - as a crutch to avoid learning (to be avoided);
  - as scaffolding to assist learning (to be gradually withdrawn);
  - as a window into mathematics (to be encouraged);
  - as a tool for thinking (to be developed);

- pupils should be taught how to use their calculators efficiently;
- pupils should develop metacognitive knowledge of their own strengths and weaknesses to aid them in strategy choice.

11 Learning with and about ICT

INTRODUCTION

The key skills of literacy, numeracy, and ICT (Information and Communication Technology) are considered to underpin the learning of all school subjects. In recognition of their importance, all teachers are expected to consider themselves as teachers of key skills in addition to any other specific subject or pastoral responsibilities they may hold. In this chapter we focus on your role as a teacher of mathematics using ICT and as a teacher of the ICT key skill. Clear thinking is required to distinguish between the demands of ICT as a key skill, as a subject in its own right with its own attainment targets and as a tool which you should use to improve the learning of mathematics, and we hope that you will learn to make such distinctions in your planning.

Computers have been in use in UK schools for about 30 years and since the 1980s the UK has been apparently at the forefront of a technological revolution. Unfortunately, in spite of the enthusiasm of technological zealots, most commentators agree that the computer has failed to make any significant impact in school settings (e.g. Selwyn 1999b; Harris 1999).

> The UK has a higher ratio of computers per schoolchild than almost any other country, including the US. Yet despite this lead and the fact that Information Technology has been on the agenda for almost 30 years, it is not clear that IT has made a significant impact on educational standards . . .
>
> (Lovegrove and Wilshire 1997: 1)

In spite of what appears to be a natural affinity between IT and mathematics, computers are hardly ever used in mathematics lessons although practice varies from school to school (Beaton *et al.* 1996; Cox 1997). In primary schools, the most common usage is word processing (DfEE 1998) and in secondary schools the number of teachers using computers in their teaching has hardly changed over the years and remains 'at about 32 per cent' suggesting that one of the most costly resources in schools may be significantly underutilized (Harris 1999).

The debate on the nature and purposes of ICT in schools has largely gone by default in the public domain with vocational and pedagogical aims confused. Politicians and members of the public often appear too ready to believe that computers in the classroom are *inherently a good thing*, no matter what their use (Stevenson 1997). This stands in stark and illogical contrast to a readiness by many politicians to reject the use of calculators out of hand.

The Dearing (1993) review placed IT 'at the heart of the curriculum' as a cross-curricular skill. However, demands that pupils should be given opportunities to develop and apply their IT capability in each subject run counter to the *subject culture* of the National Curriculum. Even at the start of the 1990s many teachers were not convinced about the value of IT for the teaching of their subjects. Furthermore, teachers were often being expected to use and pass on skills and knowledge which they did not have themselves. Teachers who learned their mathematics before the 1990s are unlikely to be aware of the ways in which ICT can contribute to their subject. Given the shortage of up-to-date hardware in many schools in the early 1990s, the failure to achieve radical change is not surprising (Tanner 1992a; Strack 1995; Kennewell *et al.* 2000).

However, in recent years, computers have become a familiar feature of many UK homes and a survey of Welsh schools in 1998 revealed that 61 per cent of primary and secondary pupils had access to a home computer, with no significant difference by sex. Analysis by social class (as judged by newspaper purchase) revealed a range of between 50 per cent (*Sun, Mirror,* etc.) and 84 per cent (*The Times, Guardian,* etc.) of households with a PC/Mac-type computer (Kennewell *et al.* 2000).

Large increases in expenditure on ICT for teaching and learning, introduced by the new Labour Government, has now improved the pupil-to-computer ratio to 18 to 1 in primary schools and 9 to 1 in secondary schools (DfEE 1999c). Prior to the significant training opportunities provided in 1999–2000, already 90 per cent of primary staff and 85 per cent of secondary staff reported having had some training in the use of IT. More importantly, 65 per cent of primary staff and 61 per cent of secondary staff claimed to feel confident in the use of ICT in the curriculum.

Although computers in school may have failed to fulfil their promise in the past, we now seem to be approaching a moment of critical change. At last we are reaching the stage at which adequate resources exist in combination with a computer-literate teaching profession. The award of qualified teacher status now demands high levels of personal IT skill as well as knowledge of how to use ICT in teaching. We expect that ICT will make an ever-increasing contribution to education during the next few years and begin to fulfil its true potential as a teaching and learning tool.

Objectives

By the end of this chapter you should understand:

- the wide ranging nature of ICT as: a key skill, a subject in its own right, and a tool for teaching;
- that ICT capability depends on higher order knowledge and skills and that these underpin both ICT and mathematics;
- how ICT can be used in mathematics as a tutor of techniques or a tool to develop mathematical thinking;
- how to use three examples of common generic software to develop math-

ematical thinking and ICT capability: in particular, graph plotters, spreadsheets, and databases;
- some of the issues arising when planning to use ICT in a mathematics lesson.

WHAT IS ICT?

The 'C' in ICT was added to the more familiar IT to reflect the increasing importance of e-mail and the Internet. There is a suggestion that the term ICT is associated with the use of technology for other purposes whereas the term IT is
reserved for the study of the technology itself. Some confusion in terminology
remains so we will use ICT to cover both the subject, its application, and the programme of study from now on. However, there are three aspects of ICT which
need to be distinguished (Kennewell *et al.* 2000).

A key skill

The ICT key skill should be taught by all teachers. Key skills are generally learned
indirectly whilst aiming to learn another subject. When key skills are learned in
this way, they are learned in conjunction with an appropriate context, making it
more likely that they will be learned in a form which is useful and useable in that
other subject. Any definition of ICT capability should include a demand that
pupils are able to employ technology appropriately in learning mathematics,
and solving mathematical problems. The term ICT is intended to suggest the *use*
of the knowledge skills and understanding of IT outside of its own subject discipline. *ICT capability in mathematics* would imply a capacity to recognize when it
would be appropriate to use ICT to assist in exploring mathematical situations
and the solution of mathematical problems.

A specialist discipline

IT or ICT can represent a subject discipline in its own right. However, the knowledge and skills associated with ICT are very different in character from the forms
of knowledge found in more traditional subjects such as history or science.
Although ICT includes some low-level basic skills, routines, and techniques, the
subject deals in concepts which are not software or platform specific. Progression
in ICT requires the development of higher level knowledge, strategies, and processes, in order to identify opportunities, to solve problems, and to evaluate solutions in areas outside of ICT. Thus the higher levels of ICT demand interaction
with other subject disciplines. It is only in interaction with other subjects and
with real-life problems that either the *key skill* or the *discipline* can be seen to exist.

A resource for teaching and learning

Since the early days of its introduction great claims have been made for the potential of ICT to transform the nature of learning just as it has transformed the
world of work and leisure. For example, Howe (1983) claimed that just as the

industrial revolution transformed society through its amplification of the power of the human muscle, ICT would revolutionize education through the amplification and emancipation of the human mind. Unfortunately, so far the impact of ICT in schools has been marginal rather than dramatic (Lovegrove and Wilshire 1997; Selwyn 1999a; Harris 1999).

ICT has the potential to make significant improvements to the teaching and learning experience in mathematics. Through its capacity to store data and to calculate and recalculate extremely rapidly, ICT offers pupils the opportunity to:

> use real data which had previously been considered too complex to deal with;
> explore in areas of the mathematics curriculum which were previously beyond their capabilities;
> use trial-and-error approaches which would have previously been too time consuming to gain insight into mathematical structures;
> see dynamic representations of changes in algebraic functions.

DEVELOPING ICT CAPABILITY IN MATHEMATICS

ICT in the National Curriculum places emphasis on the development of a range of tools and techniques, which can be used effectively:

> to explore, analyse, exchange and present information and to support their problem solving, investigative and expressive work ... being discriminating about information and the ways in which it may be used and making informed judgements about when and how to apply aspects of ICT to achieve maximum benefit ...
>
> (QCA 1999)

Progression in ICT capability depends on two groups of factors, the first relating to the application of ICT to the solution of problems; and the second depending on the range of problem contexts, sources, and tools applied (Kennewell *et al.* 2000). Clearly mathematics is a significant domain in which problem solving with ICT should be experienced and thus teachers of mathematics should ensure that their pupils become ICT capable in the context of mathematics.

ICT capability in the context of mathematics requires not only technical knowledge and skills in the domain of ICT, but also an awareness of how that knowledge base interacts with the pupils' own mathematical knowledge base, so that effective choices can be made. The choice of an effective strategy for a problem is dependent not only on knowledge of the mathematical and ICT strategies which have been learned but also on one's awareness of that knowledge and the realization that its use would be appropriate. Pupils must develop an awareness of the power and limitations of software in combination with their awareness of mathematical processes. In addition to this awareness, however, ICT capability also includes a predilection to apply ICT solutions to mathematical problems.

To become ICT capable in mathematics, then, is not merely about developing a secure knowledge of ICT skills, techniques, processes, and strategies which are appropriate in mathematical contexts; it also includes learning to consider the possibility of ICT solutions to mathematical problems and the development of a disposition to construct such solutions when it is appropriate to do so. Thus ICT capability in mathematics involves an interaction between technical facts and processes, strategic knowledge within both ICT and mathematics, metacognitive self-knowledge, and affective aspects of mind including self-confidence and a disposition to use technology (Kennewell *et al.* 2000). The development of such higher level skills and knowledge is dependent on experiencing both the effective teaching of mathematics using ICT and the construction of ICT-based solutions to mathematical problems.

Higher order skills

To be ICT capable in mathematics demands higher order skills such as:

- recognizing when the use of ICT might be appropriate or effective;
- planning how ICT resources, techniques, and processes are to be used in a task;
- conjecturing, discussing, and testing the strategies and data to be used;
- monitoring the progress of problem-solving activities;
- making and testing hypotheses;
- evaluating the outcomes of using ICT for a task;
- explaining and justifying the use of ICT in producing solutions to problems;
- reflecting on the learning which might have occurred during the task.

(Kennewell *et al.* 2000)

Task 11.1 Reflecting on mathematical thinking, numeracy, and ICT

Look back at the three components necessary for learning to think mathematically which we listed at the beginning of Chapter 7. Compare them with the definitions of numeracy which we offered at the start of Chapter 9 and what it means to be ICT capable in mathematics.

What similarities do you notice? Try substituting 'mental methods' for ICT in the reference from Kennewell *et al.* (2000) above.

Is ICT capability in mathematics just another form of numeracy?

We suggest to you that the development of numeracy and the development of ICT capability in mathematics are two parallel aspects of learning to think mathematically. Both are based on the development of higher order knowledge and skills, which we suspect are truly cross-curricular.

Higher order knowledge and skills are unlikely to be learned without significant teacher intervention and support, but they must be developed in an environment which encourages exploration and offers a substantial degree of personal autonomy. Opportunities must be presented: to decide which software to use and how to use it, to make plans, to monitor progress during extended tasks, to evaluate and reflect on solutions and the contribution made by ICT.

(Kennewell *et al*. 2000)

However, the dominant pedagogy in schools probably does not encourage such personal autonomy, and all too often ICT activities in school focus on showing pupils how to do a particular task using a particular ICT tool (Benzie 1997: 56).

IT interference factor

If a task is to be worthwhile and learning is to occur, there must be a gap between the pupil's current knowledge and that required by the task. When ICT is used, the pupil may find difficulties in the mathematical task or problem situation itself, or the software and/or its application to the problem. The 'IT interference factor' or cognitive overhead is determined by the difficulty involved in using the ICT (Birnbaum 1990). There is a double bind here. If the cognitive overhead is very large, the pupil will have little processing power left to think about the mathematics involved in the problem, thus limiting the potential for mathematical development. On the other hand, if there are few difficulties involved in either the use of the software or in its application to the problem situation, it is unlikely that ICT capability would be developed further by the lesson. Planning to strike an appropriate balance is often difficult and clear thinking about the aims of activities and the reason for using ICT is necessary. When software is generic in character – like spreadsheets, databases, or graph plotters – and you are likely to use it in a number of different contexts in mathematics and elsewhere, you may decide that a higher level of cognitive overhead is acceptable in the early stages. We regard this as similar to teaching pupils about protractors – you have to teach about the tools of the trade. When the cognitive overhead is very high and the potential for future use limited, you may decide that the use of ICT is inappropriate.

TUTOR, TOOL, TUTEE

Taylor (1980) classified computer usage in school as: tutor, tool, or tutee depending on whether the computer taught the pupil, the pupil used the computer as a tool, or the pupil 'taught' the computer by programming it. This classification remains useful and we use it below to consider how ICT may be used in the teaching of mathematics.

Tutor

From their earliest introduction into schools, attempts have been made to turn computers into substitute teachers. Integrated Learning Systems (ILS) have brought such ideas to an advanced state, incorporating instruction about facts and techniques, continuous assessment and recording, and individualized learning programmes. Unfortunately they are usually based on a similar pedagogy to the old programmed learning courses which proved to be such a dismal failure in the 1960s. They tend to take a serial, atomistic view of learning based on the (unlikely) prediction of all possible misconceptions (dubiously) linked to particular incorrect responses. They emphasize *facts*, *right answers*, and *correct methods*, ignoring intuition and stifling imagination. The National Numeracy Strategy (DfEE 1999a) respects students' idiosyncratic methods. The two approaches appear to be mutually exclusive. The jury is still out on whether such systems can be used to develop mathematics or numeracy effectively. Small-scale studies (e.g. Smith 2000) seem to indicate that at best, if they are used well, they may do no harm (aside from the expense). However, they are unlikely to contribute positively to the development of ICT capability or mathematical thinking because of their highly directive nature.

Tutee

At the other end of the scale from tutor, the computer may be used as tutee – a thing for the pupil to teach or program. Since the earliest days of computer use in schools claims have been made that benefits in pupils' thinking would result from their use (e.g. Papert 1980; Pea 1985). For example, it was claimed that pupils who programmed in Logo would learn to think like a computer, reorganizing and strengthening their own thinking (Pea 1985). Furthermore, it was suggested that because Logo was based on mathematical logic, by immersing themselves in a mathematically rich Logo environment, pupils would learn mathematics in a more natural and effective way (Papert 1980). Enthusiasts created 'Logo Worlds' for pupils to explore freely, following open-ended investigations. Sadly, then as now such pedagogy was very much against the dominant form prevailing in schools. Sadly, although there is much anecdotal evidence that programming a computer to perform mathematical processes forces pupils to organize and perhaps formalize their mathematical thinking, hard evidence for the development and transfer of such thinking skills has not been forthcoming.

Logo is still used in many schools when teaching geometry, but not on the scale originally intended. Programming *per se* has now been removed from the mathematics curriculum and Logo is used only as a tool in support of other topics, such as when writing short programs to generate regular polygons to teach angle rules.

Tool

Open-ended software – such as graph plotters – or generic software – such as spreadsheets or databases – may be seen as adjustable tools of great utility in mathematics. Developing a suitable problem formulation for such tools is often non-trivial and may be described as para-programming. Helping pupils to develop such formulations for themselves would usually be considered to be a significant part of the teacher's role.

When such tools are applied by pupils to problems arising naturally in the context of mathematics, it is possible that ICT capability *may* be developed, although that may not have been the intention of the teacher or pupil selecting the tool. The power of such tools lies in their ability to perform routine repetitive operations swiftly and accurately and allow the adjustment of parameters in an exploratory fashion. This provides an opportunity to free the mind from routine tasks to focus on higher level mathematics.

USING ICT TOOLS TO EMANCIPATE THE MATHEMATICAL MIND

To illustrate how mathematical and ICT knowledge and skills can be developed in parallel, using generic 'tool'-type software, we now offer three short-lesson ideas using graph plotting, spreadsheet, and database software.

Using graph-plotting tools

There are several places in the KS3/KS4 curriculum where pupils are required to make links between the form of equations and the shapes of algebraic graphs. One example is the straight line graph $y = mx + c$ which now appears in the NNS extension orders for Y7. A possible approach to this topic using a graphic calculator was suggested in Chapter 10.

You should notice that graphic calculators and graph-plotting computer software – such as Omnigraph or Coypu – are alternative forms of ICT. The lesson described in the last chapter could have been performed using computers, although the classroom dynamics would have been slightly different. As an example of the use of a computer graph plotting we offer a lesson on exploring the effect of different constants on the shape of trigonometrical functions.

Exploring trigonometrical functions

The class was a Y10 top set of thirty pupils. The lesson was in a computer suite of eighteen PC computers with Omnigraph software. The aim of the lesson was to explore the effect of the constant term a in functions such as: $a \sin x$; $\sin ax$, $\sin(x + a)$, $a \cos x$, $\tan ax$, etc.

The lesson began with the teacher standing by one of the computers which was linked to a large-screen monitor. All the class were told to move into a position from which they could see the screen. Some moved their chairs into a semicircle around the computer, others stood behind the chairs. (Obviously a data projector would have been better, but the school did not have one.) The teacher then logged on to Omnigraph, while pupils noted any steps they had forgotten since last time. He then set up the axes to show an appropriate range for the task ($-400 < x < 400$; $-4 < y < 4$). He then asked:

Who can show me what $y = \sin x$ would look like on these axes?

Several hands went up and one was given a white-board pen to draw on the big-screen monitor. The enter key was then pressed, the graph shown, the answer checked, and the screen wiped. Several further questions were asked about the values of x and y at significant points on the curve. Again, pupil predictions were followed up by pointing with the mouse to check.

What do you think $y = 2 \sin x$ will look like?

A range of suggestions were made and again a volunteer was chosen to draw a curve.

The teacher then worked through a range of other examples such as $\cos x$, $-\cos x$, $3 \cos x$, $\sin(x + 90)$, $\tan x$, $\tan 4x$. He then set his first task:

OK, I think you're getting the hang of that now. In a moment I'll ask you to go back to your machines and work in pairs to investigate the effect of placing a constant term. You'll have to devise a plan to work to.

Let's do this the usual way – everyone think in silence for a minute about what a good plan might be . . .

The teacher continued through the usual 'start–stop–go' procedure and set the class working, warning them to keep a record of every graph they produced on a sheet of small blank grids he had prepared.

The class worked enthusiastically on the task, exploring the patterns, making predictions, and jotting down notes and sketches.

In the plenary, he was pleased to discover that although different groups had devised different plans, all had worked systematically and had controlled variables. Between the class, all the rules had been found. He then set homework:

Tomorrow, I'm going to set you some challenges. I'll give you some curves on the computer screen and your task will be to try and match them to an equation. So tonight's homework is to look back through all your results and think about the results you have just heard from the other groups and try and write some notes which will help you.

The second lesson began with a short discussion about the notes which different members of the class had made. He then gave out a worksheet shown in Figure 11.1.

The class used their notes to try and type in the answer which would cover the curve first time. Some were interested to find more than one solution to a question.

In the plenary after the challenge questions, the teacher formalized the tacit knowledge which had been gained over the two lessons by constructing a set of notes based on the pupils' suggestions.

Reflecting on the task afterwards he commented:

They are a good class and they loved the challenges. Some of them were still using trial and error to solve some of the challenges, but it was tempered with sound intuitions about the sort of solution which would be likely. I think that by the end of the lesson they all understood the rules we had written.

Type in these functions and try and find a simpler function to produce the same curve:

1   $y = \dfrac{\sin x}{\cos x}$ 2 $y = \dfrac{\tan x}{\sin x}$ 3 $y = \dfrac{\tan x}{\cos x}$

4   $y = \dfrac{\sin 2x}{\sin x}$ 5 $y = \dfrac{2}{\cos x}$ 6 $y = \cos^2 x - \sin^2 x$

7   $y = 2 \sin x \,.\, \cos x$ 8 $y = \dfrac{\sin 2x}{\cos x}$ 9 $y = \dfrac{[2 \sin x \,.\, \cos x]}{\cos 2x}$

10   $y = \dfrac{\sin x + \cos x}{\sqrt{2}}$ 11 $y = \dfrac{\cos x - \sin x}{\sqrt{2}}$ 12 $y = \dfrac{\sin x + \sqrt{3} \,.\, \cos x}{2}$

Figure 11.1 Graphing trigonometrical functions.

The nice thing about this lesson is the way the ICT provides instantaneous, non-judgemental feedback when you make a sensible guess. You just could not do work like this without the support that the ICT gives you during the learning process.

I feel sorry for those kids whose teachers still try to teach this by doing rough sketches on a blackboard. It must be so much harder for them.

Using spreadsheets to investigate number series

These can be quite short tasks to complete, with several different number series investigated in one lesson with pupils from between years 5 and 9. We like to begin by investigating several simple number series to familiarize the pupils with the software and its potential before moving on to more complex relationships. We have given you spreadsheet templates for one easy task and one harder task overleaf. You will find further examples in Tanner and Jones (1995a), but they are very easy to make up for yourself (Figures 11.2–11.4).

The tasks which follow require no theoretical knowledge about spreadsheets on the part of the pupils. Any spreadsheet package is suitable. The lessons are not about spreadsheets although pupils will have gained many spreadsheet skills by the time the tasks are completed. The spreadsheet is used as a tool to do mathematics. The tasks exploit the power of spreadsheets to offer instantaneous recalculation of a set of numbers. The mathematical content of the tasks is determined by outcome and includes the concepts of decimal place value, variables, spotting patterns, and constructing formulae. Strategic skills include 'trial and improvement', 'pattern spotting', and 'generalization'.

The main part of each task requires only that pupils are able to enter data into one cell of the spreadsheet. Some of the extension tasks require pupils to set up a formula on the spreadsheet. Experience in the classroom leads us to suggest that individual groups of pupils can be shown this skill quickly at the point at which it is required in the lesson. (Not all pupils will reach the extension task.) We will now describe in detail a lesson using the harder task.

Target 1

	A	B	C	D	E	F
01		Input	3			
02			C1+1			
03			C2+2			
04			C3+3			
05			C4+4			
06		Output	C6+5	Target		
07						

Target 2

	A	B	C	D	E	F
01			5			
02		Input	7			
03			C1+C2			
04			C3+C2			
05		Output	C4+C3	Target		
06						
07						

Figure 11.2 Spreadsheet templates.

Target 2

This task is based on Lucas numbers – Fibonacci numbers with a non-zero start. It requires no prior knowledge of spreadsheets. The task is progressive in difficulty and differentiates by outcome.

The task may be introduced using 'start–stop–go', allowing the pupils to read the task and then explore the formulae on screen in pairs. A whole-class brain-storm then ensures that all groups are able to engage with the task before they begin in earnest. Part 1 of the task develops the strategy of 'trial and improve-ment'. During part 1, pupils' ideas of the number system are challenged by targets which progressively demand the introduction of decimal and negative inputs. Pupils are led to extend their number system gradually and eventually have to make trial-and-improvement decisions such as 'What number is a little bit smaller than -2.65? Is it -2.66 or is it -2.64?'.

Part 1 of the task develops pupils' self-confidence in using the technology and allows a 'feeling' for the sequence to develop. Significant misconceptions about number may be revealed during the 'trial and improvement' period allowing teachers opportunities for critical teaching.

Target 1

Load the file Target 1.
Copy the series of numbers into your book.

Input	3
	4
	6
	9
	13
Output	18	Target

Part 1

1   Write down what is happening to the numbers. Look at the formula in each cell if you are not sure.
2   Your first target is to get 21 as an output number. Guess what input number would give 21 as an output number and use trial and improvement until you get it.
3   Now try and get these target numbers in the same way. Keep a record of your answers.

    a   48   b   195   c   15   d   12

Part 2

Your next target is to find a rule to connect the input and output numbers. You have to choose which input numbers to investigate.

How should you set out your working? Write down a plan for this investigation.

Try to write your rule in algebra if you can.

Extension

1   Try to enter a *formula* into the next space on the ladder which will continue the series. Write down your formula.
2   *Can you think of another formula that would work?* Write it down.
3   Try entering your second formula into a cell near your first formula to check if both are the same. *Why do both the formulas work?*

Figure 11.3 A simple spreadsheet task.

Target 2

Load the spreadsheet file Target 2.
Copy down this series into your book.

	5	
Input	7	
	12	
	19	
Output	31	Target

Part 1

1   Write down what is happening in the series. Look at the formula in each cell if you are not sure.

2   Try changing the INPUT number to get these OUTPUT numbers. (Notice that the INPUT number is the SECOND number in the series.)

    a   19   b   22   c   20   d   21
    e   10   f   7   g   6   h   5

Part 2

3   Try to find a rule connecting the input and output numbers.

4   Try changing the first number in the series. *How does this affect the rule you found?* Investigate.

5   Try to find the connection between the two **bold** numbers and the output number.

Extension

Continue the series by entering a formula into the next cell in the ladder.

Investigate this new situation.

Explain why your formulas work.

Figure 11.4 A slightly harder spreadsheet task.

After a class reporting-back session, we suggest that the start–stop–go process should be used again, to introduce pupils to part 2 of the task.

Because of the way the task is introduced, able pupils, having found a formula for the starting number of 5, go on to produce a table of formulae for different initial values. The overall solution obtained in this way can also be explained by looking at the underlying structure of the question. Able year-8 pupils can often achieve this during a 1-hour lesson. Otherwise, looking for the underlying structure is a good homework task. The extension demands that formulae be entered into the spreadsheet, thus formalizing the result.

Using a database to introduce simple statistical ideas

This section includes activities of a slightly different type to those covered so far. It includes suggestions for whole-class discussions and activities which involve the creation and use of a computer database. The task makes use of the power of the computer to merge pupil files to create a large dataset for investigation.

The task is called 'Couch Potato' and it encourages pupils to design a database and plan a survey in order to test a contentious statement. 'Kids today have an unhealthy lifestyle!' Survey data collected by pupils is merged into a large database which is then interrogated and explored to justify or disprove the statement. Basic ideas about sampling, surveying, and correlation are developed.

Why use a computer?

Teachers have often asked their classes to collect real data in order to motivate pupils while teaching statistics. This data has often been displayed in thirty distinct bar charts as a result of the difficulty of collating the data from thirty separate surveys into one dataset. The questions asked about the data collected have often been limited to the mundane because of the size of the individual samples and the limited format of the data collected.

The advent of simple, user-friendly databases has changed this situation. It is now possible to use computers to merge the data from individual pupils to create a large data file which can be used to answer real questions.

The ability of computers to draw a range of graphs and to sort data quickly and easily allows pupils to concentrate on statistics instead of on the mechanics of plotting yet another bar chart. Using computers, pupils are able to explore large datasets to draw conclusions and communicate findings. The activity usually takes four lessons to complete and we describe below how one teacher approached it with her mixed ability Y8 group.

Task 11.2

Using a database for Couch Potato, read the worksheet in Figure 11.5 and consider how you would approach the task if you were

a   a Y8 pupil;
b   a teacher about to introduce the task.

In her form tutorial Jo had to discuss what the following graphs meant:

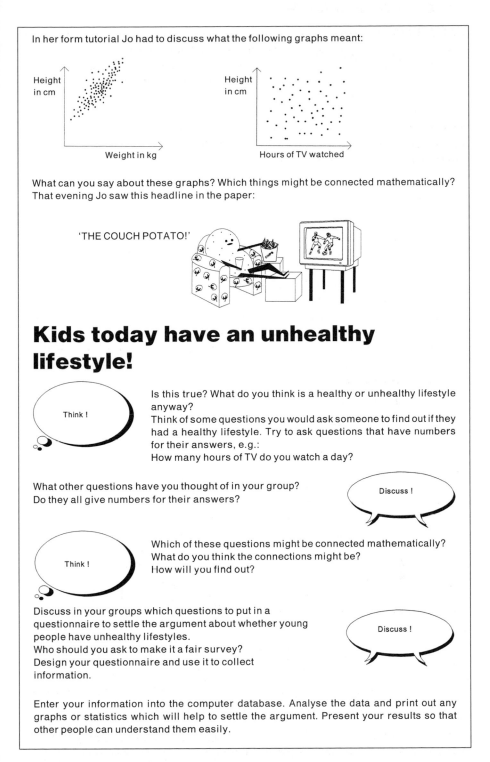

What can you say about these graphs? Which things might be connected mathematically? That evening Jo saw this headline in the paper:

'THE COUCH POTATO!'

Kids today have an unhealthy lifestyle!

Think !

Is this true? What do you think is a healthy or unhealthy lifestyle anyway?
Think of some questions you would ask someone to find out if they had a healthy lifestyle. Try to ask questions that have numbers for their answers, e.g.:
How many hours of TV do you watch a day?

What other questions have you thought of in your group?
Do they all give numbers for their answers?

Discuss !

Think !

Which of these questions might be connected mathematically?
What do you think the connections might be?
How will you find out?

Discuss in your groups which questions to put in a questionnaire to settle the argument about whether young people have unhealthy lifestyles.
Who should you ask to make it a fair survey?
Design your questionnaire and use it to collect information.

Discuss !

Enter your information into the computer database. Analyse the data and print out any graphs or statistics which will help to settle the argument. Present your results so that other people can understand them easily.

Figure 11.5 The Couch Potato.

Couch Potato

Lesson 1 – no computers

She began the lesson by claiming to have read in the newspaper that 'Kids today have an unhealthy lifestyle'. She claimed that teachers are fit and full of life (!) whilst pupils spend their time lounging around playing video games. This provoked some discussion in the class and led to her framing the question for the lesson 'How could we prove whether this was true or not?'

She discussed the statement with the class with particular reference to the sort of question which might be asked in a survey to find out if the statement is valid. The worksheets were given out and the process of 'start–stop–go' was followed – she demanded that the pupils think in silence, individually, about how they would approach the task for a few minutes before discussing it in small groups and planning the questions in a whole-class brainstorm to the board.

She did not know exactly what questions she would include in the survey prior to the start of the lesson. She worked off the suggestions made by the class, encouraging those with a numerical content and the possibility of interesting correlations. The class finally agreed on a list of ten questions which would be asked. The field names and types were then discussed with the class. Every pupil carefully copied down a correctly spelt version, noting whether each field was numeric or alphanumeric.

Sampling was then discussed using 'start–stop–go'. In the discussion at the board which followed, issues which arose included 'Who to ask?', 'How can we be sure our sample is typical?', stratified sampling procedures, safety issues, etc.

Homework was then set to collect responses from ten people each by next lesson. Emphasis was placed on banning door-to-door surveys – the class were keen and overambitious. Only friends and relatives were to be asked.

Lesson 2 – setting up the database in the computer room

In this lesson, the aim was for the class to work in pairs to set up a new database and type in their data items. The teacher explained that she sometimes missed this step out for less able classes and prepared the database for them herself so that they just had to enter their data. (And if access was difficult even this could occur during lunchtimes and after school.)

Each pair of pupils needed a separate user identity. The teacher brought along a stock of 'data she had collected herself' for absentees, etc.

Pupils who finished early examined their own dataset and began to consider what results might be of interest and if any points might be proved. At the end of the lesson, some of these insights and approaches to analysis were shared with the class in a plenary.

After the lesson

The teacher entered the network at network-manager level and moved all the files into one user area. She then merged the files into one large database which was then distributed around the network ready for next lesson.

Lesson 3

The teacher began the lesson by reminding the class of the contents of the database and the original question. Each pupil was then asked to think in silence about what fields they would look at first and with what purpose. This was then discussed in small groups before a brainstorming discussion at the board. Significant teacher input was required at this stage to help the class understand the sort of query which would produce interesting results.

The class then began to explore a large, real dataset attempting to test the original statement and seeking additional conclusions. They were highly motivated by the task which was unlike their typical schoolwork in that it was real and about them as a group and as individuals.

The teacher stopped the class at intervals to discuss the kinds of enquiry which were producing interesting or useful results. She also encouraged them to print out graphs which would help them to make a wall display which would be completed for homework. The class were then given a week to complete their displays ready for a presentation session.

Lesson 4

This lesson is critical for formalization of the learning involved. All pupils were asked by the teacher to say a few words about what they had done during the investigation and to describe one major result which they had found. Selected groups of pupils were asked to present their results in more detail to ensure that maximum value was gained from the task.

The teacher arranged the order of presentation to ensure that the less able groups were able to gain credit for the more obvious results leaving the harder analyses to their more able peers.

Groups presented their findings to the class, standing by their posters and pointing out key features. In every case the teacher demanded that groups explained why they had chosen to use a particular sort of graph and what advantages they felt it brought.

Class discussion followed presentations and focused on the validity of findings and the appropriateness of the graphs chosen. General rules about the use of various forms of data presentation were discussed and noted.

The session ended with the teacher asking pupils to summarize what they had learned about survey and sampling procedures, statistical analysis, the relative merits of different forms of presentation and graphical display. Finally the class were asked to vote on which presentation should receive gold, silver, and bronze awards of mathematical merit along with small chocolate prizes.

The class could not have attempted this task in any meaningful way without the computer. Their use of the computer made them operate at a much higher mathematical level than they would have been capable of in a more traditional lesson. We believe that this lesson demonstrated the power of the computer to 'amplify and emancipate the power of the human mind' as claimed by Howe (1983), making a valuable addition to the scheme of work for year 8.

SOME ISSUES WHICH ARISE WHEN USING ICT IN MATHEMATICS

Unless you are particularly fortunate to be in a very well-resourced school, access to computers is often a problem. Because of the demands made by specialist-subject IT lessons, computer rooms are often booked far in advance and you will need to plan carefully to gain access.

This is far from satisfactory. If the demands of ICT as a key skill are to be met, pupils need to be able to *make a decision* to use ICT in the solution of a problem. This may not always be planned in advance if the pupil autonomy is real. There is a real need for access to computer facilities close to the mathematics area which can be booked at short notice.

Many schools are beginning to plan their ICT resource with such access in mind and it is becoming more common to find a small suite of eight to ten computers provided as a resource under the control of the mathematics department. This is adequate for pupils working in groups of three or four on teacher-directed tasks like those above.

If such a facility is not available for you to use, we suggest that in the longer term you try to gain access to computers by offering to teach ICT key skills in your mathematics lessons. We have just described three sets of lessons which involve core mathematical content and use generic software which would otherwise be taught out of context in a specialist ICT lesson. You might even be able to gain more curriculum time as well as access to computer resources.

In the shorter term, even one computer in your classroom can be a valuable resource for interactive whole-class teaching purposes. This can be particularly effective if it can be linked to a large high-level TV display. It has the advantage of being in your own domain, aiding setting up and short-notice planning. Don't turn down the offer of old equipment as a stopgap if it will do the job. Some quite effective graph-plotting software runs on old technology.

Task 11.3 Gaining access

Find the booking system for computer resources in your school. Book sufficient slots to enable you to use all three tasks in this chapter with at least one of your classes.

Trainee teachers must gain access to ICT resources in order to meet the requirements of their courses. In order to gain qualified teacher status you must be able to demonstrate your ability to use ICT to support your teaching.

CONCLUSION

All teachers should be teachers of the ICT key skill. All children should have the right to experience the use of ICT in the field of mathematics. It is the duty of teachers of mathematics to ensure that they gain such experience.

The use of ICT in mathematics teaching has the potential to allow children to work at much higher levels than would normally be the case. We certainly think that there are some areas of the curriculum which should not be taught without it.

Summary

- Using ICT can enhance the teaching of mathematics;
- recognizing opportunities to use ICT in mathematics is a part of ICT capability;
- ICT can remove drudgery and scaffold pupils to higher levels of attainment;
- ICT can provide an effective tool for thinking;
- all trainee teachers must demonstrate their ability to use ICT in support of their teaching to gain qualified-teacher status.

12 Assessment and learning

Examinations date back to Imperial China around the eighth century BC, when they were introduced to eliminate nepotism and to provide a mechanism for the selection of candidates for state positions (Gipps 1990). Assessment in education today embraces a range of strategies and its purposes range from selection to accountability and, most importantly, the enhancement of the teaching and learning processes.

In this chapter we shall focus on ways in which teachers may use assessment to improve the teaching and learning of mathematics. After a discussion of the different purposes of assessment, we shall explore how assessment can be integrated into the planning, setting, and marking of pupils' work. The nature of formative assessment, the value of effective feedback, and the need for pupils to be involved in the assessment process will be considered in detail. We shall also discuss how the recording and reporting of pupils' attainment can be made manageable and effective.

Objectives

By the end of this chapter you should:

- know the different purposes for which assessments may be made;
- understand the importance of assessment for enhancing teaching and learning;
- appreciate the variety of assessment techniques available and be able to use them appropriately;
- understand the value of effective feedback in the learning process;
- be familiar with the assessment, recording, and reporting requirements of your school.

Task 12.1 Modes of assessment

What does the term 'assessment' mean to you? Make a list of five different ways in which you could assess a pupil's mathematics in addition to the formal examinations mentioned above.

Assessment is often assumed to involve marking so we expect that your list included homework, written tests, mental tests, classwork exercises, and possibly investigations or project work. These formal activities are the more obvious forms of assessment but did you also consider the questioning, discussion, or observation of pupils which occurs during lessons? Such activities provide valuable information about a pupil's understanding of mathematics.

The method you choose to assess pupils will depend on why the assessment is being undertaken. Why do teachers assess pupils? Who else would be interested in the results of the assessment?

PURPOSES OF ASSESSMENT

Information from the assessment of pupils' work is of interest to the pupils, their teachers, their parents, other teachers, and others who have an interest in a pupil's future (e.g. employers, colleges, local and national government). Each of these groups will have different uses for the assessment information and therefore any system of assessment must serve many purposes (see DES/WO 1988: para. 6.2).

As a teacher, your prime purpose for assessment is to facilitate pupils' learning. No one improves just by being assessed. Improvement only occurs if assessment leads to some action which enhances the pupils' understanding. The main emphasis of teacher assessment, on a day-to-day basis, will be for formative or diagnostic purposes.

Teachers' main purposes for assessment include:

1   to discover what a pupil knows, understands, and can do;
2   to analyse how a pupil is learning;
3   to identify and reward achievement;
4   to identify specific difficulties;
5   to give the pupil an appreciation of his/her achievement;
6   to evaluate the success of their own teaching;
7   to plan future work for individuals or groups;
8   to motivate pupils and hold them accountable.

These purposes are mostly formative in character but summative data is required for some purposes (e.g. reporting), so a teacher's list would also include:

9   to provide information about a pupil's current knowledge, skills and understanding for reporting or predicting;
10   to satisfy legal requirements.

But, most important of all, assessment must provide a means of communication between teachers and pupils. It is through assessment that teachers gain feedback on their teaching and pupils gain feedback on their learning. Unless this channel of communication is effective, both teaching and learning will suffer.

With increased attention being paid to the results of national tests, and external examination statistics being published to assess the performance of schools, the potential value of assessment for the pupils is often overlooked. All too often assessment is seen as an impersonal, formal process which is *done to* pupils. Their progress is measured, attributed a grade or score, and this is then reported to others. The assessment process appears to have little value for the pupils themselves. However, if assessment is to enhance learning then its formative purposes must be emphasized. The pupils need to appreciate how the assessment may contribute to their learning and become involved in acting on the information which the assessment has provided.

Assessment, therefore, can be undertaken for a variety of reasons. To what extent can any assessment system meet all of these purposes?

Task 12.2 Purposes for assessment

Look back at your responses to the first task in this chapter where you identified five different ways in which you could assess pupils' mathematics. What would be the main purpose for undertaking each of those assessments?

On a day-to-day basis the main purpose of assessment is formative – to improve the teaching and learning process. The need for summative information occurs toward the end of a module of work and, in particular, at the end of a key stage. Summative information can be used to evaluate and compare standards of pupils, teachers, or schools. It is these aspects of assessment which receive media coverage, for example, when reporting the latest standards at GCSE, etc. It is through the use of effective formative assessment, however, that those standards will be improved. We shall now explore how assessment can be used to enhance teaching and learning.

USING FORMATIVE ASSESSMENT TO IMPROVE LEARNING

Teacher assessment of students' work is essentially an ongoing and informal activity consisting of asking questions, observing activities or evaluating progress. For such assessments to be formative there must be feedback into the learning process. The importance of formative assessment in the teaching and learning process has been demonstrated by several researchers.

In a review of such research undertaken by Black and Wiliam (1998) they concluded that increased use of formative assessment in classrooms produced significant improvements in pupils' learning. They suggested that the size of the improvement would be sufficient to lift England to fifth place in the TIMSS international league tables (see Chapter 9) and would equate, for the average student, to an improvement of two grades at GCSE. This improvement was found to benefit lower attainers in particular, with an increase of three grades for the weaker students in comparison with one grade for higher attainers.

Research has identified the use of questioning and discussion, the involvement of pupils in the assessment process, and the quality of feedback, as key elements for effective formative assessment. We shall now explore ways in which these elements can be planned into classroom teaching.

Assessing through questioning and discussion

Effective teaching can only take place with the continuing assessment of pupils' responses to the lesson (DES 1985). Teachers can assess the pupils' understanding of and involvement in the lesson in a variety of ways – by observing the pupils' facial expressions, by looking at their written work, by listening in to discussions, or by direct questioning.

In Chapters 5 and 6 we discussed the variety of purposes for which teachers could ask questions and the types of misconceptions which many pupils hold. For formative assessment purposes the questions asked should probe for misconceptions, and the responses should indicate to the teacher what the pupil should be taught next.

Wiliam (1999a: 16) provides an example of a 'rich mathematical question which provides a window into the pupil's thinking':

$$3a = 24$$
$$a + b = 16$$

Pupils often assume that they have the wrong answer because a and b both have the value 8. Selecting such questions uncovers misconceptions as part of the teaching process.

The following example came from a lesson on place value taught to a year-7 class by one of our student teachers:

> Write in figures: Half a million

One pupil answered 1,000. When questioned he replied that as one million has six noughts then half a million would have three noughts in it. A logical, if erroneous, rationale!

This question probes pupils' understanding of place value and, more fundamentally, their sense of the size of numbers. Subsequent activities would need to develop and reinforce these concepts, for example:

> Put a million of something on the wall.
> Have you lived one million seconds?
> When was one million days ago?

Similar opportunities to assess pupils' thinking can be created if you ask pupils to explain their approaches to a problem. For example, following a lesson on finding squares and square roots of numbers, the next lesson was started by asking pupils to consider the statement:

> The square root of a number is always smaller than the number itself.

Listening to the pupils' responses allows the teacher to assess the effectiveness of the previous lesson and to adjust the planned lesson accordingly.

The benefits of such forms of interaction for pupils' learning are well documented in the literature. Finding suitable tasks and questions can take time, however, and this needs to be part of your lesson planning. Japanese teachers spend much of their lesson preparation time devising such activities (Wiliam 1999a). In the RSN project (Tanner *et al.* 1999), effective ideas were discussed during mathematics departmental meetings thereby sharing expertise and good practice. You will also be able to identify examples of useful questions and tasks when you observe your mentor and other experienced teachers.

Task 12.3 Planning questioning

For a topic that you are to teach:

1   write a question or a statement for discussion which will provide you with useful information about the pupils' prior knowledge, any misconceptions which they hold, the extent to which they have understood the work so far, etc.;

2   suggest what incorrect responses the task might generate and plan how you would proceed given each of the responses (you might find it helpful to reread Chapters 5 and 6 here);

3   discuss your plans with your mentor or the class teacher before you teach the lesson.

If the tasks were sufficiently probing you should have gained insight into the pupils' understanding and difficulties. The extent to which you were able to predict the pupils' responses indicates how accurately you had been assessing their progress. Accurate assessment is necessary if you are to pitch subsequent work within the pupils' zone of proximal development (Vygotsky 1978) – their learning zone. Questioning and discussion with the pupils encourages them to reflect on what they have learned and to identify which aspects of it you consider important enough to assess.

Involving pupils in the assessment process

Several researchers have demonstrated the value of involving pupils in their own assessment (Schoenfeld 1987; Gipps 1994; Tanner and Jones 1994b; Black and Wiliam 1998). Pupils need to know two things – what criteria their work is being assessed against, and how to self-assess their own work.

Teachers explain the learning objectives at the start of a lesson to clarify to the pupils what it is that they are meant to be learning. Similarly, sharing the assessment criteria for a task with the pupils will help them to focus on those aspects of their learning which you consider to be important. At one level this can be interpreted just as discussing with the pupils how the submarks are allocated within a question so as to persuade them to show their workings (compare this with the marking of the trigonometry question in Chapter 5).

Another effective strategy is to ask the pupils to write a question to test the work which has just been taught. The questions are judged on the extent to which they meet the assessment criteria for the topic. The best of the questions can then be used as the basis for the topic test.

Discussing the assessment criteria at the end of the task helps to explain how it is to be assessed. Holding the discussion towards the start of the task, however, gives the pupils the opportunity to demonstrate which of the criteria they can attain now that they understand their importance!

With more open-ended, problem-solving tasks the criteria used to evaluate them are more difficult to interpret. Discussion with the pupils is needed to negotiate with them what the criteria actually mean for their work. Whilst the National Curriculum level descriptors may be used as a starting point it is usually necessary to create task-specific examples for the criteria to be meaningful. Showing pupils examples of good-quality work can be helpful in illustrating how the criteria are interpreted, and can be used to develop their skills of peer and self-assessment (Jones 1992).

In our research into improving mathematical thinking skills we found that pupils who were taught to monitor and to reflect on their progress through assessing their own work and that of others outperformed their comparison classes in tests of general mathematical attainment (Tanner and Jones 1997).

When working on investigations or open-ended tasks the project class was stopped at intervals for selected groups to report on their progress. This shared good practice and teachers used questioning to emphasize key strategies such as the need to work systematically. Listening to how others had approached the problem, and the progress they had made, prompted pupils to contrast the reports with their own work and to identify ways in which it could be improved. Pupils were then encouraged to modify their plans if they thought that they could be improved.

Towards the end of the investigation, groups were selected to present their draft report to the class. The 'ground rules' were carefully established – the purpose of reporting back was to improve each group's work through discussion and constructive criticism. Pupils could ask for explanations of points which they did not understand – 'How did you know ...? Why did you do ...? Will that always be true?'; but any criticism had to be justified with reasons and, preferably, accompanied by suggestions for improvement. Each activity had an 'assessment framework' which indicated the criteria against which the reports would be assessed. The discussion during the presentation helped pupils to understand how the criteria would be interpreted. Following the presentation all pupils were encouraged to produce a final draft of their work, which was then submitted for formal marking.

The grades achieved following redrafting were usually higher than would have been achieved unaided but this formative assessment was part of the teaching process, not a summative judgement. The teacher formed a professional judgement about how much help each pupil had needed to produce that level of work.

Their performance in the next investigative task would indicate how much had been learned.

A vital question which had to be answered was: 'If I were to do this investigation again what would I do differently?' This encouraged 'looking back' and allowed consideration of the elegance of different solutions, economy of approach to a task, etc. Assessing the work of others helped students to identify the nature of a good solution and reporting back made them concentrate on what was important in their own work. By learning to assess the work of others, students learned to reflect on and assess their own.

Similar findings on the value of peer and self-assessment are reported by Black and Wiliam (1998). Learning is improved when pupils reflect on what they have learned during the lesson.

Wiliam (2000: 21) suggests encouraging reflection by:

- appointing a pupil to act as a 'rapporteur' during the plenary to summarize the main points of the lesson and to answer any questions from other pupils;
- asking pupils to indicate, perhaps by using tick boxes, the degree to which they feel that they have understood each of the lesson objectives.

Other strategies include asking pupils:

- to identify warnings which they would give to other pupils about to start the same task;
- to mark the work of an imaginary pupil which contains standard errors and to explain why the errors were made;
- to identify what is important for them to remember from today's lesson.

Such strategies also provide immediate feedback to you as the teacher on the effectiveness of your teaching. The feedback provides you with an insight into the extent to which the pupils have understood the concepts, and which aspects were easy or difficult, what further practice is required, etc. You are then able to adapt future lessons to match the pupils' level of attainment and understanding.

Task 12.4 Involving pupils

For a topic that you are to teach choose a suitable strategy to involve the pupils in their assessment. Plan how you will organize this in the classroom. Discuss your plan with your mentor and adapt it if necessary. Try out the strategy and evaluate its impact. What insights did you gain into the pupils' thinking? How effective was it for the pupils?

Remember that if pupils are not used to evaluating their own work it may take time for them to accept the process and learn how to do it effectively. It is often easier to begin by assessing other pupils' work than trying to assess their own.

For any assessment to be formative it has to provide feedback to the pupils which they can use to improve their learning. In what ways can you provide feedback to pupils and what types of feedback are most useful for them?

Providing effective feedback

Task 12.5 Using feedback

What types of feedback do you remember receiving when you were learning mathematics in school?

List five different ways in which you could give feedback to pupils on their work.

What might be the effect of each type of feedback on the pupils' learning, and their attitude to mathematics?

Teachers can give feedback in a variety of ways:

- a mark out of a given total;
- a grade, which may be related to NC levels, GCSE grades, or school descriptors;
- a general comment (e.g. 'untidy work'), which can be oral or written;
- an instruction (e.g. 'show your workings');
- a specific target which indicates what needs to be done next in order to improve (e.g. 'revise your 7× table';
- correction of errors (e.g. in calculation, spelling, method).

A mark or a grade is essentially a summative judgement; it tells you how you did. If the mark was a high one you might feel pleased or, conversely, if the mark was low, discouraged. The mark will confirm or challenge your perception of your mathematical ability. However, it tells you nothing about where you went wrong or how your performance could be improved.

There is evidence to suggest that feedback based on grades or marks can have a detrimental effect on performance (see Wiliam 1999b). Pupils can attribute their success or failure to themselves (i.e. to their own ability, or to the amount of effort they put into the task). Pupils whose feedback consisted of praise and grades increasingly attributed their performance to their ability in mathematics, and performed no better on subsequent tasks than pupils who were given no feedback. Similarly, where pupils were given both grades and comments, the impact of the grade appeared to dominate. However, pupils who received just comments on their work attributed their performance to their degree of effort, and improved their performance in comparison with the other three groups.

Wiliam suggests that feedback based on grades or marks promotes a view of mathematical ability as a fixed entity. If pupils believe that mathematical ability is fixed then each task is seen as an opportunity either to confirm their ability or to fail. There is no point, therefore, in attempting a task which appears too difficult and pupils will avoid engaging with the task preferring to be thought lazy rather than stupid. If, however, ability is seen as 'trainable', something which can be increased with effort, then tasks which are difficult are viewed by the pupils as opportunities to 'learn to get cleverer' and, therefore, will be attempted (Wiliam 1999b:11).

Feedback, therefore, should promote a view of ability in mathematics as being trainable, rather than fixed, and should indicate what needs to be done in order to improve.

Setting clear targets for pupils can be helpful here. Teachers in the high-performing schools studied in the Raising Standards in Numeracy project (Tanner *et al.* 1999) frequently set short-term targets for their pupils; for example:

> Look back at how to label the sides of a right-angled triangle, then redo questions 1 and 2 by next week.

Targets can be used to identify difficulties or to set a challenge to extend the pupils' understanding. They must clearly identify what the pupils need to do next. Such target setting can help to motivate pupils as it structures their learning into small, clearly specified and achievable steps. This also promotes a view of ability in mathematics as something which they can develop. Some teachers also awarded 'merits' when pupils achieved significant personal targets.

For feedback to be most effective it should be given as soon as possible after the task is completed. Prompt marking can identify errors before they become ingrained through use. Marking an exercise in class is often more effective than returning the work, albeit with lengthy comments, after a long period of time has elapsed. If the assessment is done during the teaching of the topic there are often further opportunities for the pupils to implement the advice given in the feedback. This will help to reinforce their learning.

Assessments undertaken for formative purposes have the most impact on learning but the assessment structure within a school must address all the purposes which assessment must meet. We shall now consider ways in which assessment can be planned into the teaching process.

PLANNING FOR ASSESSMENT

It is obviously not possible to assess everything that a pupil does. Just as you have to prepare your lessons, assessment also has to be planned for maximum effectiveness.

Most schools now have policies on assessment which should include guidance on:

- planning for everyday assessment, marking work, and providing feedback to pupils;
- using the outcomes of assessment to identify strengths and weaknesses and to inform future teaching;
- recording assessments;
- planning for statutory assessments at the end of a key stage;
- reporting to parents;
- monitoring and evaluating policies and procedures.

(after ACCAC 1999: 3 and 14)

Your department might also have produced a departmental policy which exemplifies how the more general school policy will be implemented in mathematics. Within these frameworks you have to decide what you will assess, when, and how.

What should be assessed?

WYTIWYG is a useful acronym which helps to determine what should be assessed – *What You Test Is What You Get*. Pupils judge what you value in their work by the assessments that you make.

Assessment should reflect broad classroom approaches to the teaching and learning of mathematics (DES 1985). Assessments which focus only on recall and memorization, such as the repetition of standard algorithms or tables tests, undervalue the need to be able to apply those skills to problems. If you value creativity and imagination you should assess creativity and imagination. We have to ensure that we assess that which is important rather than that which is convenient.

The validity and reliability of the assessments should also be considered. An assessment is reliable if the same result would be obtained by another assessor. Tests of recall are very reliable as the answers are either right or wrong. Their validity is not very high, however, as such tests do not assess everything that is important in mathematics. Assessments made purely for summative purposes may emphasize reliability at the expense of validity.

When planning your assessments you should include a variety of tasks which address all your main objectives for the pupils' mathematical development.

Task 12.6 Familiarizing yourself with your school policies

Use your school or departmental assessment policies to answer the following for each of the classes that you teach:

a   How often should you try to collect in pupils' books when you are teaching a class full time?

b   Is all work marked by the teacher or only selected pieces? Is some work marked by the pupils themselves? Is any marking done in the lesson?

c   How detailed is marking expected to be? Will just a tick or cross suffice? Are you expected to correct every mistake (e.g. spelling)?

d   What kind of comments will you be expected to make on pupils' work? How long are your comments expected to be?

e   Are you expected to record marks or grades after marking work? How and where?

f   How often is homework expected to be set and marked? How long is the homework expected to last?

Questions which test pupils' knowledge of facts and skills such as '$38 \times 7 =$' must be accompanied by other questions which probe pupils' understanding of what multiplication means and when it should be used. Open questions such as 'Find five different equations with a solution $x = 3$' allows pupils to demonstrate what they know about equations. The ceiling of difficulty for such tasks is set by the pupils and not by the teacher's perceptions. Such open questions are particularly useful when a class has a wide range of ability.

The answers to these questions will depend on your individual departmental routines but before you start taking responsibility for a class you should be clear as to how you will assess and record pupils' work.

SETTING AND MARKING PUPILS' WORK

Pupils' performance can be assessed in a variety of contexts (e.g. during lessons, through homework tasks, in tests, or in more formal examinations). Assessment opportunities in each of these contexts need to be planned. You should also consider how the work will be marked and whether your assessments should be recorded.

Not all work can be marked in detail; you have to decide which aspects should be marked by you. Marking which merely indicates whether an answer is right or wrong fails to guide the pupil's further study and so is a waste of a teacher's valuable time. Marking a limited number of indicative pieces of work thoroughly, with detailed formative comments, contributes far more to the pupil's learning. Much routine work may be marked in class by the pupils themselves.

Let us now examine where opportunities for assessment arise and which strategies for assessment would be most appropriate.

Classwork

During lessons you may wish to assess pupils' oral contributions or their written work. As we discussed earlier, assessing pupils during lessons may involve questioning, discussion, or presentations by pupils. It would not be possible to record every interaction which occurs but, over time, you should build up a picture of each pupil. You should note any unexpected features of a pupil's work to follow up later. Planning to target a different group of pupils each lesson is one strategy to ensure that you assess every pupil closely.

Pupils benefit from fast feedback on their work especially when they are working on new tasks. After the majority of the class have attempted the first few questions in an exercise then they need to check their answers. Similarly, at the end of the exercise you need to evaluate the level of understanding before you move on. There are several options for marking work in class:

- the teacher marks each individual pupil's work in turn;
- the teacher calls out the answers;
- pupils are chosen to call out the answers;
- pupils volunteer to answer;
- pupils mark their own work;

- pupils swap books and mark another's work;
- pupils explain their solutions on the board;
- the class marks a solution on the board (see Chapter 5 for a fuller description).

Marking the work of each individual takes too long in a lesson – the last pupils could have completed the entire exercise incorrectly before you get to them. Asking pupils to volunteer to give the answers can give you an indication of their confidence – if the majority of the class are eagerly waving their hands then they could probably do that question! Selecting pupils allows you to target individuals (e.g. to praise their efforts or to probe suspected difficulties). If you are to call on pupils to answer then they need their own books in front of them – there is little benefit in calling out someone else's error.

In addition to providing feedback to the pupils, assessing during a lesson allows the teacher to judge the level of understanding of the class. A show of hands 'Who had every question correct? Who had just two wrong?' will indicate whether or not to proceed. Rather than risk public humiliation for any pupils with several incorrect answers, experienced teachers will scan for pupils who did not raise their hands, note any worried expressions, and move around the class to check unobtrusively on anyone they suspect might have had difficulties. Pupils should, of course, be encouraged to show their work to you if they need further help before attempting their corrections.

Pupils' exercise books should be checked on a regular basis – your departmental policy will probably indicate the minimum frequency. We would suggest that you aim to mark on a weekly basis. Glancing quickly through self-marked work allows you to identify any important errors to be followed up, either as a class or individually. You should also check for inconsistent performance between contexts (i.e. between the standards a pupil achieves in class and in tests).

Investigative tasks

The criteria against which such tasks are to be assessed should be discussed with the pupils in advance. For formative purposes your comments should indicate a strength, a weakness, and set a target for improvement. In preparation for external examinations, the external criteria should be used and marks awarded against these in addition to the comments. Most departments have examples of assessed tasks and hold moderation discussions to ensure consistency of marking across staff. You might also find SEAC (1993) helpful.

Homework

The duration and frequency of homework varies according to the age and ability of the pupils, and differing school policies. Homework can be set for a variety of purposes as the extract from a school homework policy illustrates in Figure 12.1.

For which purposes do you usually set homework? What do your homework tasks include?

If homework is to be set following a lesson then it should be planned in advance and should have a clear purpose. Telling pupils to 'finish off the exercise' is often just a lazy way of setting some homework which the teacher has forgotten to

By expecting pupils to complete a homework task we hope to:

- target aspects of the mathematics curriculum on a regular basis (e.g. learning of key facts);
- provide an opportunity for pupils to discuss their mathematics with parents;
- develop pupils' study skills (e.g. meeting deadlines).

Homework tasks should include:

- regular practice of number skills;
- short focused tasks to develop investigative skills (e.g. working systematically, justifying, proving, etc.);
- consolidation of current work;
- revision of previous work;
- revision for tests and examinations.

In Key Stage 3, two homeworks of 30 minutes should be set each week, although this may vary according to the ability of the group.

Figure 12.1 Guidance on homework.

plan! Although it might punish pupils who have been wasting time (and you should have dealt with them during the lesson!) it also penalizes slower workers who are not able to complete the task in the notional time allowed. The more able pupils are likely to have completed the majority of the exercise and so will end up with little or no homework. Parents who are trying to support the school by checking that their child is doing homework as indicated by the homework timetable find themselves in a difficult position when their child regularly claims 'I finished it off during the lesson so I left my book in school'. You would be better advised to have a different exercise prepared for homework and then, if necessary, require the timewasters to complete their classwork as well.

Before you set homework consider when it is to be submitted and how it is to be marked. Suppose the homework is to consolidate ongoing work. You could tell the pupils to complete it by the next lesson. The lesson would then start by going through the homework. If unexpected problems arise with the work then your planned lesson will have to be revised swiftly to address the difficulties. The alternative is that you collect the books in to mark before the lesson. You can then amend your planning in the light of the pupils' achievements.

Some departments issue pupils with homework books as well as classwork books. This allows you more time to mark homework without having to get the books back to the pupils for the next lesson. Remember, however, for feedback to be effective, work should be marked and returned to the pupils swiftly. Try to spread out your marking so that you do not end up with five sets of books all to be marked on one night!

In order to be able to track pupils who do not submit work make a note in your class register of when the work was set and when it was due in. You will then be able to check quickly which pupils were absent and which ones have 'forgotten'.

Tests

Tests can provide a quick check on factual knowledge – asking pupils to write down the formulae for finding the area of a rectangle, parallelogram, trapezium, etc.; or a more formal exploration of their degree of understanding of a concept (e.g. in an end-of-topic test). When the test is given will affect pupils' performance.

If the test is given at the end of the topic then the pupils have no immediate opportunity to use feedback from their errors to improve their learning. If the test is set toward the end of the topic then errors can be corrected and new learning reinforced in the subsequent lessons.

Giving warning of the test, and including some revision questions as part of homework, will help to reinforce pupils' learning. Unless revision takes place, learning, as indicated by test performance, appears to deteriorate with time. Even concepts which appeared to be well understood during the teaching often seem to be forgotten after a period without use. Pupils normally do better on tests given immediately after teaching than if the test is delayed until, say, 2 weeks later.

Delayed tests may provide more reliable information for summative purposes but formative purposes are best served by more immediate assessments.

In order to obtain a complete picture of a pupil's attainment in mathematics a variety of forms of assessment should be used. This attainment then has to be recorded and reported as appropriate.

RECORDING AND REPORTING PUPILS' WORK

The main reasons for recording pupils' attainments are:

- to inform the planning of future work;
- to enable teachers to make judgements against National Curriculum and other external criteria;
- to help teachers and pupils be aware of progress;
- to inform reporting to parents.

(after SEAC 1991: 2)

Most record keeping can be done in your mark book as an integral part of your marking and preparation for teaching.

A limited selection of other aspects of pupils' work (e.g. coursework tasks, presentations), which may be required for formal summative assessments may be kept in a portfolio. Pupils should be involved in selecting the sample of their best work. The portfolios are often discussed as part of the departmental moderation process. Portfolios, together with other information about a pupil's progress, should be sent on to the next teacher or, most importantly, to the next school.

Task 12.7 Using and reporting assessment information

Discuss with your mentor:

1 How does your school utilize the information received on pupils' prior progress?
2 What information is sent on to the pupil's next teacher or school?

Many secondary schools use the information received from KS2 tests and teacher assessments to plan their teaching groups for year 7 and to identify pupils with special needs. Teachers need information about their pupils' prior attainments and weaknesses so that they may plan suitable work. The lack of such information can lead to unnecessary repetition of work already understood.

Schools have to report formally to parents annually: your school may also send interim reports at key points during the year (e.g. after the first half-term in year 7) to indicate how well the pupil has settled in to the new school. Parents' evenings are also usually held annually for each year group.

Task 12.8 Reporting on achievements

1   Find out from your school policies or your mentor when reporting takes place for each class that you teach. Obtain a copy of the report form(s) and discuss with your mentor the type of comments you would be expected to write. What other information will the report contain?

2   When do parents' evenings occur? What happens at them? What sort of information will you need to prepare?

Reports provide summative information about the standards achieved by the pupil. They may also contain National Curriculum levels or, if external examinations are forthcoming, predicted grades. For the reports to be useful they should also indicate the pupil's main strengths and weaknesses and indicate strategies for improvement.

You should expect to discuss your comments further during the parents' evening. Having examples of the pupil's work available to show to parents can be helpful. Some teachers prepare for a parents' evening by ensuring that they have at least one positive comment and one target to suggest for each pupil. Be precise when commenting on the pupil – 'She finds algebra difficult' is less helpful than 'She needs to revise expanding brackets'. Most parents are keen to help their children and appreciate your advice. Many mentors encourage their trainee teachers to prepare for and to attend parents' evenings during their training.

CONCLUSION

Assessment may serve many purposes and involve a range of techniques. For teachers and pupils, the main purpose of assessment is to improve learning. Involving pupils in the assessment process helps to communicate to them what you consider to be important in their work and helps them to demonstrate their achievements. It is not only pupils who should be self-assessing their progress, however. Good teachers also monitor their effectiveness and plan for improvement. We shall consider such issues in the final chapter.

Summary

- Assessments should be planned and address all your main teaching objectives.
- there should be a balance between teacher-marked and pupil-marked work;
- teachers should mark pupils' books regularly;
- marks and grades can adversely affect learning. Poor marks discourage pupils by lowering their self-esteem. Good marks may lead to complacency;
- feedback is more effective for formative purposes when specific comments are made.

Formative assessment can enhance learning through:

- the provision of effective feedback which conveys an image of mathematical ability as trainable and clearly identifies steps which the pupils can take to improve their performance;
- the effective use of questioning to identify and to address difficulties;
- the use of peer and self-assessment to encourage pupils to reflect on their own learning and to identify aspects which they have not fully understood.

13 Evaluating and developing your teaching

This chapter is intended to be of interest to experienced teachers as well as to trainees and recently qualified staff.

For experienced mentors or team leaders, the discussions and activities could be used to support the development of your inexperienced colleagues and, in particular, to encourage your mathematics staff to develop as a team.

As a trainee or a newly qualified teacher, the successful completion of your initial-training course means that your teaching will have been assessed as meeting satisfactory standards of competence. This does not mean that your lessons will no longer be observed or your teaching assessed. Schools are now inspected regularly and a major focus of an inspection is to assess the quality of the teaching. More importantly, perhaps, you need to continue to improve your teaching skills, and to assess the impact of your teaching on pupils, as part of your professional development from being a competent teacher to being an 'advanced skills' teacher.

In the early stages of their development, novice teachers often improve rapidly learning new techniques and skills day by day. After a time, however, most novice teachers reach 'the plateau' (Furlong and Maynard 1995). At this stage lessons are reasonably well controlled and learning is occurring, but things can still be improved. Our aim in this chapter is to help you move off the plateau and scale the peaks! We shall focus on how you can judge how effective you are as a teacher, and which aspects of your teaching could be improved.

In Chapter 12 we discussed how assessment could be used to help pupils improve their learning. Similar principles can be used to help you to assess and improve your teaching. Good teachers see themselves as learners and use a variety of strategies to reflect on their effectiveness and to inform their self-assessments.

In this chapter we shall look at ways in which you can evaluate your impact on the pupils' learning and their views of mathematics. Any evaluation is based on information and we shall identify the types of feedback on your teaching which are most helpful. The most effective teachers do not work in isolation, however, and working as part of a mathematics team can enhance the professional development of all its members. Finally we shall consider the importance of making a professional development plan and how short-term target setting can contribute to this.

Objectives

By the end of this chapter you should:

*   understand the importance of continuing to develop your teaching skills;
*   be aware of strategies to improve your skills of self-assessment;
*   appreciate the importance of working as a self-monitoring team;
*   understand the advantages and the difficulties associated with using data to monitor pupils' attainment;
*   be able to plan for your personal career development.

WHAT HAVE YOU TAUGHT PUPILS ABOUT LEARNING AND MATHEMATICS?

During a lesson-planning session a PGCE (Post-Graduate Certificate of Education) student was asked by a colleague how he could be so confident in the assumptions he was making about the pupils' prior knowledge. His reply was:

Of course they know it – I taught it to them.

Unfortunately, as you will have already discovered, just because you have taught something it does not mean that the pupils have learnt it! Or, at least, what you think you have taught is not always the same as what the pupils have learned.

Towards the end of our PGCE course, we expect our students' focus to change from concentrating on their teaching performance to assessing what effect that performance has had on the pupils' learning. In order to do this you need to be able to distinguish between those superficially successful lessons in which the pupils are kept busy, on task and may even be enjoying the activities, and those which maximize pupils' learning.

In Chapter 2 we identified the different elements of mathematical knowledge (e.g. facts and conventions, skills and routines, mathematical processes and thinking), and discussed how pupils could be led to develop an instrumental or a relational understanding of a topic. Instrumental understanding is certainly easier to teach and to learn in the short term but it does not provide a basis for developing higher order thinking skills. Where has the emphasis been placed in your teaching? Have you created an impression of mathematics as a subject where what is important is the memorization of facts and the repetition of routines? Or have you fostered a perception of mathematics as a fascinating, creative subject which requires imagination, systematic working, persistence, and co-operation? For as HMI (Her Majesty's Inspectors) stated:

If these personal qualities are missing there is something fundamentally wrong with the mathematics curriculum whatever the levels of achievement attained by the pupils.

(DES, 1985: 51)

Task 13.1 Analysing the emphases in your teaching

Choose a lesson which you taught recently and which you thought went well. Analyse the relative proportions of time which were spent on teaching:

> facts and conventions;
> skills and routines;
> conceptual structures;
> techniques and results;
> mathematical processes and thinking.

How typical of your teaching is this? Which aspects of mathematical thinking are under-represented? Identify two of these as targets and plan how you could incorporate them in your lessons during the next week.

In addition to monitoring what images you are conveying of mathematics, you should also consider how you are teaching your pupils to learn. Do your pupils expect to have to think about their mathematics, or do they wait for instructions each time they meet a different problem. For example, what would happen if you were interrupted during an explanation of a problem? Would the class just sit there quietly waiting for you to be able to continue, or would they try to work out for themselves what the next step should be? In other words, have you taught them to think or merely to follow? Reviewing the answers to such questions for a range of classes will help you to assess the extent to which your pupils are developing as independent learners.

So far our discussions have been based on your self-analysis. There are other useful sources of information which can contribute to your evaluations.

ASSESSING THE EFFECTIVENESS OF YOUR TEACHING

Information on your teaching can range from informal comments from pupils or other staff to quantitative data collected for formal, evaluative purposes. Each type of data can be helpful.

Using the pupils' views

After teaching in schools for many years we were pleasantly surprised when we started lecturing in university at how often our students were asked to comment on our teaching and to evaluate the quality of the courses they were studying. Pupils can also provide insightful comments on which aspects of your teaching they find most effective.

Good teachers monitor their pupils for informal feedback – such as the level of interest shown during different phases of a lesson, the enthusiasm they show for mathematics, or the degree of care taken over their work. More formal comments can be obtained at the end of a term or the school year. Questionnaires similar to that shown in Table 13.1 can be used to gather pupils' views.

Table 13.1 Gathering pupils' views.

Learning maths			
Class _____ **Boy/Girl** _____			
How good are the following activities in helping you to learn maths?	Very helpful	Sometimes helps	Doesn't usually help
Listening to me explain to the class			
When I explain to you individually			
When I ask you to answer a question			
Listen to other pupils answer questions			
Explaining your ideas to the whole class			
Explaining your ideas to a small group			
Discussing ideas as a small group			
Working on your own			
Reporting back your findings to the class during the lesson			
Having to summarize the main points at the end of the lesson to the class			
Listing what you've learned in your 'Dear Diary'			
Doing questions just like the examples on the board			
Doing questions which are all slightly different to the examples			
Trying difficult problems which you have to think about and sometimes get stuck on			
How hard do you usually work:	Very hard	Quite hard	Not very hard
in maths lessons			
at your maths homework			
Was the amount of homework	Not enough	About right	Too much
Which maths topic did you find hardest? Why?			
Which maths topic did you enjoy the most? Why?			
Which maths topic did you like the least? Why?			
Complete this: I would learn maths better if we did more did less			
How much did you learn in my lessons Why?	More than usual	Usual	Less than usual
Did you enjoy my lessons Why?	More than usual	Usual	Less than usual

As well as providing useful feedback to the teacher, the questioning contributes to the pupils' self-knowledge by encouraging them to reflect on what they have learned and which learning strategies they have found most effective. You could adapt the questionnaire provided in Table 13.1 to focus on particular activities or teaching strategies.

Task 13.2 Gathering information from pupils

Choose a class with whom you have developed a good rapport and you consider your teaching to be effective. Ask them to complete the evaluation questionnaire. This should be done anonymously although it might be interesting to explore any gender differences. Tell them that the purpose of the questionnaire is to identify ways in which they could learn more effectively.

Collate the results for each question.

To what extent did the pupils' views reflect your impressions? Were there any gender differences? Would you get similar findings with older, younger pupils, lower sets, . . .?

The results of the questionnaire will probably identify some aspects of your teaching which could be enhanced. You may be able to set yourself some targets and work independently to achieve them. Alternatively, you may benefit from working in collaboration with others. For example, comparing your results with those from a similar class taught by a colleague could indicate different strengths and suggest opportunities for supportive mutual development.

Learning from your colleagues

Although some self-improvement may be achieved independently, many teachers find it helpful to enlist the support of their mentor or a trusted colleague. Asking a colleague to observe your lessons can, just as when you were training, provide a fresh perspective on your strengths and help to identify the sources of any difficulties. Being observed, teaching can, of course, be quite stressful so it is important to establish in advance the focus of the observation and the nature of the feedback. Agree, also, whether the observation will be confidential. The relationship between the observer and the observed need not be hierarchical. We have found this focused observation to be particularly effective when the two teachers consider themselves to be of equal status (i.e. both are learners with the aim of enhancing their practice).

After the observation you and your observer should set clear objectives. You also need to discuss strategies for attaining these objectives within a reasonable timescale.

Suitable topics for observation could include:

- your use of open questions and encouragement of extended responses from pupils;

- maintaining the pace of the lesson during transitions;
- maintaining an appropriate noise level during the exercise phase;
- your provision of constructive feedback to the pupils during a reporting-back session – the observer could be introduced to the pupils as the audience for their reports;
- your management of a particular group of pupils with whom you experience difficulty.

The final observation could be followed up by you observing the lessons of other teachers who find those pupils less difficult to deal with.

Sharing practice is good practice. Pupils respond favourably to departments and year groups that act as *teams*, sharing the celebration of achievement, for example:

> *Some of this work is so good that I am going to ask Mr Smith to come and listen to a couple of your presentations next lesson.*

Such collaboration between staff was a common feature of the outperforming mathematics teachers in the Raising Standards in Numeracy (RSN) project (Tanner *et al.* 1999). The teachers worked as part of a self-reviewing team with the intention of improving their own practice. For example, new teaching approaches, such as those introduced by the National Numeracy Strategy, would be planned collaboratively by a small group and then tried out with their classes. The teachers then fed back to the mathematics-team meeting. Some of the lessons were videoed and significant excerpts used for discussion.

The purposes of the strategies described so far have been formative – to help you to develop your own practice. At intervals, however, especially during your early years of teaching, you should seek more evaluative appraisals. After all, if your head of department or another senior member of staff, is concerned about some aspect of your teaching then you need to know that as soon as possible so that you can take steps to improve. More positively, asking your mentor or team leader to comment on your performance encourages them to review your capabilities, and to identify your strengths as well as weaknesses. Following the review, you should ensure that together you have identified strategies by which you may improve. The form shown in Table 13.2 is useful as a prompt sheet for reviews of teachers' performance.

The RSN teachers also monitored their teaching practices more formally. The head of department, and sometimes the head teacher, would monitor the work of a random selection of pupils on a regular basis. The monitoring would look for evidence that the work was set and marked according to departmental or school policy and, in particular, that effective use was made of formative feedback.

A final source of information on your effectiveness is to examine how well your classes have performed in comparison with other comparable groups. Test and examination scores can be used in a variety of ways to monitor performance and to set targets for improvement.

Table 13.2 Evaluating your professional practice.

Focus	Strengths/targets:
Subject knowledge	
• Pupils' common mistakes and errors	
• ICT and its role in teaching	
Planning	
• Structure and effectiveness of planning	
• Choice, variety, and differentiation of tasks	
• Effective use of assessment information	
• Setting targets for pupils' learning	
Teaching and class management	
• Questioning	
• Listening and responding constructively	
• Attention to errors and misconceptions	
• Teaching with enthusiasm and motivating pupils	
• Management of time and pace	
• Monitoring and intervening	
• High expectations for work and behaviour	
• Relationships with pupils	
Assessing, recording, and reporting	
• Systematic assessment and recording of pupils' work	
• Providing feedback and setting targets	
• Use of assessment to improve teaching	
Wider professional role	
• Critical evaluation of own teaching	
• Other professional activities	
• Personal and professional conduct	

After Rowe (2000).

The use of numerical data

One method of judging your teaching effectiveness is to compare the performance of your classes with groups of a similar standard in the school. Many departments set common end-of-topic tests or common questions across examination papers. Pupils' performance on such questions should be reviewed to check that they are working at the correct level or placed in an appropriate set.

You can use such data to identify strengths and weaknesses in your teaching (e.g. questions which your pupils answered less well than other classes).

The results of external examinations – GCSE or KS tests – should be considered against past performance. Are you doing better or worse than last year? Are you meeting the national targets? The raw scores do not give the whole picture, however; obviously some schools will be expected to do better than others.

A considerable body of research now exists to counter the claim that schools have uniform effect, indicating instead that individual schools can exert an influence over and beyond the qualities of their incoming pupils, their families and even the social determinants of gender, class and race.

(Mortimore *et al.* 1994: 316)

In some contexts, being satisfied with achieving the national norms is not sufficient. If you are teaching in a school where the pupils achieved above target levels on entry, and benefit from parental support and encouragement to do well, then just to achieve national targets with such pupils would represent under-achievement. On the other hand, if you are teaching in an area where the social factors are not so supportive of education, there is a danger that your expectations will be artificially low and you will not expect your pupils to achieve as highly as they are capable. In either case you need to know what would be a realistic, challenging but achievable target for your classes. Such information should be available from the senior staff.

Most schools now are data rich about their pupils. In addition to in-school data such as homework marks, test and examination scores, the results of external assessments such as end-of-key stage tests are available. Many schools also use 'standardized tests' based on tests of cognitive ability (CATs) or measurements of pupils' reading ages. These tests have been trialled on large, representative samples of pupils and can provide an indication of an individual's performance in comparison with the 'average' pupil of the same age. Such data can be used to indicate the value added by the school over and above the result which could have been expected given the pupil's prior performance.

Information systems such as YELLIS (Year Eleven Information System) and PIPS (Performance Indicators in Primary Schools) (Hulme *et al.* 1998) provide predictions of pupils' performance at the end of a key stage given their performance on a baseline test at the start. The RSN schools used a range of baseline tests such as reading scores and SAT data alongside social factors based on postcodes to predict likely and possible outcomes for their pupils. These were used with the teachers' knowledge of the pupils to set challenging but attainable targets for pupils and for classes.

Such data can be used to monitor for underperformance by pupils or, indeed, by teachers or subjects. It can also provide an indication of teaching effectiveness by comparing the actual score achieved by a pupil with the predicted score.

In the RSN schools, the reasons for any anomalous outcomes were explored and the adoption of strategies which appeared to have been effective encouraged across the department. They also compared the pupils' results within mathematics with those in other subjects to assess their effectiveness as a subject department.

When you receive the results of such tests you should reflect on why the results are as they are. Thinking about individual pupils can help you to identify those who underperformed and those who did better than expected. Can you suggest strategies which would have prevented the underperformance? What can you learn from those pupils who did better than you expected? Such self-evaluation should help to identify your own targets for improvement.

PLANNING YOUR PROFESSIONAL DEVELOPMENT

At the end of your training, the completion of your Career Entry Profile (CEP) required you to identify your strengths and also areas in need of development. Formulating targets and action plans for achieving them is an effective method of promoting your professional development. In the early days of your teaching career you are likely to focus on short-term targets such as developing your strategies for managing more difficult classes or developing your use of questioning. It is important, however, to have thought through your longer term objectives. Answering the questions:

> *Where do I want to be in 5 years' time?*
> *What do I have to do to get there?*

will help you to plan your career development. Do you want to be a team leader, to teach A level, to develop your expertise with pupils with special needs, etc.? Knowing where you want to get to will help you to choose appropriate courses.

You might not think so now, but unless you are careful, your hard-won professional knowledge will gradually begin to seem a little jaded. Like most professionals, you have a duty to stay up to date with the latest ideas and approaches. It is not only a matter of updating; it is also a matter of keeping the fire of enthusiasm burning. You need to ensure that updating and reinvigorating is a continuous process. You should consider joining a professional association such as the Association of Teachers of Mathematics (ATM) or the Mathematical Association (MA). Both of these organizations are dedicated to improving the standard of mathematics teaching in schools and publish journals containing interesting lesson ideas and discussions about the teaching of your subject. Both hold annual conferences which can be a stimulating source of new ideas and help to keep you up to date.

Professional development is becoming more formalized with the introduction of qualifications and courses for intending head teachers and standards for subject leaders. Courses are usually provided by your school, your local-education authority, or by universities. Many of these courses carry accreditation towards higher degrees.

Task 13.2 Researching the opportunities

Contact the MA and the ATM and ask for the name of the secretary of the local branch. How often do they meet?

Ask your staff development officer about training opportunities in your LEA.

Make enquiries of your local university and discover the name of the person responsible for mathematics education.

Call them and ask about the opportunities available in your area for maths clubs, training courses, higher degrees, collaborative research.

Ask if there are any Teacher inquiry Groups (TIGs) running in your area.

Our own experience suggests that longer term courses leading to higher degrees are a very effective method of focusing your professional development. Most universities offer MA or MEd programmes for teachers which address immediate professional concerns but also allow you to stand back and reflect in supported discussion with colleagues.

CONCLUSION

We would not have been able to write this book without the professional collaboration of practising teachers. Our research is based on genuine classroom practices which we have shared with teachers who have generously invited us into their classrooms to work together trying out new approaches.

Teacher Inquiry Groups (TIGs) are sometimes funded by research agencies and run during the day, with supply cover provided. Often, however, they are unfunded and consist of a group of dedicated professionals meeting together after school, trying to improve their own practice through action research.

Action research usually involves professional teachers working in partnership with academics to develop their own practice. You might consider which professional issues you would like to research with the support of an action-research network and contact your local higher education institution for support. Many of the teachers we worked with in the PAMP and RSN projects welcomed the challenging questions they were asked to ponder during the research. Several commented on the value they gained from being part of an action-research group debating their teaching practices with other teachers and academics.

We believe that research which is grounded in the classroom and under the control of teachers is far more significant in improving the education of children than studies conducted in the glorious isolation of an ivory tower. You should consider playing your part in developing professional knowledge.

All good teaching involves action research and all good teachers are self-critical reflective researchers. We hope that this book will have provided practical support and also stimulated you to reflect on your practice with the intention of improving it.

Bibliography

ACAC (Awdurdod Cwricwlwm ac Asesu Cymru = Curriculum and Assessment Authority for Wales)/SCAA (School Curriculum and Assessment Authority) (1995) *GCSE: Regulations and Criteria*, London: HMSO.

ACCAC (Awdurdod Cymwysterau Cwricwlwm ac Asesu Cymru = Qualification Curriculum and Assessment Authority for Wales) (1999) *Making Effective Use of Assessment Information: Key Stages 1–3*, Cardiff: Qualification, Curriculum and Assessment Authority for Wales.

ACCAC (Awdurdod Cymwysterau Cwricwlwm ac Asesu Cymru = Qualification Curriculum and Assessment Authority for Wales) (2000) *Mathematics in the National Curriculum in Wales*, Cardiff: Qualification, Curriculum and Assessment Authority for Wales.

André, T. (1989) 'Problem solving and education', in B. Moon, and P. Murphy (eds) *Developments in Learning and Assessment*, pp. 60–74. London: Hodder & Stoughton/OU.

Andrews, P. (1997) 'A Hungarian perspective on mathematics education', *Mathematics Teaching* 161: 14–17.

APU (Assessment of Performance Unit) (1991) *Mathematics Monitoring (Phase 2)*, Slough: National Foundation for Educational Research.

Askew, M., Bliss, J., and Macrae, S. (1995) 'Scaffolding in mathematics science and technology', in P. Murphy, M. Selinger, J. Bourne, and M. Briggs. (eds) *Subject Learning in the Primary Curriculum*, pp. 209–17, London: Routledge/OUP.

Askew, M., Rhodes, V., Brown, M., Wiliam, D., and Johnson, D. (1997) *Effective Teachers of Numeracy: Final Report*, London: King's College.

ATM (1989) *Using and Applying Mathematics*, Derby: Association of Teachers of Mathematics.

Ausubel, D. P. (1968) *Educational Psychology: A Cognitive View*, London: Holt, Rinehart & Winston.

Ausubel, D. P. (1969) *School Learning*, New York: Holt, Rinehart & Winston.

Backhouse, J., Haggarty, L., Pirie, S., and Stratton, J. (1992) *Improving the Learning of Mathematics*, London: Cassell.

Bauersfeld, H. (1988) 'Interaction, construction and knowledge: alternative perspectives for mathematics education', in D. Grouws, T. Cooney, and D. Jones (eds) *Effective Mathematics Teaching*, pp. 27–46, NCTM, Reston, VA: Lawrence Erlbaum.

Bauersfeld, H. (1994) 'Theoretical perspectives on interaction in the mathematics classroom', in R. Biehler, R. Sholz, R. Straesser, and B. Winklemann (eds) *The Didactics of Mathematics as a Scientific Discipline*, pp. 133–146, Dordrecht: Kluwer.

Beaton, A., Mullis, I., Martin, M., Gonzales, E., Kelly, D., and Smith, T. (1996) *Mathematics Achievement in the Middle School Years: IEA's Third International Mathematics and Science Study*, Chestnut Hill, MA: Boston College.

Bell, A. (1993a) 'Principles for the design of teaching', *Educational Studies in Mathematics* 24(1): 5–34.

Bell, A. (1993b) 'Some experiments in diagnostic teaching', *Educational Studies in Mathematics* 24(1): 115–37.

Benzie, D. (1997) 'Information Technology: is our definition wide of the mark?' In D. Passey, and B. Samways (eds) *Information Technology: Supporting Change Through Teacher Education*, pp. 55–61, London: Chapman & Hall.

Berry, J. and Graham, T. (1991) 'Using concept questions in teaching mathematics', *International Journal of Mathematics Education, Science & Technology* 22(5): 749–57.

Berry, J. S., Savage, M. D., and Williams, J. S. (1989) 'Case studies in modelling in mechanics: Part 1', *Teaching Mathematics and its Applications* 8(3): 128–34.

Bierhoff, H. (1996) *Laying the Foundations of Numeracy*, London: Institute of Social and Economic Research.

Birnbaum, I. (1990) 'The assessment of IT capability', *Journal of Computer Assisted Learning* 6: 88–97.

Black, P. J. and Wiliam, D. (1998) 'Assessment and classroom learning', *Assessment in Education: Principles Policy and Practice* 5(1): 7–73.

Blanchard, J. (1993) 'Keeping track: criterion-based peer-assessment by pupils', *British Journal of Curriculum and Assessment* 4(1): 37–42.

Boaler, J. (1993a) 'Encouraging the transfer of "school" mathematics to the "real world" through the integration of process and content, context and culture', *Educational Studies in Mathematics* 25: 341–73.

Boaler, J. (1993b) 'The role of contexts in the mathematics classroom: do they make mathematics more real?' *For the Learning of Mathematics* 13(2): 12–17.

Brown, A. (1987) 'Metacognition, executive control, self-regulation and other more mysterious mechanisms', in F. H. Weinhart, and R. H. Kluwe (eds) *Metacognition, Motivation and Understanding*, pp. 65–116, Hillsdale, NJ: Lawrence Erlbaum Associates.

Brown, M. (1981a) 'Number operations', in K. Hart (ed.) (1981) *Children's Understanding of Mathematics: 11–16*, pp. 23–47, London: John Murray.

Brown, M. (1981b) 'Place value and decimals', in K. Hart (ed.) (1981) *Children's Understanding of Mathematics: 11–16*, pp. 48–65, London: John Murray.

Brown, M. (1999) 'Is more whole-class teaching the answer?' *Mathematics Teaching*, 169: 5–7.

Bruner, J. S. (1968) *Towards a Theory of Instruction*, Cambridge, MA: Harvard University Press.

Bruner, J. S. (1985) 'Vygotsky: an historical and conceptual perspective', in J. V. Wertsch (ed.) *Culture, Communication and Cognition: Vygotskian Perspectives*, pp. 21–34, Cambridge: Cambridge University Press.

Burton, L. (1994). Clashing epistemologies of mathematics education: can we see the 'wood' for the 'trees'? *Curriculum Studies* 2(2): 203–19.

Butt, P. (1999) 'So much better in the old days?' *Micromath* 15(2): 30–3.

CCW (Curriculum Council for Wales) (1989) *Mathematics in the National Curriculum: Non-statutory Guidance for Teachers*, Cardiff: HMSO.

CCW (Curriculum Council for Wales) (1992) *Mathematics in the National Curriculum: Non-statutory Guidance for Teachers*, Cardiff: HMSO.

Centre for Innovation in Mathematics Teaching (CIMT) (1997) *Mathematics Enhancement Project (MEP)*, Exeter: University of Exeter.

Charles, C. M. (1998) *Building Classroom Discipline*, Harlow: Addison-Wesley Longman Inc.

Cobb, P. and Bauersfeld, H. (eds) (1995) *The Emergence of Mathematical Meaning: Interacting in Classroom Cultures*, Hillsdale, NJ: Lawrence Erlbaum Associates.

Cobb, P., Wood, T., Yackel, E., and Perlwitz, M. (1992) 'A follow-up assessment of a second-grade problem centred mathematics project', *Educational Studies in Mathematics* 23(5): 483–504.

Cobb, P., Boufi, A., McClain, K., and Whitenack, J. (1997) 'Reflective discourse and collective reflection', *Journal for Research in Mathematics Education* 28(3): 258–77.

Cockcroft, W. H. (1982) *Mathematics Counts*, London: HMSO.

Cornelius, M. (1985) 'From Jeffery syllabus to Cockcroft report part 1', *Mathematics in Schools* 14(4) 31–4.

Costello, J. (1991) *Teaching and Learning Mathematics 11–16*, London: Routledge.

Cox, M. (1997) *The Effects of Information Technology on Student's Motivation (Final Report)*, Coventry: National Council for Educational Technology.

Crawford, D. (1997) 'Learning probability – misconceptions and all', *Mathematics Teaching*, 159: 23–9.

Crowther, G. (1959) *15 to 18: A Report of the Central Advisory Council for Education*, London: HMSO.

Daugherty, R. (1994) *National Curriculum Assessment: A Review of Policy 1987–1994*, London: The Falmer Press.

Daugherty, R., Thomas, B., Jones, G. E., and Davies, S. (1991) *GCSE in Wales: A Study of the Impact of the General Certificate of Secondary Education on the Teaching of History, Geography and Welsh*, Cardiff: Welsh Office Education Department.

Dearing, R. (1993) *The National Curriculum and Its Assessment*, London: School Curriculum and Assessment Authority.

DES (1979) *Aspects of Secondary Education*, London: HMSO.

DES (1985) *Mathematics from 5–16: Curriculum Matters*, London: HMSO.

DES (Department of Education and Science)/WO (Welsh Office) (1988) *National Curriculum: Task Group on Assessment and Testing: A Report*, London: HMSO.

DES (Department of Education and Science)/WO (Welsh Office) (1989) *Mathematics in the National Curriculum*, London: HMSO.

DES (Department of Education and Science)/WO (Welsh Office) (1991) *Mathematics in the National Curriculum (1991)*, London: HMSO.

DfEE (Department for Education and Employment) (1998) *Teaching: High Status, High Standards*, London: Department for Education and Employment.

DfEE (Department for Education and Employment) (1999a) *The National Numeracy Strategy: Framework for Teaching Mathematics*, Cambridge: Cambridge University Press.

DfEE (Department for Education and Employment) (1999b) *The Standards Website*. Online at http://www.standards.dfee.gov.uk (6 April 2000).

DfEE (Department of Education and Employment) (1999c) *Information and Communications Technology in Maintained Primary and Secondary Schools in England: 1999*, London: HMSO.

DfEE (Department of Education and Employment) (2000) *The National Numeracy Strategy: Framework for Teaching Mathematics Year 7*, Cambridge: Cambridge University Press.

DfEE (Department for Education and Employment)/QCA (1999a) *The National Curriculum for England: ICT*, London: HMSO.

DfEE (Department for Education and Employment)/QCA (1999b) *The National Curriculum for England: Mathematics*, London: HMSO.

DFE (Department for Education)/WO (Welsh Office) (1994). *Code of Practice on the Identification and Assessment of Special Educational Needs*, London: HMSO.

DFE (Department for Education)/WO (Welsh Office) (1995) *Mathematics in the National Curriculum*, London: HMSO.

Dickson, L., Brown, M., and Gibson, O. (1984) *Children Learning Mathematics: A Teacher's Guide to Recent Research*, London: Holt, Rinehart and Winston.

Dubinsky, E. (1991) 'Constructive aspects of reflective abstraction in advanced mathematics', in L. P. Steffe (ed.) *Epistemological Foundations of Mathematical Experience*, pp. 160–202, New York: Springer-Verlag.

Elton, R. (1989) *Discipline in Schools: Report of the Committee of Enquiry*, London: HMSO.

Feuerstein, R. (1979) *The Dynamic Assessment of Retarded Performers*, Baltimore, MD: University Park Press.

Flavell, J. H. (1976) 'Metacognitive aspects of problem solving', in L. B. Resnick (ed.) *The Nature of Intelligence*, pp. 231–5, Hillsdale, NJ: Lawrence Erlbaum Associates.

Flavell, J. H. (1987) 'Speculation about the nature and development of metacognition', in F. E. Weinhart and R. H. Kluwe (eds) *Metacognition, Motivation and Understanding*, pp. 21–30, Hillsdale, NJ: Lawrence Erlbaum Associates.

Fontana, D. (1994) *Managing Classroom Behaviour*, Leicester: British Psychological Society.

Foxman, D. (1985) *Mathematical Development: Review of the First Phase of Monitoring: Report on the Series of Annual Surveys of the Mathematical Performance of 11 and 15 year olds held from 1978–1982 Inclusive*, London: HMSO.

Fullan, M. (1991) *The New Meaning of Educational Change*, London. Cassell.

Fullan, M. (1993) *Change Forces: Probing the Depths of Educational Reform*, London: The Falmer Press.

Furlong, J. and Maynard, T. (1995) *Mentoring Student Teachers: The Growth of Professional Knowledge*, London and New York: Routledge.

Gagne, R. M. and Briggs, L. J. (1974) *Principles of Instructional Design*, London: Holt, Rinehart & Winston.

Galpin, B. and Graham, A. (eds) (1997) *Tapping into Mathematics with the T1-83 Graphics Calculator*, Harlow: Addison-Wesley.

Galton, M., Simon, B., Kroll, P., Jasman, A., and Willcocks, J. (1980) *Inside the Primary Classroom*, London: Routledge and Kegan Paul.

Gardiner, T. (1995) 'Mathematics hamstrung by long divisions', *The Sunday Times*, 22 January 1995: 20.

Geen, A. (1998) *Educational and Professional Studies: A Reader*, Cardiff: Relay Publications.

Gipps, C. (1990) *Assessment: A Teacher's Guide to the Issues*, London: Hodder & Stoughton.

Gipps, C. (1994) *Beyond Testing: Towards a Theory of Educational Assessment*, London: Falmer Press.

Gipps, C. and Murphy, P. (1994) *A Fair Test: Assessment, Achievement and Equity*, Buckingham: Open University Press.

Girling, M. (1977) 'Towards a definition of basic numeracy', *Mathematics Teaching* 81(5): 4–5.

Glaser, R. (1995) 'Expert knowledge and the process of thinking', in P. Murphy, M. Selinger, J. Bourne, and M. Bridges (eds) *Subject Learning in the Primary Curriculum*, pp. 274–88, London: Routledge/OUP.

Goulding, M. (1997) *Learning to Teach Mathematics*, London: David Fulton Publishers Ltd.

Graham, A. (1982) 'Calculator games in the primary school', *Mathematics Teaching* 101: 14–15.

Graham, T. and Berry, J. (1992) 'Sixth form students intuitive understanding of mechanics concepts', *Teaching Mathematics and its Applications* 11(3): 106–11.

Graham, T. and Berry, J. (1993) 'Students' intuitive understanding of gravity', *International Journal of Mathematics Education, Science & Technology* 24(3): 473–8.

Graham, T., Rowlands, S., Jennings, S., and English, J. (1999) 'Towards whole class interactive teaching', *Teaching Mathematics and its Applications* 18(2): 50–60.

Gray, S. S. (1991) 'Ideas in practice: metacognition and mathematical problem solving', *Journal of Developmental Education* 14(3): 24–8.

Green, D. and Pope, S. (eds) (1993) *Graphic Calculators in the Mathematics Classroom*, Leicester: The Mathematical Association.

Greer, B. and Mulhern, G. (1989) *New Directions in Mathematics*, London: Routledge.

Griffiths, M. (1999) *Teaching Numeracy in the Primary School*, Cardiff: National Assembly for Wales/BBC Wales.

Groves, S. (1994) 'Calculators: a learning environment to promote number sense', *Proceedings of the American Research Association*, New Orleans, USA, 1(14): 33–40.

Hardy, T., Haworth, A., Love, E., and McIntosh, A. (1986) *Points of Departure 1*, Derby: Association of Teachers of Mathematics.

Hargreaves, D. H. (1972) *Interpersonal Relations and Education*, London: Routledge and Kegan Paul.

Harris, S. (1999) *INSET for IT: A Review of the Literature Relating to Preparation for and Use of IT in Schools*, Slough: National Foundation for Educational Research.

Hart, K. (1981) *Children's Understanding of Mathematics: 11–16*, London: John Murray.

Hart, K. (1984) *Ratio: Children's Strategies and Errors; A Report of the Strategies and Errors in Secondary Mathematics Project*, Windsor: NFER-Nelson.

Hart, K. (1988) 'Fractions', *Mathematics 11–16: Some Research Findings*, Leicester: The Mathematical Association.

Hembree, R. and Dessart, D. (1992) 'Research on calculators in mathematics education', in J. Fey and C. Hirsch (eds) *Calculators in Mathematics Education*, pp. 23–32, Reston, VA: National Council for Teachers of Mathematics.

Holt, M. (1996) 'The making of Casablanca and the making of the curriculum', *Journal of Curriculum Studies* 28(3): 241–52.

Howe, J. (1983) 'Towards a pupil centred classroom', in R. Walker, J. Nisbet and C. Hoyle (eds) *Computers in Education*, pp. 27–63, London: Kogan Page.

Howe, M. (1999) *A Teacher's Guide to the Psychology of Learning*. London: Blackwell Publishers.

Hulme, J., Defty, N., Bryant, L., and Fitz-Gibbon, C. (1998) *The YELLIS Handbook: Performance Indicators for Schooling of Students Aged 14–16*, University of Durham: Curriculum Evaluation and Management Centre.

Johnson, D. C. (1978) 'Calculators: abuses and uses', *Mathematics Teaching*, 85: 50–6.

Johnson, D. C. (ed.) (1989) *Children's Mathematical Frameworks 8–13: A Study of Classroom Teaching*, Windsor: National Foundation for Educational Research-Nelson.

Johnston-Wilder, S. and Pimm, D. (1999) 'Using information and communications technology', in S. Johnston-Wilder, P. Johnston-Wilder, D. Pimm, and J. Westwell (eds) *Learning to Teach Mathematics in the Secondary School*, pp. 144–68, London: Routledge.

Johnston-Wilder, S., Johnston-Wilder, P., Pimm, D., and Westwell, J. (eds) (1999) *Learning to Teach Mathematics in the Secondary School*, London: Routledge.

Jolliffe, F. R. (1988) 'Two sampling misconceptions', *Teaching Statistics* 10(1): 16–19.

Jones, K. (1999) 'Planning for mathematics learning', in S. Johnston-Wilder, P. Johnston-Wilder, D. Pimm, and J. Westwell (eds) *Learning to Teach Mathematics in the Secondary School*, pp. 84–102, London: Routledge.

Jones, S. (1992) 'The assessment of mathematical modelling', unpublished M.Ed. dissertation, University of Wales, Swansea.

Jones, S. and Tanner, H. (1997). 'Do calculators count?' *Micromath* 13(3): 31–5.

Jones, S. and Tanner, H. (1998) 'The effective use of calculators in the teaching of numeracy', paper given at Proceedings of the Conference of the Mathematics Education Research Group of Australia – 21 (Brisbane), Vol. 1, pp. 287–94.

Kennewell, S., Parkinson, J., and Tanner, H. (2000) *Developing the ICT Capable School*, London: Routledge/Falmer.

Kerslake, D. (1986) *Fractions: Children's Strategies and Errors; A Report of the Strategies and Errors in Secondary Mathematics Project*, Windsor: National Foundations for Educational Research-Nelson.

Keys, W., Harris, S., and Fernandez, C. (1996) *Third International Mathematics and Science Study: First National Report. Part 1, Achievement in Mathematics and Science at Age 13 in England*, London: NFER.

Kilpatrick, J. (1987) 'What constructivism might be in mathematics education', paper given at Proceedings of the 11th Psychology of Mathematics Education Conference, Montreal, pp. 3–27.

Kitchen, A. (1998) 'Using calculators in schools', *Micromath* 14(2): 25–9.

Kounin, J. S. (1970) *Discipline and Group Management in Classrooms*, New York: Holt, Rinehart and Winston.

Küchemann, D. (1981) 'Algebra', in K. M. Hart (ed.) *Children's Understanding of Mathematics: 11–16*, pp. 102–19, London: John Murray.

Kyriacou, C. (1986) *Effective Teaching in Schools*, Hemel Hempstead: Simon & Schuster Ltd.

Lakatos, I. (1976) *Proofs and Refutations*, London: Cambridge University Press.

Lave, J. (1988) *Cognition in Practice*, Cambridge: Cambridge University Press.

Lave, J. (1992) 'World problems: A microcosm of theories of learning', in P. Light and G. Butterworth (eds) *Context and Cognition: Ways of Learning and Knowing*, pp. 74–92, Hemel Hempstead: Harvester Wheatsheaf.

Lave, J., Smith, S., and Butler, M. (1988). 'Problem solving as an everyday practice', in R. Charles and E. Silver (eds) *The Teaching and Assessing of Mathematical Problem Solving*, pp. 61–81, Reston, VA: National Council of Teachers of Mathematics.

Lerman, S. (1999) 'Doing research in mathematics education in time of paradigm wars', paper given at Proceedings of the 23rd Conference of the International Group for the Psychology of Mathematics Education, Haifa, Vol. 1, pp. 85–92.

Lester, F. and Kroll, D. L. (1990) 'Teaching students to be reflective: a study of two grade seven classes', paper given at *Proceedings of the 14th Psychology of Mathematics Education Conference*, Vol. 5, No. 1, pp. 151–8.

Love, E. and Mason, J. (1992) *Teaching Mathematics: Action and Awareness*, Milton Keynes: Open University Press.

Love, E. and Mason, J. (1995) 'Telling and asking', in P. Murphy, M. Selinger, J. Bourne, and M. Briggs (eds) *Subject Learning in the Primary Curriculum*, pp. 252–267, London: Routledge/OUP.

Lovegrove, N. and Wilshire, M. (1997) *The Future of Information Technology in UK Schools*, London: McKinsey & Co.

McManus, M. (1989) *Troublesome Behaviour in the Classroom: A Teacher's Survival Guide*, London; Routledge.

Mason, J. (1988) 'Modelling: What do we really want pupils to learn?', in D. Pimm (ed.) *Mathematics, Teachers and Children*, pp. 201–15, London: Hodder & Stoughton.

Mason, J., Burton, L., and Stacey, K. (1982) *Thinking Mathematically*, London: Addison Wesley.

Mathematical Association (1992) *Mental Methods in Mathematics: A First Report*, Leicester: The Mathematical Association.

Miles, T. and Miles, E. (1992) *Dyslexia and Mathematics*, London: Routledge.

Mitchell, G. (1997) *Practical Strategies for Individual Behaviour Difficulties at Stages 1 and 2 of the Code of Practice*, London: David Fulton.

Mitchell, P. (1997) '0.4971 and all that – is there life after the calculator?', *Teaching Mathematics and its Applications* 16(4) 177–80.

Mortimore, P., Sammons, P., and Thomas, S. (1994) School effectiveness and value added measures. *Assessment in Education* 1(3): 315–31.

NCC (National Curriculum Council) (1989) *Mathematics in the National Curriculum: Non-statutory Guidance for Teachers*, York: HMSO.

Neumark, V. (1995) 'For the love of maths', *Times Educational Supplement*, 8 September 1995: 5.

Newman, D., Griffin, P., and Cole, M. (1989) *The Construction Zone: Working for Cognitive Change in School*, Cambridge: Cambridge University Press.

Noss, R. (1998) 'Numeracy is not enough', Online at http://www.ioe.ac.uk/rnoss/numeracy.html (18 February 1998).

Nunes, T., Schliemann, A. D., and Carraher, D. W. (eds) (1993) *Street Mathematics and School Mathematics*, New York: Cambridge University Press.

OHMCI (1996) *Behaviour and Discipline in the Secondary Schools of Wales*, Cardiff: Office of Her Majesty's Chief Inspector of Schools in Wales.

Oldknow, A. (1998) 'Real data in the mathematics classroom', *Micromath* 14(2): 14–20.

Orton, A. (1992) *Learning Mathematics: Issues, Theory and Classroom Practice*, London: Cassell.

Orton, A. and Wain, G. (eds) (1994) *Issues in Managing Mathematics*, London: Cassell.

Papert, S. (1980) *Mindstorms: Children, Computers and Powerful Ideas*, Brighton: Harvester.

Pea, R. D. (1985) 'Beyond amplification: using the computer to reorganise mental functioning', *Educational Psychology*, 20(4) 167–82.

Peer, L. (1996) *Winning with Dyslexia: A Guide for Secondary Schools*, London: British Dyslexia Association.

Phillips, M. (1996) *All Must Have Prizes*, London: Little, Brown & Company.

Piaget, J. (1937) *La construction du réel chez l'enfant*, trans. M. Cook (1971) *The Construction of Reality in the Child*, New York: Basic Books; Neuchâtel, Switzerland: Delachaux et Niestlé.

Piaget, J. (1972) *The Principles of Genetic Epistemology*, London: Routledge & Kegan Paul.

Piaget, J. (1980a) 'Afterthoughts', in M. Piatelli-Palmarini (ed.) *Language and Learning: The Debate Between Jean Piaget and Noam Chomsky*, pp. 278–84, London: Routledge & Kegan Paul.

Piaget, J. (1980b) 'The psychogenesis of knowledge and epistemological significance', in M. Piatelli-Palmarini (ed.) *Language and Learning: The Debate Between Jean Piaget and Noam Chomsky*, pp. 23–34, London: Routledge & Kegan Paul.

Pimm, D. and Johnston-Wilder, S. (1999) 'Different teaching approaches', in S. Johnston-Wilder, P. Johnston-Wilder, D. Pimm, and J. Westell (eds) *Learning to Teach Mathematics in the Secondary School*, pp. 56–83, London: Routledge.

Pozo, J. I. and Carretero, M. (1992) 'Causal theories, reasoning strategies and conflict resolution by experts and novices in Newtonian mechanics', in A. Demetriou, M. Shayer, and A. Efklides (eds) *Neo-Piagetian Theories of Cognitive Development: Implications and Applications for Education*, pp. 231–55, London: Routledge.

Prawat, R. (1989a) 'Promoting access to knowledge, strategy and disposition in students: a research synthesis', *Review of Educational Research* 59(1): 1–41.

Prawat, R. (1989b) 'Teaching for understanding: Three key attributes', *Teaching and Teacher Education* 5(4): 315–28.

Prawat, R. (1991) 'The value of ideas: The immersion approach to the development of thinking', *Educational Researcher* 20(2): 3–10.

QCA (1999) *Qualifications 16–19: A Guide to the Changes Resulting from the Qualifying for Success Consultation*. Sudbury: Qualifications and Curriculum Authority.

Reid, G. (1998) *Dyslexia: A Practitioner's Handbook*, Chichester: John Wiley & Sons.

Resnick, L. B. (1987) *Education and Learning to Think*, Washington, DC: National Academy Press.

Reynolds, D. (1998a) *Numeracy Matters: The Preliminary Report of the Numeracy Task Force*, London: Department for Education and Employment.

Reynolds, D. (1998b) *The Implementation of the National Numeracy Strategy: The Final Report of the Numeracy Task Force*, Sudbury: Department for Education and Employment Publications.

Robertson, J. (1981) *Effective Classroom Control*, London: Hodder & Stoughton.

Rowe, M. (2000) *PGCE Secondary Course Handbook*, Swansea: University of Wales.

Salomon, G. and Globerson, T. (1987) 'Skill may not be enough: the role of mindfulness in learning and transfer', *International Journal of Educational Research* 11(6): 623–37.

Salomon, G. and Perkins, D. N. (1989) 'Rocky roads to transfer: rethinking mechanisms of a neglected phenomenon', *Educational Psychology* 24: 113–42.

SCAA (School Curriculum and Assessment Authority) (1994) *Mathematics in the National Curriculum: Draft proposals*, London: HMSO.

SCAA (1997a) *The Teaching and Assessment of Number at Key Stages 1–3*, London: School Curriculum and Assessment Authority.

SCAA (1997b) *The Use of Calculators at Key Stages 1 to 3*, London: School Curriculum and Assessment Authority.

Schoenfeld, A. H. (1985) *Mathematical Problem Solving*, New York: Academic Press.

Schoenfeld, A. H. (ed.) (1987) *Cognitive Science and Mathematical Education*, Hillsdale, NJ: Lawrence Erlbaum Associates.

Schoenfeld, A. H. (1992) 'Learning to think mathematically: problem solving, metacognition and sense making in mathematics', in D. A. Grouws (ed.) *Handbook of Research on Mathematics Teaching and Learning*, pp. 334–70, New York: Macmillan.

Schoenfeld, A. H. (ed.) (1994) *Mathematical Thinking and Problem Solving*, Hillsdale, NJ: Lawrence Erlbaum Associates.

SEAC (School Examinations and Assessment Council) (1991) *Teacher Assessment at Key Stage Three: An In-service Resource, Mathematics*, London: HMSO.

SEAC (School Examinations and Assessment Council) (1993) *KS3: Pupils' Work Assessed: Mathematics*, London: HMSO.

SED (Scottish Education Department) (1979) *Issues in Educational Assessment*, Edinburgh: HMSO.

SEC/OU (Secondary Examinations Council/Open University) (1986) *Mathematics GCSE: A Guide for Teachers*, Milton Keynes: The Open University Press.

Selwyn, N. (1999a) 'Differences in educational computer use: the influence of subject cultures', *The Curriculum Journal* 10(1) 29–48.

Selwyn, N. (1999b) 'Why the computer is not dominating schools: a failure of policy or a failure of practice?', *Cambridge Journal of Education* 29(1): 77–91.

Shuard, H., Walsh, A., Goodwin, J., and Worcester, V. (1991) *Calculators, Children and Mathematics*, London: Simon & Schuster.

Silver, E. A. (1987) 'Foundations of cognitive theory and research for mathematics problem solving instruction', in A. H. Schoenfeld (ed.) *Cognitive Science and Mathematics Education*, pp. 33–61, Hillsdale, NJ: Lawrence Erlbaum Associates.

Silver, E. A. (1994) 'On mathematical problem posing', *For the Learning of Mathematics* 14(1): 19–28.

Simon, H. A. (1978) 'Information processing theory of human problem solving', in W. K. Estes (ed.) *Handbook of Learning and Cognitive Processes*, pp. 271–95, London: J. Wiley & Sons.

Simon, H. A. (1980) 'Problem solving and education', in D. T. Tuma and F. Reif (eds) *Problem Solving and Education: Issues in Teaching and Research*, pp. 81–96, Hillsdale, NJ: Lawrence Erlbaum Associates.

Simon, H. A. (1989) 'The scientist as problem solver', in D. Klahr and K. Kovotsky (eds) *Complex Information Processing: The Impact of Herbert A. Simon*, pp. 375–98, Hillsdale, NJ: Lawrence Erlbaum Associates.

Skemp, P. R. (1976) 'Relational understanding and instrumental understanding', *Mathematics Teaching* 177: 20–6.

Smith, S. (2000) 'The effect of using Successmaker on numeracy: a case study', unpublished M.A.(Ed) dissertation, University of Wales Swansea.

SMP (School Mathematics Project) (1985) *SMP (11–16) Book G1*, Cambridge: Cambridge University Press.

Stenhouse, L. (1975) *An Introduction to Curriculum Research and Development*, London: Heinemann Educational.

Stevenson, D. (1997) *Information and Communications Technology: An Independent Inquiry*, London: Independent ICT in Schools.

Strack, G. (1995) 'Curriculum constraints and opportunities', in B. Tagg (ed.) *Developing a Whole-school IT Policy*, pp. 9–26, London: Pitman.

Straker, A. (1997) *National Numeracy Project*, Reading: National Centre for Literacy and Numeracy.

Stigler, P. G., Gonzales, P., Takako, K., Knoll, S., and Serrano, A. (1999) *The TIMSS Videotape Classroom Study: Methods and Findings from an Exploratory Research Project on Eighth Grade Mathematics Instruction in Germany, Japan and the United States, NCES99-074*, Washington, DC: US Government Printing Office.

Szalontai, T. (1995) 'Changing educational framework in the teaching of mathematics in Hungary', *Teaching Mathematics and its Applications*, 14(4): 149–55.

Tanner, H. (1987) 'The teaching of investigations and problem solving in mathematics', unpublished M.Ed dissertation, University of Bristol.

Tanner, H. (1989) 'Managing perceptions through action research: introducing investigations and problem-solving – a case study', *School Organisation* 9(2): 261–9.

Tanner, H. (1991) 'The Information Technology Curriculum and Mathematics', *Applications of Mathematics in the National Curriculum*, November, 87–91, Institute of Mathematics and its Applications, Southend.

Tanner, H. (1992a) 'Developing the use of IT within mathematics through action research', *Computers and Education* 18(1–3): 143–8.

Tanner, H. (1992b) 'Teacher assessment of mathematics in the National Curriculum at Key Stage 3', *Welsh Journal of Education* 3(2) 27–34.

Tanner, H. (1997) 'Using and applying mathematics: developing mathematical thinking through practical problem solving and modelling', unpublished Ph.D. Thesis, University of Wales, Swansea.

Tanner, H. and Jones, S. (1993) 'Developing metacognition through peer and self assessment', in T. Breiteig, I. Huntley, and G. Keiser-Messmer (eds) *Teaching and Learning Mathematics in Context*, pp. 228–41, London: Ellis Horwood.

Tanner, H. and Jones, S. (1994a) 'The development of metacognitive skills in mathematical modelling', in G. Wain. (ed.) *British Congress on Mathematical Education, 1993: Research Papers*, pp. 76–80, Leeds: University of Leeds.

Tanner, H. and Jones, S. (1994b) 'Using peer and self assessment to develop modelling skills with students aged 11 to 16: A socio-constructive view', *Educational Studies in Mathematics* 27(4): 413–31.

Tanner, H. and Jones, S. (1995a) *Better Thinking, Better Mathematics*, Swansea: University of Wales Swansea.

Tanner, H. and Jones, S. (1995b) 'Developing metacognitive skills in mathematical modelling – a socio-constructivist interpretation', in C. Sloyer, W. Blum, and I. Huntley (eds) *Advances and Perspectives in the Teaching of Mathematical Modelling*, pp. 61–70, Yorklyn, DE: Water Street Mathematics.

Tanner, H. and Jones, S. (1995c) 'Teaching mathematical thinking skills to accelerate cognitive development', *Proceedings of the 19th Conference of the International Group for the Psychology of Mathematics Education (PME19), Recife, Brazil*, Vol. 3, pp. 121–8.

Tanner, H. and Jones, S. (1997) 'Teaching children to think mathematically', in E. Pehkonen (ed.) *Solving Open-ended Problems*, pp. 106–20, Helsinki: University of Helsinki.

Tanner, H. and Jones, S. (1999a) 'Dynamic scaffolding and reflective discourse: the impact of teaching style on the development of mathematical thinking', *Proceedings of the 23rd Conference of the International Group for the Psychology of Mathematics Education (PME23), Haifa*, Vol. 4, pp. 257–64.

Tanner, H. and Jones, S. (1999b) 'Scaffolding metacognition: reflective discourse and the development of mathematical thinking', paper given at Proceedings of the British Educational Research Association (BERA-99), Brighton. Online at http://www.leeds.a-c.uk/educol/bera99.htm (1 April 2000).

Tanner, H. and Jones, S. (2000) 'Scaffolding for success: reflective discourse and the effective teaching of mathematical thinking skills', in T. Rowland and C. Morgan (eds) *Research in Mathematics Education Volume 2: Papers of the British Society for Research into Learning Mathematics*, pp. 19–32, London: British Society for Research into Learning Mathematics.

Tanner, H., Jones, S., and Treadaway, M. (1999) 'Schools that add value: raising standards in mathematics', paper given at Proceedings of the British Educational Research Association (BERA-99), Brighton. Online at http://www.leeds.ac.uk/educol/bera99.htm (1 April 2000).

Taylor, R. (1980) *The Computer in the School*, New York: Teachers' College Press.

Von Glasersfeld, E. (ed.) (1991) *Radical Constructivism in Mathematics Education*, Dordrecht: Kluwer Academic.

Vygotsky, L. S. (1962) *Thought and Language*, Cambridge, MA: The MIT Press.

Vygotsky, L. S. (1978) in M. Cole, V. John-Steiner, S. Scribner, and E. Souberman (eds) *Mind and Society: The Development of Higher Psychological Processes*, Cambridge, MA: Harvard University Press.

Walkerdine, V. (1988) *The Mastery of Reason: Cognitive Development and the Production of Rationality*, London: Routledge.

Watkins, C. (1997) *Managing Classroom Behaviour: A Bit Like Air Traffic Control*, London: Association of Teachers and Lecturers.

Watzlawick, P. (ed) (1984) *The Invented Reality*, New York: Norton.

Welsh Office Education Department (1998a) *How Is Your Child Doing at Primary School?* Cardiff: Welsh Office.

Welsh Office Education Department (1998b) *How Is Your Child Doing at Secondary School?* Cardiff: Welsh Office.

Wheatley, G. H. (1991) 'Constructivist perspectives on science and mathematics learning', *Science Education* 75(1): 9–21.

Wheatley, G. H. (1992) 'The role of reflection in mathematics learning', *Educational Studies in Mathematics* 23(5): 529–41.

Wiliam, D. (1992). 'Some technical issues in assessment: A user's guide', *British Journal of Curriculum and Assessment* 2(3): 11–20.

Wiliam, D. (1999a) 'Formative assessment in mathematics, Part 1: Close questioning', *Equals: Mathematics and Special Educational Needs* 5(2): 15–18.

Wiliam, D. (1999b) 'Formative assessment in mathematics, Part 2: Feedback', *Equals: Mathematics and Special Educational Needs* 5(3): 8–15.

Wiliam, D. (2000) 'Formative assessment in mathematics, Part 3: The learner's role', *Equals: Mathematics and Special Educational Needs* 6(1): 19–22.

Williams, J. and Ryan, J. (2000) 'National testing and the improvement of classroom teaching: Can they coexist?', *British Educational Research Journal* 26(1): 49–73.

WJEC (Welsh Joint Education Committee) (1999) 'GCSE results 1999'. Online at http://www.wjec.co.uk/wjecpress99.html (10 December 1999).

Wood, T. (1994) 'Patterns of interaction and the culture of mathematics classrooms', in S. Lerman (ed.) *Cultural Perspectives on the Mathematics Classroom*, pp. 149–68, Dordrecht: Kluwer Academic.

Wood, D., Bruner, J., and Ross, G. (1976) 'The role of tutoring in problem solving', *Journal of Child Psychology and Psychiatry* 17(2): 89–100.

Wragg, E. C. (1993) *Class Management*, London: Routledge.

Index